European Union in Changing International Order

Edited by

Jayaraj Amin

2013

Kaveri Books

New Delhi - 110 002

First Published in 2013

ISBN : 978-81-7479-122-1

Published by
Kaveri Books
4832/24, Ansari Road, Darya Ganj
New Delhi-110002 (India)
Tel: 011-23288140, 23245799
Telefax: 011-2382 8140
E-mail : kaveribooks@vsnl.com
web : www.kaveribooks.com

Typeset in Times New Roman at
Delta Book World, New Delhi - 110 002

PRINTED IN INDIA

Preface

European Union (EU) today is a major international actor with dominant economic influence not with standing of current economic crisis. Increasing gradually is the impact of its political moves and global reach with wider ramifications. The nature and developments in EU, hence, is of immense significance both in terms of theoretical underpinning and practical implications to the countries within EU as well as outside. Internally moving beyond the specific sectoral integration, EU today has flexed its muscles into the terrain that traditionally belonged to nation-states though not without contestation. This has brought to the fore a large number of issues including identity, citizenship, security, concept of welfare state, and relation between supranational and sovereign national entities among others, with divergent perspectives. *Deepening* of integration implied additional responsibility and susceptibility to the consequences of the ill-conceived actions of others as it has now become evident with financial crises affecting some European countries and pressure on others to share the burden. *Widening* to include twenty-seven countries has raised the apprehension to hold on in the cacophony of voices articulated in European defence, relations with the US and NATO, subsidies and ethnic minorities among others or on the increasing pro-active role of some European countries in the global crisis situation – be it the West Asian region, Afghanistan or responses to selective pro-democracy movements elsewhere. Despite the compromised Lisbon Treaty EU is at cross-roads and the future direction seems uncertain.

Externally, the EU has become a major economic entity and a global actor in its own right, but the image of EU is not uniform. EU considers itself as a supporter of market economy and liberal democracy. But EU's actual practice and record of its professed free trade is seen cynically in some quarters of the world especially, in the developing world so as its global politically motivated moves in conflict situations. But at the same time, EU's reliance on soft power approach is seen as a hope in this critical juncture the world is passing through. EU's significant experiment in harmonisation of policies and its perception of security through cooperation between memberstates has come to inspire others especially other regional organisations. Hence, the developments in the EU are of tremendous significance and consequence, affecting the way the world deals with and perceive politics, culture, economics, and international relations.

South Asia is closely related to Europe and this relationship has come to influence not merely its economic and political patterns but also its perceptive modes, inextricable from its identity. EU, as it brings together within its fold a number of countries with significant politico-cultural implications and massive resources, impacts South Asia as much as other regions and countries in divergent ways holding out a promise as well as a challenge. For the countries of South Asia, in particular India, an opportunity is on the anvil to tap resources, share ideas, and shape destiny based on common concerns and democratic perceptions. EU-India strategic partnership is a step in this direction among a host of other initiatives. Nevertheless, countries of South Asia and within it, different regions have divergent perspectives of Europe and have come to network with Europe in their own distinct ways. This is also true of EU countries and their regions that have differentiated linkages with countries and regions of South Asia. Naturally the developments in EU, as much as the developments in South Asia, are of consequence to the pattern of EU-South Asia relations, networks, and perceptions even as broad consensus exists among major constituencies to evolve mutually beneficial policies and global perspectives and premium is laid on dialogues and discussions. No doubt every move of EU is of consequence, and is therefore, subjected to critical reflection.

The contributors to this volume explore various dimensions of the issues and concerns of EU. The book is divided in to four sections. The first section on *the nature of EU* examines the trends in EU development and development strategies, identity, culture, and citizenship in the backdrop of theoretical positions. The second section on *developments in EU* reviews the implications of global and European financial crisis on EU and European Companies, European responses, and the debate on admission of Turkey into EU. The third section on *EU and the World* analyses the external priorities of EU, its perspectives towards China, India and China vis-a-vis EU; and, EU – India strategic engagement. The fourth section on *EU-South Asia- India* evaluates the specific aspects of EU's relation with South Asia and India, EU position in multilateral trade negotiations; and, EU linkages with specific regions within India.

In the materialisation of this project I am supported by many and I deem it necessary to acknowledge them. I am personally indebted to Prof. Rajendra K. Jain, Centre for European Studies, Jawaharlal Nehru University, New Delhi for all his support in the academic activities and publication of this book. I acknowledge with gratitude the support of India-European Union Study Centre Programme (IESCP) and its Team Leader, Mr. Ulrich Podewils in completing the project and in the materialisation of this book. My sincere gratitude to Prof. Hartmut Elsenhans, Leipzig University for his support and encouragement to my intellectual pursuits.I also thank my colleagues in the department of Political Science; Prof. Mallikarjunappa, Department of Business Administration; and, Mr. P V Mohan for their support at different levels. I am grateful to Ms Mamatha Rao for her help in the neat organisation of the book.

Dr. Jayaraj Amin

Contents

Section-III: EU and the World

Section-IV: EU-South Asia-India

Section-I
The Nature of European Union

1

European Union as a Global Player: In Perception and Action

B. Krishnamurthy & S. Jeeva

Realists consider states as the main actors in international politics and the considerable influence of traditional state-centric approaches to international relations and the related tendency to focus attention upon a limited range of external activities considered to comprise the 'high politics' of traditional foreign policy, led to the rejection of entities like European Union (EU) as actors in international politics. The way in which the Europeans attempted to cooperate and conduct their external relations with non-member third parties confused international political analysts so much that they pointed out that the then European Community (EC) had failed miserably in playing its collective role in global politics. Since then, there is considerable debate among scholars of international relations whether EC (and the present EU) is a global actor or not. In the present chapter, an effort is made to critically follow both sides of the debate; to establish that the EU is emerging as a global player of considerable influence and to critically analyse its multidimensional/multifaceted activities in contemporary international politics.

Any study on the EU as an international actor and a global player of significance has to concentrate on certain issues and has find answers for the following questions:

- What the EU is and is not?
- What the EU seems to be?
- What it does in the international arena?

- What it is likely to become?
- How far is it effective and acceptable to other international actors, the international community, and world citizens, at large?

1. What the EU is and is not?

It is well said that the "factor shaping the international role of the EU is not what it does or what it says, but what it is."[1] While analysing the EU and the role its plays in international politics, it is quite necessary to understand and appreciate what the EU is and especially, what it is not.

(a) Legal Personality

Public International Law focuses upon the inter-state system and has developed a formal concept of actorness in international politics in terms of the notion of a legal personality. This legal personality/actorness not only confers the right to participate in international politics, but also to be held responsible by other actors and to incur obligations. Articles 210 and 211 of the Treaty of Rome or the Treaty establishing the European Community (TEC) of 1957 give the EC 'legal personality' under international law. Article 281 of the TEC expressly regulated the legal personality of the EC. As such, its rights and obligations, its legal capacity depend on its functions and the purposes for which it was set up. Subsequently, the European Court of Justice ruled that it has limited competences in the sphere of international relations, while the member states are believed to have unlimited competences. The EC's powers rest on the principle of *competence d'attribution* - "the Community only holds those powers ... confirmed upon it by the Treaty." Article 113 and its derivations give the EC a potentially vast scope since it also has an implied power wherever it has the necessary internal powers and those needed for the performance of its duties and this concept is known as the principle of "parallel powers."[2] As such, the Community had legal personality and in that capacity played the role of a major international actor with extensive involvement in international trade, international organizations, and multilateral arrangements.

However, the Maastricht Treaty or the Treaty on European Union (TEU) of 1992, which provided for the creation of the EU and established the Community as the first of its three pillars, did not accord legal personality to the Union. Hence the EU, unlike the Community, was not empowered to conclude international agreements. This proved to be a source of confusion to third parties as it left the international personality of the Union incomplete. The Constitutional Treaty agreed by the member states in June, 2004, accorded legal personality to the Union (Article I-7). As the Dutch and subsequently the French voters rejected it in 2005, the Union's claim for legal personality remained unfulfilled. Article 47 of the Lisbon Treaty TEU(L), which entered into force on December 1, 2009, thus conferred a legal personality on the Union and also the right to conclude international agreements.

This acquisition of a legal personality by the EU was a logical consequence of the amendment of the three-pillar structure, since the Union replaced and succeeded the EC. The fact that the EU's legal personality is now formally recognised under Article 47 "simplifies its status and appears as an important step towards legal certainty." In other words, the EU became indisputably an actor under international law. As a consequence, the diplomatic representation came under the Union's authority: the Commission's delegations became the Union's delegations under the authority of the High Representative and are part of the European External Action Service (EEAS). As such, these amendments clearly strengthen the EU's status as an international actor, and, furthermore, it clarifies the question concerning the Union's diplomatic relations and the status of its institutions, which solidifies the EU's position in the international arena under international law.[3]

Article 216 (1) of the TFEU contains an explicit provision on the conclusion of international agreements in the scope of the responsibilities of the EU: "The Union may conclude an agreement with one or more third countries or international organisations where the Treaties so provide or where the conclusion of an agreement is necessary in order to achieve, within the framework of the Union's policies, one of the objectives referred to in the Treaties, or is provided for in a legally binding Union act or is likely to affect common rules or alter their scope." Again, Article 216 (2) of the TFEU stipulates that international "agreements concluded by the EU are binding upon the institutions of the Union."

Moreover, the Union's authority to conclude international agreements on the CFSP is explicitly regulated by Article 37, Chapter 2 on "Specific Provisions on the Common Foreign and Security Policy" of the TEU (L), according to which, "The Union may conclude agreements with one or more States or international organisations in areas covered by this Chapter." The procedure for the conclusion of an international agreement within the framework of the CFSP is still based on unanimity, and thus differs from the general procedure for the conclusion of international agreements based on qualified majority. Nevertheless, with the explicit treaty making authority within the scope of the CFSP, the EU "acquired for the first time an external legal instrument to execute the CFSP, which goes beyond the instruments for coordination of the Member States' external activities within the EU framework."[4]

(b) Actor and Actorness

Any actor in international politics would be an entity capable of formulating purposes and making decisions and thus engaging in some form of purposive action.[5] Actor capability is the 'capacity to behave actively and deliberately" in relation to other actors in the international system. Again, an international actor "can be said to be an entity which is delimited from others, and from its environment; autonomous in the sense of making its own laws and decisions and possesses certain structural prerequisites for action on the international level, such as legal personality, a set of diplomatic agents and the capability to conduct negotiations with third parties."[6] The concept of autonomy has been accorded central importance in the approach to actorness. Alongside autonomy, the ability to perform significant and continuing functions having an impact on inter-state relations, and the importance accorded to them and to their actions by third parties too count while evaluating the actorness of the concerned entity. On this ground, Cosgrove and Twitchtt conclude that the EC had become "a viable international actor" even by late 1960s.[7] From 1970s various efforts have been made to increase the profile and scope of the EC's actorness.

(c) Mixed/Multifaceted Actor

In 1970s, while the Realists still held the view that 'states' are 'sole' actors in international politics, other scholars developed pluralist approaches to international relations and portrayed 'mixed actor' system or even a 'global' political system, in their effort to conceptualize a world greatly complicated by the emergence of complex interdependence between and among states. In its external relations, the Community/Union acts as an intergovernmental organization and under this framework, it has been disaggregated and appears as several actors – at one level as a collectivity and at another as numerous - as many as the constituent member states. The EC/EU in foreign policy is solely intergovernmental and is therefore no more than the sum of what the members states severally decide.

In this regard, Merle argues that to be autonomous, international actors must be capable of playing "a specific role independent of their constituent members." In consequence he dismisses the EC as an actor on the grounds that the decision-making procedures of the Council of Ministers were subject to unanimity.[8] Subsequent introduction of qualified majority voting (QMV) means that the EC has become a (disaggregated) actor in those areas where QMV applies. The extent to which outsiders are puzzled as to whether they should negotiate with the Community/Union or with separate member states, demonstrates the political 'mixity' under the EC/EU framework. Moreover, actorness was attributed to the European Commission, the executive body of the Community/Union, which, on this count, is labelled as "the new variety of international actors."[9] John Ruggie's notion of the EU as a "multiperspectival polity" captures something of the complexity of the EU's external personality, which contributes for considering EU to be a multifaceted actor.[10] On the other hand, Reinhardt Rummel refers to the EU as a collective international actor, which conducts a composed foreign and security policy that integrates multiple elements all at once that are national, intergovernmental, and communitarian in nature and scope.[11]

(d) Actor *sui generis*

It is noted by several foreign policy analysts that it is difficult to compare the EC/EU with other state and non-state actors in the global system as it is an actor *sui generis* – unique, in terms of its character, identity/personality, conception, and evolution. During the Cold War, the Community's preference for persuasion and 'neutrality' distinguished it from other actors.[12] The EU's preferred policy instruments also distinguish it from other international actors, notably the US. Though the EU may not be so unique in its choice of foreign policy objectives, the way it pursues them does distinguish it from other international actors who are pursuing similar objectives. In this connection, Karen Smith maintains that, "What it does is less unique than how it does it."[13] Again, she adds: "What is also clearly unique about the EU's approach is that is based on legal texts, the human rights clauses in (legal) agreements and regulations on aid."[14]

Though not quite as structured as the fifty American states, the EU is a unique experiment in international cooperation. It is not quite one country yet, but not fully 27 separate ones, either - more tightly knit, by far, than the United Nations. It is essentially organized as a network that involves the pooling or sharing of sovereignty.[15] The EU is also projected as a non-traditional, unorthodox, but rule-based and supposedly value-driven international actor, which plays First-of-its-kind Role on the World Stage. Some scholars emphasize the *sui generis* characteristics of EU's decision making process, its cross-pillar interactions among different hierarchies, and the crucial role member states play in sensitive areas. Based on these observations, they affirm the EU as a unique actor on one hand and an incomplete, fragmented, and impotent actor, on the other. Philip Gordon is categorical when he maintains: "So long as the United States is willing to remain engaged in European security and in NATO, and unless some unforeseen and overwhelming common external challenge were to emerge, the EU is likely to remain a fragmented and incomplete international actor."[16]

(e) Not an International Actor

In early 1980s, Hedley Bull argued that Europe "is not an actor in international affairs, and doesn't seem likely to be one."[17] His contention was that the Europeans would need to develop a military capability through the Western European Union, if they were ever to be taken seriously on the great issues of international politics.

(f) International Actor in part

On the other hand, in 1990s, Christopher Hill maintained that the EC is a genuine international actor in some respects but not all.[18]

His analysis and conviction clearly brought out the dilemma in which the leaders and bureaucrats of the Community found themselves in their relations with third countries.

(g) International actor

The EU lacks a number of attributes traditionally associated with actors in the international arena – most conspicuously, the kind of centralized authority - 'traditional' nation-states usually possess.[19] Considering the fact, that the "EU is neither a state nor a non-state actor, and neither a conventional international organisation nor an international regime," it is difficult to define it as a great power in the classical sense. Nonetheless, due to its significant presence in nearly all international matters - economical, humanitarian or conflict issues - it can clearly be considered as a power on the international stage. By virtue of its economic size, policy scope, and political profile, the EU is a leading global actor and it maintains more than 150 diplomatic missions and offices in every continent of the world.[20] Roy Ginsberg maintains that the EU's external political and economic influence to be substantial. Again, taking the cumulative impact of EU on international political and economic scenario into consideration, he pooh-poohs the conventional depiction of the international relations scholars of the EU as "economic giant and political pigmy."[21]

Some scholars talk about EU becoming an actor of global influence even without taking recourse to becoming a state. It is argued by commentators that full political integration is not required for the EU to wield international influence and that its apparent weaknesses constitute its real strengths and that the EU represents something new, worthy of the twenty-first century and potentially a more successful type of international actor than the traditional ones. The fact that Europe is the global power that has signed most of the forty documents that constitute the basis of global governance: European member states have signed thirty-four of those treaties and texts, compared to eleven for the US, sixteen for China, and fifteen for India, needs to be taken note of, as it is worthy of emulation.[22]

(h) EU Actorness under Construction

Taking all these positive as well as negative factors into consideration, Bretherton and Vogler maintain that EU 'actorness' is under construction, and elaborate on the "opportunity, presence and capability" of the Union in international politics.[23] According to them, 'opportunity' denotes factors in the external environment of ideas and events which constrain or enable actorness and signifies the structural context of action. Europe maintains a variable and multidimensional presence and cohesive impact in international affairs. The 'presence' of the Community is invariably felt in the international organizations, in international political, economic and environmental diplomacy, throughout the European sub-system and its borderlands, in the developing world, and wherever mediated solutions to international conflicts/crises are attempted. The Union's growing presence in international affairs and its ability to exert influence externally; to shape the perceptions, expectations, and bahaviour of others are factors that determine the reputation and status accorded to the EU by external audiences and in this regard, the Union fairs superbly.

Capability means cohesiveness, resources, and the operational capacity of the EU in its dealings with other powers. Again, capacity refers to the internal context of EU action or inaction and those aspects of the EU policy process which constrain or enable external action and hence govern the Union's ability to capitalize on its presence or respond to opportunity. Internal and external factors initially constrained and then permitted and promoted the development of the EU's role in global politics.

2. What the EU seems to be?

Since its inception, the EU is conceptualised as and quite proud of itself being a distinctly 'different' type of international actor.[24] Over the decades, it has been described as a 'civilian', 'soft', and of late, a 'normative' power in international politics. The EU's official texts invariably make similar claims about the Union's role in world politics.

(a) Civilian Power

From the beginning the Europeans consciously and deliberately projected the EU in its external relations as a "civilian power." François Duchene, a strong exponent of the 'civilian power' school defines this concept thus: "The European Community's interest as a civilian group of countries long on economic power and relatively short on armed force is as far as possible to domesticate relations between states, including those of its own members and those with states outside its frontiers. This means trying to bring to international problems the sense of responsibility and structures of contractual politics which have in the past been associated almost exclusively with 'home' and not foreign, that is alien affairs."[25] As such, the Europeans intended the domestication of their foreign policy and deliberately assumed a non-military norm/approach in their external relations. Laidi, however, gives a classical definition of civilian power: a political entity with "a preference for peaceful conflict settlement and the use of a binding multilateral framework to organize the international system."[26]

As Romano Prodi pronounced at the start of his presidency, the status of the EU as a global civilian power is one which is still central to a discussion of its role in international relations: "We must aim to become a global civil power at the service of sustainable global development. After all, only by ensuring sustainable global development can Europe guarantee its own strategic security."[27] The EU is also projected as a civilian power, with no intention to use force to secure the national interest of the member states but persuasion to achieve 'milieu goals.'[28]

(b) Soft Power

In the 1990s, Hill referred to Europe as a 'soft' power. This is in continuation with the earlier concept of 'civilian' power, which is determined to use its economic strength, cultural vivacity, and sterling example to influence third countries rather than the traditional use of military power to force others to fall in line with their stand. Joseph S. Nye, Jr., in his recent book "Soft Power: The Means to Success in World Politics" defines soft power as "the ability to get what you want through attraction rather than coercion or payments. It arises from the attractiveness of a country's culture, political ideals, and policies. When our policies are seen as legitimate in the eyes of others, our soft power is enhanced."[29] The EU has a vast array of "soft power" instruments such as trade concessions, development assistance, and the European Investment Bank preferential lending at its disposal, which it may use to try to alter the behaviour of non-member states and shape the international system to its liking. The

Europeans emphasize more on economics and how to use it as an instrument of integration of human beings and states at the regional as well as international levels. As an actor which has indomitable faith in its 'soft' power potentials, the EU tends to use foreign aid and development cooperation assistance to influence and to bring expected changes in the policies and attitudes of third countries.

The EU has always wielded significant soft power due to its ability to inspire the dreams and desires of others. The countries that are more likely to be attractive and gain soft power in the present age of information/communication revolution are those with multiple channels of communications that help to frame issues; whose dominant culture and ideas are closer to prevailing global norms - which now emphasize liberalism, pluralism, and autonomy - and whose credibility is enhanced by their domestic and international values and policies. The EU fits very well into this bill.

(c) Normative Power

From 1970s, norms and values began permeating European foreign policy documents and declarations. On December 14-15, 1973, a two-day meeting of the EU Heads of State and Government resulted in a declaration on Europe's international identity. The declaration referred to building a 'just basis' for international relations. The 1986 Single European Act too goaded the Community to "display the principles of democracy and compliance with the rule of law and with human rights" in its conduct of external relations. The 1988 Rhodes European Council called for a meaningful role for the EU in preserving international peace, promoting the solution to regional conflicts, demonstrating solidarity for democracy, supporting the Universal Declaration of Human Rights, strengthening the effectiveness of the United Nations, and improving social and economic conditions in less developed countries. The Maastricht Treaty went a step further by calling for the preservation of peace and security, promotion of international cooperation, fight against international crime, development of democracy and the rule of law, respect for human rights and fundamental freedoms, and support for economic and social development (Article J.1). More explicitly, the Lisbon Treaty, which presented the now defunct Constitution Treaty under a different framework, states that in international affairs the EU would be guided by and would seek to promote values such as democracy, human rights, fundamental freedoms and the rule of law on which the Union is founded (Title V, Article 21; Title V, Article 2c).

The EU is constituted as a political entity by the values, images, and principles (VIPs) which shape the discourse and practice of its relations with the rest of the world. As such, the Union plays a distinctive role in global politics and behaves according to a set of dynamic, yet identifiable, values, principles, and images of the world. Values are notions laden with an absolute positive significance for the overall order and meaning we try to give to our world. While images are the pictures we have, based on our experiences and cultural traditions of the relationship between the physical and social worlds, principles are normative propositions that translate values into general 'constitutional' standards for polity action.[30]

The EU, as Ian Manners suggests, represents neither a civilian power nor a military power, "but a normative power of an ideational nature characterized by common principles." Following this logic, the Union's normative power is "characterized by its ability to shape standards of common sense," aimed at achieving non-military aims. Manners also emphasizes on the EU's ability to shape conceptions of 'normal' in international relations. The EU has moved further towards making its external relations informed by and conditional on, a catalogue of norms which come closer to those of the European Convention on Human Rights and Fundamental Freedoms (ECHR) and the Universal Declaration of Human Rights (UDHR), than most other actors in world politics.[31] As an international norm-setter and promoter of norms, Manners identifies in the EU five core values - peace, liberty, democracy, the rule of law, and respect for human rights and four subsidiary values – social solidarity, anti-discrimination, sustainable development, and good governance.[32] Subsequently, he talks about European self-images as constituted by five European perspectives – economic, social, environmental, conflict, and political - and nine EU values and principles – sustainable peace, social liberty, consensual democracy, associative human rights, supranational rule of law, inclusive equality, social solidarity, sustainable development, and good governance.[33] Further, he elaborates on three Europes - state Europe, supranational Europe, and cosmopolitan Europe – on the basis of the European self-image. EU values and principles such as the rule of law and good governance are to be found in the combination and interaction of these three EU self-images.[34]

For Rosencrance, normative power refers to the idea of setting world standards, in contrast to empirical power, which imposes itself by conquest or physical domination.[35] Stephan Keukeleire and Jennifer MacNaughtan project the EU as a normative power- an actor whose foreign policy is driven by identity and values rather than interests – with a growing role of political conditionality in agreements with third countries, in the insertion of social clauses such as labour rights or environmental clauses in multilateral agreements, and in the creation of specific instruments to promote democracy and human rights.[36] At the same time, they point out that "while values are undoubtedly a cornerstone of EU foreign policy, the EU is just as quick to protect its narrower self interests and geostrategic interests-its policies *vis-à-vis* Russia and China being examples."[37]

3. What does the EU do in the International Arena?

Bretherton and Vogler argue the fact that there are no actors with a comparable range of interests, policies, and relationships in the contemporary international political system and attributes to the Union three broad roles –a model, as a promoter of its proclaimed values, and as an alternative to the US.[38]

(a) As a Model

While analyzing the role of the European Union in the 21st Century global politics, Pierre-Yves Monjal points out that the Europeans "are inventing on a daily basis a unique and specific model which is legally an alloy, an alliance of governmental powers which are exercised on a revolutionary mode which is quite new and which consists in the common exercise of governmental powers detained by entities that are still sovereign... Peace was thus constructed in Europe around community law, free market economy and the political will of social democrat elite to do away with the most abject forms of political and economic nationalism - wars."[39]

The EU offers itself as a model to others on the basis of its political and economic achievements and has become the world's brand-leader in peaceful political cooperation.[40] It remains a stabilizing factor and a model in the new world order, a model of regional economic integration and a Community of security and peace. The EU projects itself as a value-based Community, an ethical actor, and a champion of sustainable development representing an attractive vision to potential applicants. Moreover, contemporary discourse of the good life takes the 'European dream' as a model to identify and attempt to achieve. Leidi projects the EU as a normative model and believes that "norms are and will remain not only Europe's best shield but also its finest banner."[41]

The EU tends to export to the international system its domestic political and socio-economic development model which is based upon democratic principles, minority rights, equal opportunities and solidarity, and assumes that its model which had already proved successful in Western Europe and more recently in Eastern Europe will work wonders for the rest of the world. For this reason, principles and values such as liberty, fundamental freedoms, democracy, respect for human rights, the rule of law and good governance are included in the EU official documents and international agreements as a key dimension of EU foreign policy. Also, it is assumed that poverty reduction can only be achieved with functioning democratic institutions and accountable governments, and that democratic, pluralist governments respecting minority rights alone lead to domestic stability. After analyzing this tendency of the EU, Stefania Panebianco argues that beyond this discursive dimension of the EU foreign policy, the EU is not always able (or willing) to exert its capability to "extend its norms into the international system" and concrete action in defence of Human Rights and Democracy (HRD) lags behind overriding security and economic interests in cases of Russia and China and "the analysis of the promotion of HRD in EU relations with Russia and China shows the limits of the 'exportability' of the EU model."[42]

(b) As a Promoter of Norms and Values

Scholars opine that the EU is a norm entrepreneur and there is a strong homothetic relation between the way Europe is constructed and the way in which it sees and approaches the world.[43] Norms are standards aimed at codifying the behaviour of actors sharing common principles in order to generate collective disciplines and to forbid certain conducts in the different fields of public policies. Manners always highlights the international role of the EU as a promoter of norms which displaces the state as the centre of concern.[44] Former European Commission President Romano Prodi commented in a speech at the *Institut d'Etudes Politiques* in Paris on May 29, 2001 thus: The "essence" of the European Union is essentially all about subjecting inter-state relations to the rule of law. Europe's experience of successful multilateral governance has in turn produced an ambition to convert the world. Europe "has a role to play in world 'governance,' adds Prodi, "a role based on replicating the European experience on a global scale. In Europe the rule of law has replaced the crude interplay of power . . . power politics have lost their influence." And by "making a success of integration we are demonstrating to the world that it is possible to create a method for peace."[45] As such, the transmission of the European miracle to the rest of the world has become Europe's new *mission civilisatrice* (civilizing mission). The European ambition is to convert the world by their solid and laudable example.

The European promotion of norms and values in the international political arena has created a new and distinctive wave. The 'European way' is attractive today because of the values underpinning it: the balanced model of a prosperous and cohesive society, the notion that dialogue and compromise can overcome historical barriers, the voluntary self-restraint of national powers, the emphasis on global public goods and on delivering them more effectively through a joint effort, and the commitment to sustainable development.[46]

(a) As an Alternative to the US

Charles Kupchan points out that the EU whose wealth rivals that of the US is "in and of itself a counterpoise to America."[47] Jacques Derrida as well as Jeremy Rifkind too find EU as a counter-hegemonic alternative to the US.[48] Reid calls EU the new super power and predicts the decline of the US.[49] The developing world tends to accept the EU as a protector in preference to the US, since it perceives the EU as a "positive influence" in the international politics and a second western voice to balance the American bellicosity. There is overwhelming hope that the EU, as a counter-hegemonic alternative will be able to restrain the all-powerful US, which is considered as a behemoth and a menace to world peace, through its unilateral actions.

Philip H. Gordon maintains: "An EU of nearly 400 million people and a combined gross domestic product (GDP) of more than $8 trillion that was able to unite its diplomatic and military potential could easily challenge the United States' current status as "lone superpower."[50] However, he subsequently recants and holds on the view that "the United States' current status as the world's "lone superpower" may well be challenged in the twenty-first century, but not by the European Union."[51] This self-contradiction is the outcome of the fact that the EU remains an enigma, less understood and least appreciated by some foreign policy observers and scholars, both European and non-European, since the EU is a unique experiment in international politics.

The EU itself is the best example of institutionalized multilateralism, of the sharing of sovereignty for a common purpose, and it is but natural for the Union to preach and practice multilateralism, in both domestic and foreign fronts.[52] Multilateralism and reliance on international organizations comes naturally to EU nations that individually are comparatively weak. As such, the EU is playing a crucial role in international politics by advocating multilateralism and supporting the UN in all its endeavours. The European Security Strategy puts succinctly the Union's determination to uphold the UN system and to contribute to its success. The EU attempts to formulate a common position on any issue of international importance and to take joint action, so that it would not develop into a crisis threatening world peace.[53]

Again, the prospect of the EU membership is deliberately used as a successful "soft power" instrument. Chris Patten refers about influencing third countries through the lure of membership in the 'privileged club' that the EU is made out to be.[54] As such, the most successful EU foreign policy has been its own expansion. In the 1980s, the prospect of joining, played a critical part in ensuring a smooth transition from dictatorship to democracy in Greece, Spain, and Portugal. In the 90s it transformed the East European countries as they moved from communist central planning to liberal democracy. The countries of the Western Balkans have been pacified and stabilised after the bloody 1990s, thanks mainly to their hopes of gaining EU membership. And Turkey has made wholesale changes in its politics, economics, and society largely to boost its chances of joining the Union.[55] Indeed, judged in terms of success in exporting its values to its backyard, the EU has done much better with its neighbours than the United States has with Central and South America, largely because of the charm of membership.[56] Membership has thus proved a brilliant way of entrenching liberal democracy in Europe's neighbourhood.

The EU has developed the image of a soft, civilian power and purveyor of funds for development cooperation in international politics. In the South, the EU is regarded as a relatively unbiased interlocutor, in that it has distanced itself from the colonial ties of individual member states.[57] Through the Lomé system, the Mediterranean preferences, and trade and commercial agreements with regional organizations such as ASEAN and the Contadora countries, the EU maintains institutionalized relations with most of the poorer countries of the world.[58]

The EU's increasing clout internationally stems from several factors, from the vastly greater amount of money that the EU spends on foreign aid as compared to the United States to the strongly secular values it promotes. "There are about 80 countries around the world that cover 1.5 billion people for whom the European Union is the most important and critical player," points out Mark Leonard, Director for foreign policy for the London-based Center for European Reform. The EU is delivering change - its tactics of trying to reform Turkey and the Balkans by dangling the incentive of EU membership, or in trying to negotiate with Iran over nuclear regulation, is more suited to the twenty-first century than the "hard power" of unbridled military force of yester decades. This strategy is quite appropriate, since Europe has significant trade ties with Iran and considerably more applicable soft power influence than the US. The EU soft power induces nations to alter sometimes passionately held beliefs and objectives to meet the EU norms and standards. Systems of law and governance are willingly altered and protectionist barriers against producers in other EU states are pulled down in response to EU requirements. The European Union has tremendous soft power and attracts nations from far and near.

Though hesitation to develop their military might permeated the Europeans for a quite long time, the developments of the 1990s and the realization that interaction of the two types of power – hard and soft - are today "inextricably intertwined" an intelligent combination of both could bear fruit, forced them to come out of the cocoon. The TEU signalled the intent of the member states of the Union "to move beyond a civilian power Europe and to develop a defence dimension to the international identity of the Union." Article 11 of the TEU is quite specific: "[W]ithout the backing of force and a willingness to use it, 'Europe' is unlikely to become a normative power, telling other parts of the world what political, economic and social institutions they should have."

Through its common European Security and Defence Policy (ESDP) and subsequent developments, the Union developed its military and civilian capabilities so as to enable it to perform the Petersburg Tasks – humanitarian and rescue tasks, peacekeeping tasks and combat-force tasks in crisis management, including peacemaking.[59] More than 7,000 European troops are operating under the EU flag, keeping the peace in Bosnia-Herzegovina and other operations are taking place in the South Caucasus, Africa, and elsewhere. The Union is making good progress in of building up its military capabilities, where the traditional European underperformance hindered the EU's ability to be as effective as it should have been. Within the framework of the EU Rapid Reaction Force, the first of the planned thirteen battle groups have already been setup. The European Defence Agency was also established to get better value for money in defence procurement and to increase the amount of usable military capabilities that the European governments have at their disposal. Civilian-military cooperation has been brought to a new operational level through the creation of a civilian-military cell. All these measures are expected to enable the Union to increase its crisis management capabilities so that it can successfully address the complex, multi-faceted security crises of the 21st century.[60]

However, all is not well with the EU in its role as a global player. It suffers from shortcomings and its role is severely and severally restricted by factors, both internal and external, which are beyond its control. The EU faces major problems that will negatively impact both its hard and soft power like an aging population, rigid labour markets, stagnant economic system, and failure to assimilate immigrants. Again, the system on which the European political cooperation is based on too restricts the capabilities of the EU. Not only in terms of substantive resources like financial and military power but also in terms of the ability to take decisions and stick to them, the EU is still far from being able to play the role expected of it from its *demandeurs*.[61] The failure of the EU in the Balkans, most notably in Bosnia and Kosovo, illustrates this "capabilities –expectation" gap.[62] In this regard, scholars also refer to the rhetoric and performance gap as well as the gap between preaching and practice, which eventually makes the European foreign policy more rhetorical.

The recent militarization of the EU is not without criticism with some scholars like Zielonka arguing that it weakens the EU's 'distinct profile' of having a civilian international identity.[63] However, Karen Smith suggests that the acquisition of military power would represent the culmination of a 'statebuilding' project in Europe and integration process would recreate the state on a grander scale.[64] Again, it is believed that the EU may take recourse to military force only as a last resort.

In the end, it may be concluded that the EU does not appear to be such a unique international actor and its objectives are less of the product of unique internal dynamics or its 'constitutive values' and are more a reflection of the global *zeitgeist*, only the way in which it pursues them does distinguish it from other international actors.[65]

4. What is it likely to become?

In the decades to come the EU is expected to develop into a union of about thirty-five states capable of making substantial contributions to international peace, stability, and security. Current political, economic, and social trends point towards increasing importance for soft power in international relations. This trend augurs well for the EU, which projects itself as a soft power, in spite of its developing military might of late, since it is believed that EU by its construction, temperament, and aptitude will never take recourse to 'power politics.' The fact that the EU is the cause and effect of the post-war trend of 'no' to war as an instrument of state policy remains a source of hope for peace in Europe, and for the world at large.

5. How far the EU is effective and acceptable to other international actors, international community, and world citizens?

The EU has realized the dream of its founders and the way forward. It has ensured uninterrupted peace and prosperity to the continent, and thereby to the world, by putting a premium on international organisations, multilateralism, and multipolar world order. As such, the European Project has been an enormous success, not only for Europe, but also for the world. The lesson to be learnt is to keep the narrowly defined national interests under control and to work for the broadly based international altruism.

Joseph S.Nye, a reputed American scholar on international relations, considers Europe's focus on law and institutions as an 'asset' not only for Europe but also for the world.[66] Robert Kagan too talks about Europe's "entering a post-historical paradise of peace and relative prosperity, the realization of Kant's Perpetual Peace."[67] Generally, both the American elite as well as the common people are appreciative of Europe and its post-war peace and prosperity. Especially, Joseph Stiglitz, the American economist and Nobel laureate has high hopes on Europe, which enthuse him to maintain: "Europe has succeeded because it recognizes that the rights of individuals are inalienable and universal and it has created institutions to protect those rights. Only Europe can speak with credibility on the subject of universal human rights. For the sake of all of us, Europe must continue to speak out – even more forcibly than it has in the past." He is categorical when he pronounces: "Another world is possible. But it is up to Europe to take the lead in achieving it."[68]

Again, American Liberal Institutionalists stress on a Lockean world of nation-states which tend to pursue their national interests using both the hard and soft power at their disposal preferably, within a multilateral framework of institutional cooperation, laws, and rules. Naturally, they take into account the influence of unorthodox actors such as the EU and recognize the latter as a world player even though it is not a state with all its adjunct organs, including armed forces. The liberal institutionalists sincerely believe that EU has the clout for what it is – an economic superpower with distinct social-democratic model and an example of interstate reconciliation and cooperation - what it seems to be - an active influence in the international polity and economy, especially employing its soft power - and what it is likely to become - a post-modern harbinger of peace and prosperity.

On the other hand, the Neorealists/Neoconservatives, who stress on a Hobbesian world of contending/competing great powers locked in perpetual conflict employing hard military power, tend to take little or no account of actors other than powerful nation-states, and as such, does not recognize the EU as an actor in international politics. They maintain that states alone can have foreign and security policies, thus stressing that the EU, which is not a state in the conventional sense, cannot claim to have foreign and security policies. Thus, they chide the Europeans for pretending to have a Common Foreign and Security Policy and question the very rationale of the EU – its objectives, activities and accomplishments - in its external relations. The most atrocious part of the prediction of the American realists is that Europe without the two controlling superpowers would dissolve into anarchy.[69]

The European concept of Civilian Power, by which they intend to domesticate relations between states, is incomprehensible and as such unacceptable to the American neocons. They see it as an effort to transform the international system from the Hobbesian universe into a Lockean universe; to turn the state of nature into a norm-driven community; to turn the law of the jungle into the rule of law - of treaties and contracts and UN resolutions and in short, to remake the international system in the image of a domestic civil society. The American realists and triumphalists like Charles Krauthammer ridicule the whole idea of the international system being modeled as a domestic society as fundamental fallacy and point out: "The European conceit that relations with all nations—regardless of ideology, regardless of culture, regardless even of open hostility—should be transacted on the EU model of suasion and norms and negotiations and solemn contractual agreements is an illusion."[70] And they attribute this tendency of the Europeans not to their political sagacity but to economic rapacity and "see Europeans as pursuing economic advantage through trade with America's enemies while refusing to invest in military forces needed to confront hostile regimes."[71] Indeed, one of the complaints levelled against the EU by American leaders at various times, for example, over the politics of the Middle East or the former Soviet Union, and most recently and dramatically over the 'war against terror', is that the 'trading' interests of the EU and its members have tended to crowd out the more strategic security interests seen to be inseparable from international leadership and responsibility.[72]

Moreover, the Neocons like Robert Kagan maintain: "Europeans oppose unilateralism in part because they have no capacity for unilateralism... For Europeans, the appeal to multilateralism and international law has a real practical payoff, with little cost." Kagan goes on to claim that EU is a weak power, both militarily and morally, and that the Europeans are from the 'Venus' and so, for a pacific policy.[73] Thus, the 'goodness' of the Europeans is attributed to their 'weakness.' Kagan continues this belittling of the EU while commenting on Mark Leonard's book titled "Why Europe Will Run the 21st Century", and points out to what degree Europe will even participate in the 21st century and attributed its pathetic condition to "a steady loss of self-confidence in Europe, a turning inward and a growing pessimism about the future," and adds that "the 21st century, decidedly not run by Europe, will be a very tricky time for the United States."[74]

On the other hand, quite naturally, the EU is a welcome source of financial assistance and positive, benign power in other parts of the world. Europe, with its emphasis on communalism rather than rugged individualism, is increasingly seen as a model to be emulated by developing countries seeking to integrate traditional culture with the globalization processes.[75] With its soft power appeal and advancement in a positive direction and with its values spreading across the globe, the EU is quite acceptable to them.

A public opinion poll conducted in 2005 across twenty-three countries finds that in twenty, a majority (seventeen) or pluralities (three) of citizens think it would be mainly positive for Europe to become more influential than the US in world affairs. Currently, Europe is seen as having a positive influence across the world in twenty-two countries. On an average, in all the countries polled, 58 per cent favour Europe becoming more influential than the US in world affairs. Excluding European countries, the average is 53 per cent. It is interesting to note that the most enthusiasm for greater European influence (other than in Europe) is among US neighbours—Mexico (66 per cent), Canada (63 per cent), China (66 per cent), South Africa (63 per cent), Australia (62 per cent), and Russia (60 per cent). The only countries where a majority sees this prospect as negative are the Philippines (54 per cent), and the US. However, among Americans only 55 per cent see it as negative, while 34 per cent say it would be positive, reflecting the deep political divide among Americans over US foreign policy. Among specific major countries, France is the one most widely viewed in twenty countries as having a positive influence. When asked to evaluate the current influence of the five permanent members of the UN Security Council and Europe as a whole, twenty-two out of twenty-three countries, a majority (twenty) or plurality (two) see Europe as having a positive influence in the world. On average, 68 per cent see Europe as having a positive influence and only 13 per cent see it as negative—63 per cent to 15 per cent if European countries are excluded. Steven Kull, Director of PIPA, comments, "What is notable here is that Europe, which have engaged the world primarily through economic relations—or soft power—is widely seen as having a mostly positive influence." Doug Miller, President of GlobeScan concludes: "Our research shows that Europe's star has risen."[76]

It is noteworthy that the young generation between eighteen to twenty-nine (60 percent) are more supportive of Europe becoming more influential than the US than the older generation of sixty or more (51 per cent). Excluding Europeans, 56 per cent of young people are supportive, as compared to 45 per cent of older people. Larger percentages of young people than older people have a positive view of the influence of Europe (69 per cent vs. 64 per cent; excluding Europeans, 65 per cent vs. 57 per cent). Again, those with relatively high levels of education are more likely to have a positive view of Europe becoming more influential than the US (63 per cent) than are those with lower levels of education (53 per cent) - excluding Europeans: 57 per cent and 45 per cent. Larger percentages of those with higher education have a positive view of the influence of Europe (72 per cent vs. 64 per cent; excluding Europeans, 67 per cent vs. 55 per cent). This trend works with those with higher income levels as well. Those with higher levels of income were more likely to have a positive view of Europe becoming more influential than the US; to have a positive view of the influence of Europe.

Again, in twenty-four out of twenty-seven countries surveyed in 2007 for the BBC World Service, people mostly approve of the EU's influence in the world. Overall, an average of 53 per cent worldwide say the EU has a positive influence, while only 19 per cent consider it negative. Moreover, when asked whether they would like Europe to become more influential than the United States, the majority around the world say yes. Naturally, European public are among the most positive about the EU's global role. Even when EU member states are excluded, the union's image is rosy: in sixteen out of nineteen non-EU countries the most common opinion is that the EU plays a constructive role in world affairs. On average 48 per cent say the EU's influence is positive, while only 22 per cent say that it is negative. Two of the three exceptions are in the Middle East.[77]

Moreover, the EU policies seem to be effective and fruit-yielding. The 80,000 pages of laws the EU has developed since the common market was formed in 1957, influencing everything from genetic labelling to human rights, have allowed Europe to "syndicate" its legislation and values across the world – from Russia to Rwanda. It does this by making access to its market conditional on compliance with its mores. Even US companies have been forced to follow European regulations in at least three spheres: mergers and acquisitions, GM foods, and data privacy. Again, Europe's obsession with the law has allowed it to transform other countries. For example, Turkey renounced the death penalty to further its chance of admission into the EU just before it said no to the US on Iraq.[78]

Conclusion

On the basis of the foregoing study it may be concluded that the EU is an international actor and global player of significance. Incrementally, the EU has become part of the club of principal actors in the world. Taken together, the internal fabric and the external profile of the Community make for a new and influential player in world affairs.[79] When it comes to the instruments needed to engineer peace, the softer tools of civilian power, Europe far exceeds America and is emerging as a "quiet superpower."[80] While some international relations scholars are not recognizing the EU as a global player, since it is not a state, European scholars like Laidi maintain: "Although Europe in no way aspires to become a super state, on a world scale it is striving to obtain recognition as a "de facto super state" on which the classic attributes of power would be conferred."[81] Again, he adds: "And if it is not a super state, then Europe has no other choice then to unite on the model of a super state, may be not like others, but a super state all the same."[82]

From the very beginning, European project has been directed towards changing the structure and rules of international relations through the initiation of the European "grand strategy" of "civilisation" and "domestication" of international politics. The EU played and continues to play the role of a civilian, soft and normative power, which is expected to bring a welcome change in the way in which the game of international politics is to be played in the 21st century.

The EU's pronouncements and rhetoric are well-taken by the international community and its credentials as an international actor for good, are well-founded and well-appreciated. However, at times, its actions fall short in both domestic as well as external fronts. To be successful, the EU needs to exercise both influence through soft power and be able to deploy hard power in a targeted and strategic way, as recognised by the European Security Strategy. The European leaders have taken certain remedial measures but success depends on further meaningful result-oriented actions. Determined internal political cohesion is a necessary pre-condition for the Union to stand up to its reputation of a global norm-setter and to perform effectively as a strategic international actor.

The present day globalised world is fast changing and it contains new dangers but also many opportunities. The EU has a major contribution to make, in at least two respects. Both through what it is: a highly successful example of building peace through integration; and through what it does - by promoting global security through cooperation. A successful and effective role played by the Europeans in the global po!itics is good for Europe and the World at large. The Union's low profile diplomacy, the obsession with the rule of law, delay in taking decision rather than taking wrong decisions hastily, and being from Venus rather than from Mars are good for the EU and for the world. After all it is well said: "Devils rush in where angels free to tread."

References

1. Sonia Lucarelli, "Values, principles, identity and European Union foreign policy", Sonia Lucarelli and Ian Manners (eds.), Values and Principles in European Union Foreign Policy, Routledge; London and New York, 2006, p. 6.
2. Juliet Lodge, "European Political Cooperation: towards the 1990s", Juliet Lodge (ed.), The European Community and the Challenge of the Future, Pinter Publishers; London, 1989, pp.225-227.
3. Kateryna Koehler, "European Foreign Policy after Lisbon: Strengthening the EU as an International Actor", Caucasian Review of International Affairs,Vol.4, No. 1, Winter 2010, pp. 62-3.
4. *Ibid.,* pp. 64-5.
5. Charlotte Bretherton and John Vogler, The European Union as a Global Actor, Routledge; London, 2006, Second Edition, p.17.
6. Gunnar Sjöstedt, The External Role of the European Community, Farnborough; Saxon House, 1977, p.16.
7. C.A. Cosgrove and K.J. Twitchtt (eds.), The New International Actors: The UN and the EEC, Macmillan; London, 1970, p.12.
8. M. Merle, The Sociology of International Relations, Leamington Spa, Berg, 1987, p.296.
9. B. Hocking and M. Smith, World Politics: An Introduction to International Relations, Hemel Hempstead, Harvester Wheatsheaf, 1990, p.75.
10. John G. Ruggie, "Territoriality and beyond: problematizing modernity in international relations', International Organization, Vol. 47, No. 1, 1993, p.172.

11. Reinhardt Rummel, "West European Cooperation in Foreign and Security Policy", Annals of the American Academy of Political and Social Science, Vol. 531 in The European Community: To Maastricht and beyond, Sage Publications, Inc. in association with the American Academy of Political and Social Science Stable, January 1994, p. 117.
12. Karen E. Smith, European Union Foreign Policy in a Changing World, Polity, Cambridge; 2008, Second Edition, p. 141.
13. Ibid., pp. 233-4.
14. Ibid., p. 141.
15. R.O.Keohane, and Stanley Hoffman, The New European Community: Decision-Making and Institutional Change, Boulder, CO: Westview, 1991, p.13.
16. Philip H. Gordon, "Europe's Uncommon Foreign Policy", International Security, Vol. 22, No. 3 ,Winter 1997-1998, p.76.
17. Hadley Bull, "Civilian Power Europe: a contradiction in terms?", in R. Tsoukalis (ed.), The European Community: Past, Present and Future,London; Blackwell, 1983, pp. 149-70.
18. Christopher Hill, "The Capability-Expectations Gap, or Conceptualizing Europe's International Role", Journal of Common Market Studies,Vol. 31, No. 3, September 1993, p. 309.
19. Anne Coulon, "EU-India Understandings on Major Global Political Issues: Where do We Stand?", p. 340, www.jnu.ac.in.
20. Desmond Dinan, Ever Closer Union – An Introduction to European Integration, Hampshire; Palgrave Macmillan, 2005, Third Edition, p. 519.
21. Roy H. Ginsberg, The European Union in International Politics: Baptism by Fire, Lanham, MD: Rowman and Littlefield, 2001, passim.
22. Zaki Laïdi, EU Foreign Policy in a Globalized World – Normative Power and Social Preferences, Routledge, London and New York, 2008, p.5.
23. Bretherton and Vogler, n. 5, pp.24-29.
24. Nathalie Tocci, "When and why does the EU act as a normative power in its neighbourhood?" in What prospects for normative foreign policy in a multipolar world?, Working Paper No. 29, European Security Forum, July 2008.
25. François Duchene, "The European Community and the Uncertainties of Interdependence", K. Kohnstamm and W. Hager, A Nation Writ Large? Foreign-policy Problems before the European Community, London, Macmillan, 1973, pp. 19-20.

26. Zaki Laidi. Norms Over Force -The Enigma of European Power, Palgrave Macmillan, New York, 2008, p.38.
27. Romano Prodi, "2000-2005: Shaping the New Europe", Speech to the European Parliament, Strasbourg, February 15, 2000, Speech/00/441, p.3.
28. In this regard, Arnold Wolfers' classical distinction between "possession goals" and "milieu goals", while he evaluates foreign policies of the EU member states, is quite pertinent: "possession goals" are objectives that a state seeks to fulfil in a given context, usually at the expense of others (for example, concerning the distribution of power and influence in European institutions, a country will prefer a higher voting quota, a larger or smaller number of members of the European parliament, etc.). On the other hand, milieu goals aim at not to defend or increase possessions one holds to the exclusion of others, but attempts instead at shaping conditions beyond one's national boundaries.
29. http://www.futurecasts.com/book%20review%206-4.htm.
30. Lucarelli, n. 1, pp.1-10.
31. Ian Manners, "Normative Power Europe: A Contradiction in Terms?", Journal of Common Market Studies, 2002, Vol. 40, No. 2, pp. 239-41.
32. Ibid.,p.240.
33. Ian Manners, "The Constitutive nature of values, images and principles in the European Union", in Lucarelli and Manners , n. 1, pp. 20-38.
34. Ibid., pp.39-41. According to Manners, the three Europes are: state Europe, self-image of the EU as being constructed from liberal-democratic member states who choose to confer competence on the Union; supranational Europe, self-image of the EU as a union of states representing Kantian pacific federation as well as the supranational incarnation of European identity and cosmopolitan Europe, self-image of the EU as a union of people promoting the Kantian cosmopolitan rights of hospitality to strangers, common rights to the earth's surface, and universal community. In this respect, the cosmopolitan self-image is one in which the EU constitutes a decisive break with all previous political and legal history.
35. Laidi, n. 26, p.39.
36. Stephan Keukeleire and Jennifer MacNaughtan, The Foreign Policy of the European Union, Palgrave Macmillan, 2008, p.334.
37. Ibid.,
38. Bretherton and Vogler, n. 5, p.223.

39. Pierre-Yves Monjal, "European Union in the 21st Century World: A Successful Example of Regional Organization", B.Krishnamurthy and Geetha Ganapathy Doré (eds.), Changing World Order: India, EU and US – A Trialogue, New Delhi; Shipra Publications, 2009,p. 43.
40. Jean-Claude Trichet, "Europe Turns 50", The Wall Street Journal, March 23, 2007.
41. Laidi, n.26, p.139.
42. Stefania Panebianco, "Promoting human rights and democracy in European Union relations with Russia and China",Lucarelli and Manners, n. 1, p.131.
43. Laïdi, n. 22, p. 4.
44 Manners, n. 31, p. 236.
45. Speech by Romano Prodi, President of the European Commission, titled "For a strong Europe, with a grand design and the means of action" delivered at Institut d'Etudes Politiques, Paris on May 29, 2001,http://www.cie.gov.pl/futurum.nsf/0/89E3C36770C7CBD8C1256CAB0028A5EE.
46. Giovanni Grevi, "Reflections after the No votes: What makes the EU an international actor?", November 2005, http://www.iss.europa.eu/nc/actualites/actualite/browse/29/article/reflections-after-the-no-votes-what-makes-the-eu-an-international-actor/?tx_ttnews[page]=2&cHash=fc49b40f39
47. Charles Kupchan, The End of the American Era: US Foreign Policy and the Geopolitics of the Twenty First Century, New York, Alfred A. Knopf, 2002, p.145.
48. Jeremy Rifkind, The European Dream: How Europe's Vision of the Future is Quietly Eclipsing the American Dream, Polity Press, Cambridge, 2004.
49. R.Reid, The United States of Europe: The New Super Power and the End of American Supremacy, Penguin, London, 2004.
50. Gordon, n. 16, p.75.
51. Ibid., p.100.
52. http://europe.eu.int/comm/external_relationss/nfewss/patten/sp02_134.htm (14-06-02) Developing Europe's External Policy in the Age of Globalisation (Speech by Chris Patten, the then European Commissioner for External Relations on April 4, 2002).
53 Krishnamurthy and Doré, n. 39, pp. 178-81.
54. http://europe.eu.int/comm/external_relationss/nfewss/patten/sp02_134.htm (14-06-02) Developing Europe's External Policy in the

Age of Globalisation (Speech by Chris Patten, the then European Commissioner for External Relations on April 4, 2002).

55. B.Krishnamurthy, "Turkey's Membership in the European Union: Human Rights Factor", Journal of the Institute for Research in Social Sciences and Humanities, Vol. 2, No. 2, July 2007, pp.247-64.
56. The Economist, March 17, 2007.
57. Bretherton and Vogler, n. 5, p. 136.
58. Hill, n. 18, p. 109.
59. Krishnamurthy and Doré, n. 39, pp.175-6.
60. Javier Solana, "The Future of the European Union as an International Actor", http://www.consilium.europaeu/uedocs/cms_data/docs/pressdata/eu/articles/84347.pdf.
61. Hill, n. 18, pp. 113-6.
62. Georgi Kamov, "EU's role in Conflict Resolution: The Case of Eastern Enlargement and Neighborhood Policy Areas", June 2006.p.16 www.iehei.org/bibliotheque/memoires/2006/Kamov.pdf .
63. J. Zielonka, Explaining Euro-Paralysis: Why Europe is Unable to Act in International Politics, Macmillan, Basingstoke, 1998, p. 229.
64. Karen E. Smith, "The End of civilian power EU: a welcome demise or cause for concern?", International Spectator, 2000, Vol.35, No.3, p. 27.
65. Smith, n. 12, pp. 231-4.
66. Joseph S.Nye, "Europe's Power to Lead", February 2008, http://www.project-syndicate.org/commentary/nye54.
67. Robert Kagan, "Power and Weakness - Why the United States and Europe see the world differently", http://www.hoover.org/publications/policyreview/3460246.html.
68. Joseph E. Stiglitz, "The EU's Global Mission", http://www.project-syndicate.org/print-commentry/stiglitz85/English. (18/6/2008).
69. John J. Mearsheimer, "Back to the Future – Instability in Europe after the Cold War", International Security, Summer 1990, Vol. 15, No. 1, pp.5-56.
70. Charles Krauthammer, 'The New Unilateralism', Washington Post, June 8, 2001, p. A29.
71. William Wallace, "Europe, the Necessary Partner", Foreign Affairs,vol. 80, No. 3, May-June 2001, p.20.
72. Michael Smith, 'The framing of European foreign and security policy: towards a post-modern policy framework?", Journal of European Public Policy, Vol. 10, No. 4, p.568.

73. Kagan, n. 67.

74. Robert Kagan, "In Europe, A Slide Toward Irrelevance", June 15, 2008, http://www.washingtonpost.com/wp-dyn/content/article/2008/06/13/AR2008061302639.html.

75. Don Melvin, "Quickly, quietly the EU gains superpower status", Cox News Service, Friday, May 06, 2005, http://www.oxfordpress.com/hp/content/shared/news/world/stories/05/08_EUROPE_SUPERPOWER.html.

76. 23 Nation Poll: Who will Lead the World?, April 6, 2005, http://www.worldpublicopinion.org/pipa/articles/views_on_countriesregions_bt/114.php?lb=btvoc&pnt=114&nid=&id= The poll of 23,518 people was conducted by the international polling firm GlobeScan together with the Program on International Policy Attitudes (PIPA) at the University of Maryland. Polling was conducted by GlobeScan's network of national Research Partners from Nov. 15, 2004 to Jan. 5, 2005 with a total of 23,518 people. In eight of the countries, the sample was limited to major metropolitan areas. The margin of error per country ranged from +/-2.5-4%.

77. World Publics See European Union as a "Positive Influence",March 21,2007,http://www.worldpublicopinion.org/pipa/articles/views_on_countriesregions_bt/335.php?lb=btvoc&pnt=335&nid=&id = The BBC poll was conducted by Globe Scan and the Program on International Policy Attitudes of the University of Maryland, which publishes WorldPublicOpinion.org. Interviews took place between November 2006 and January 2007.

78. Mark Leonard and Richard Gowan, "Implementing the European Security Strategy",www.fpc.org.uk.

79. Rummel, n. 11, p.121.

80. Iskra Kirova, "The European Union, A "Quiet Superpower" or A Relic of the Past", March 30, 2007- 1:17PM PDT, http://uscpublicdiplomacy.com/index.php/newsroom/specialreports_detail/the_european_union_a_quiet_superpower_or_a_relic_of_the_past/

81. Laidi, n. 26, p.2.

82. Ibid.,p.26.

2

Being and Becoming: European Policy, Economy and Society

Subrata K. Mitra

Introduction

Europe is at cross-roads. The pace of EU enlargement and the accelerated social mobility have started challenging the stability of European society. The hardening of social attitudes towards 'foreigners,' echoes the rising sense of anxiety about the economy. Underpinning these emerging issues are the larger issues of global terrorism and Islamophobia, the international financial crisis, and emerging Asian economies that are siphoning jobs, talent, and markets away from Europe. This gives rise to several questions.

What is the idea of Europe with regard to identity, welfare, citizenship? What policies and processes are being undertaken to reach these goals? How successful are they? What course, if any, has the flow of concepts Europe- Asia; Asia-Europe taken? What can Europe teach Asia, what can it learn from the Asian context? The paper briefly describes these challenges and sets out a framework for a discussion of European responses to the challenges that Europe faces currently.

1. State of the play: facts at a glance

A brief perusal of the European press shows the extent of anxiety and rage in Europe about the state of the economy, the fear of losing rights long acquired as part of the austerity measures adapted by governments to balance their budgets and to keep the economy competitive. In particular, the presence of minorities – especially Islamic minorities – comes as a threat to the social stability, security, and integration. The following statistical details will give an idea of the presence of Islam in some West European countries with large Islamic minorities. More countries can be seen from the map of Europe, below (Maps 1 and 2).

1.1 Society and Muslim Population

FRANCE[1]

Total population: 62.3 million

Muslim population: Five to six million (8-9.6%)

Background: The French Muslim population is the largest in Western Europe. About 70% have their heritage in the former north African colonies of Algeria, Morocco, and Tunisia. France favours integration and many Muslims are citizens. Nevertheless, the growth of the community has challenged the French ideal of strict separation of religion and public life.

GERMANY[2]

Total population: 82.5 million

Muslim population: 3 million (3.6%)

Background: The majority of the Muslim population is Turkish, with many retaining strong links to Turkey. Until recently, Muslims were considered "guest workers", who would one day leave the country - a view that is changing. Steps are being taken to improve integration.

NETHERLANDS[3]

Total population: 16.3 million

Muslim population: 945,000 or 5.8%

Background: The integration of Muslims remains a concern for the Dutch government, particularly after a film-maker critical of Islam was murdered in 2004 by a radical Islamist. Netherlands favours multiculturalism, essentially the accommodation of different groups on equal terms.

DENMARK[4]

Total population: 5.4 million

Muslim population: 270,000 (5%)

Background: In the 1970s Muslims arrived from Turkey, Pakistan, Morocco, and former Yugoslavia to work. In the 1980s and 90s, the majority of Muslim arrivals were refugees and asylum seekers from Iran, Iraq, Somalia, and Bosnia. Access to housing and employment have been sources of concern for Muslims in Denmark. (A minority have citizenship).

Map 1: Muslim Populations in Europe Countries

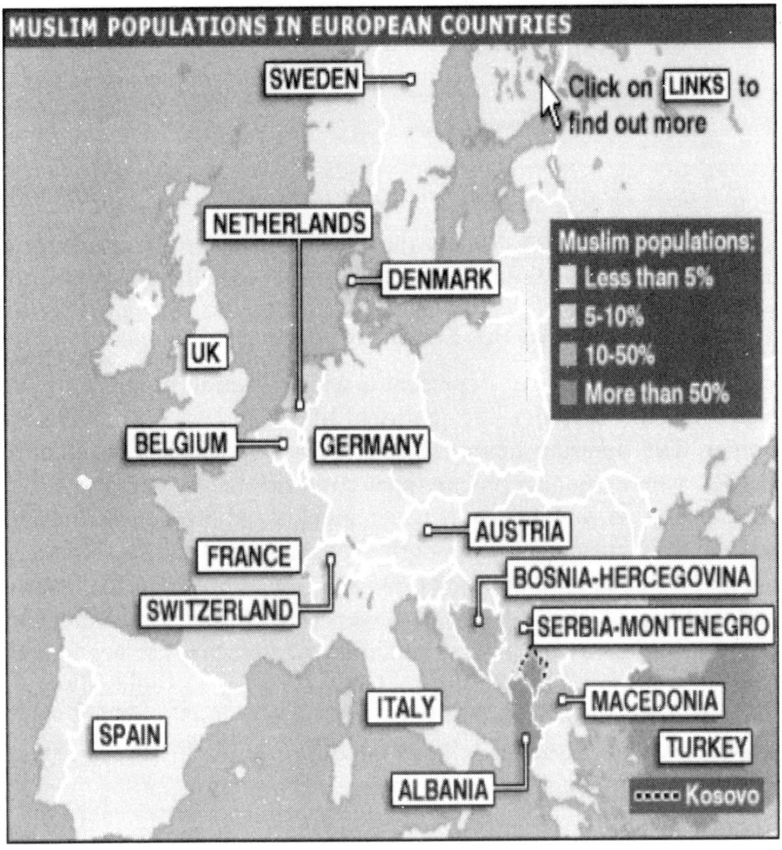

Map 2: Distribution of Muslim Population in Europe

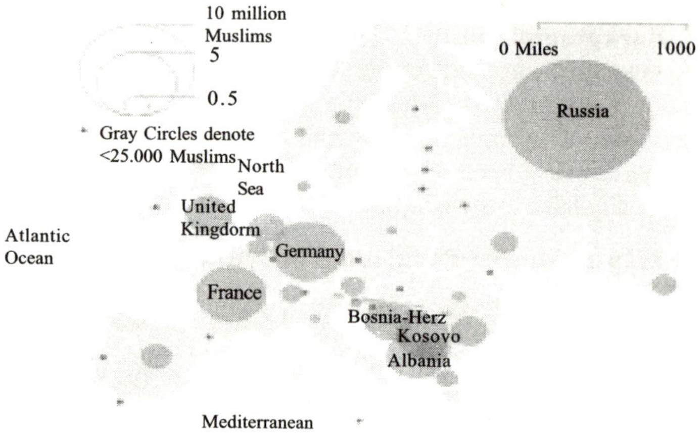

Source: Mapping the Global Muslim Population A Report on the Size and Distribution of the World's Muslim Population ANALYSIS October 7, 2009

1.2 The variation in the Economy

European countries represent a wide variation in terms of per capita income as well as the quality of life, as seen in the purchasing power. The diagram below shows the wide variation in income (EUR), where one can quickly spot countries below and above the EU average, as well the gap between income and level of purchasing power. That indicates the strength or weakness of the social safety net that the country in question provides. Not surprisingly, the culture and tradition of the welfare state lingers on in former East European countries whereas the liberal capitalist western market economies have moved on with the march of liberalisation and globalisation, without necessarily bringing down the *average* quality of life. This may, however, conceal islands of deprivation in the midst of affluence. (See diagram 1 below)

Diagram 1: GDP per capita at current market prices, 2008 (EU-27 = 100%)

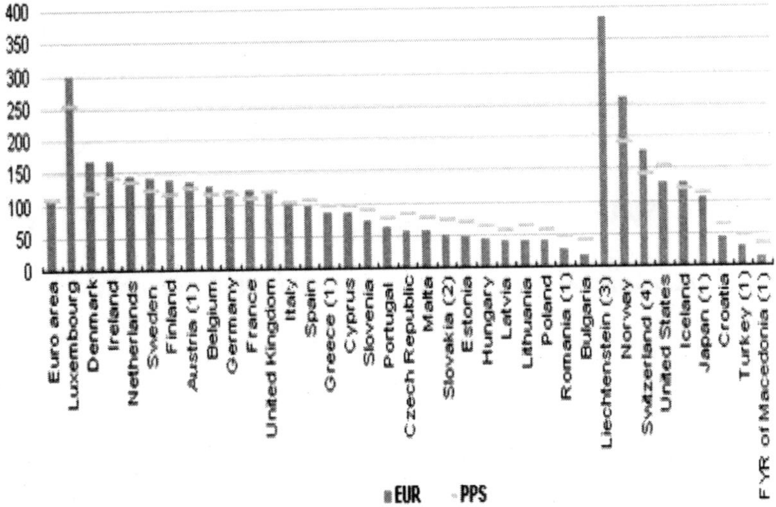

(1) Forecast. (2) Estimate. (3) 2006. PPS not available. (4) Provisional.
Source: Eurostat (nama_gdp_c and tec00001)

2. Making the French, English, Germans, etc. 'Europeans': Why does 'citizenship' work, sometimes?

In the contemporary world, globalization, which was meant to make citizenship and national boundaries increasingly less salient, has in fact revived their importance. The agenda of contemporary international politics is crowded with competing claims of the state and supra-stage agencies on the loyalty of individuals and ethnic groups. In the absence of a global political order with binding character, nation-states, acting in their capacity as the collective voice of their citizens, remain the most important agents of accountability and enforcement. The complex process through which subjects and immigrants become citizens, thus, pitches territoriality and ethnicity as competing norms for the entitlement to citizenship. Caught in this double bind, citizenship has become a contested category and a political problem of global importance. (see Figure 1)

Figure: 1

Overlapping circles of state and society

The Modern 'Post-colonial' State, Traditional Society and Citizenship: Overlapping Legal and Moral Categories

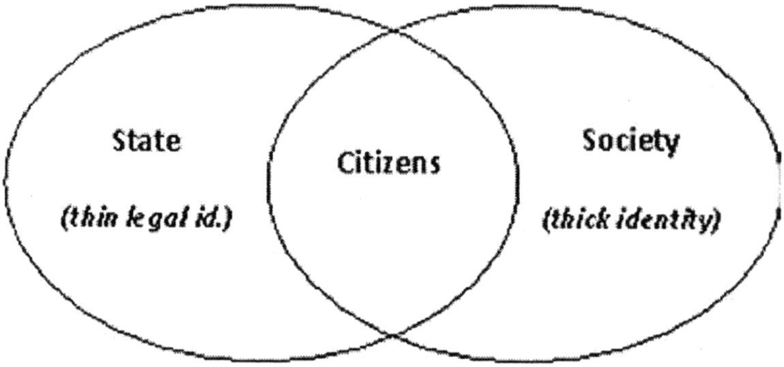

My past research on the Indian case – a federal multi-cultural state with problems of social integration, dissidence and the threat of terrorism comparable to Europe - suggests a neo-institutional model as the basic framework for the discussion of European responses to the emerging problems. (see Figure 2)

Figure: 2

Culture, Context and Strategy in Turning Subjects into Citizens: A Rational Choice, Dynamic Neo-Institutional Model

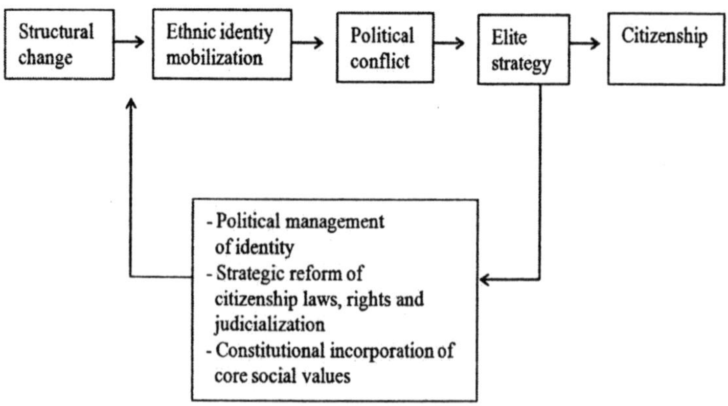

2. The challenge of citizenship in the European Union

Theories of citizenship are based mostly on the concept of national states. The European Union – uneasily situated between a federation and a confederation – is a *hybrid political entity*. As such, extending the idea of citizenship to the people of the twenty-seven European states that have come together in this novel political entity is both complex, and challenging.

In view of the above, it can be argued that citizenship in the European Union is different from what the common usage implies.[5] It is both transnational and dual in the sense that it is linked to citizenship of the member states of the European Union. Every citizen of a member state is automatically a citizen of the Union. The various types of relationships between citizenship and political frameworks, the different dimensions of citizenship, as well as the different categories of migration with respective national and EU regulations are quite complex. There are four dimensions involved in citizenship. There is a *legal dimension* which refers to the formal rights and duties of citizens and stands in the tradition of liberal thought. The *psychological dimension* refers to the sense of belonging, a person's identification with the community. It is an affective aspect and is closely linked to tradition, culture, religion, ethnicity, etc. Third, there is the *political dimension* of citizenship which refers to the participatory rights of the citizens, foremost the right to vote and contest as a candidate; it is an aspect of political philosophy. Finally, there is a *social and economic dimension* of citizenship referring to the social or welfare rights for support in situations of need.

The social, political, legal, and economic dimensions of citizenship are crucial in the context of the EU. Industrialization processes in Western societies were accompanied by social demands on the state to protect the poor and disabled. As a result the fight for social protection encompasses the market economy with free mobility within the society. Since the EU has no uniform social policy, this dimension is taken care of by the member states and, as a future project, enshrined in the Fundamental Rights of the European Union of 2000. The constitutional requirements do not insist on the equality of the conditions of life as was the case in the Federal Republic of Germany. However, the regional (Art. 130c), structural and cohesion

(Art. 130d) funds as well as the social fund (Art. 123) aim at adjusting the economic and social conditions among the member states. In the Chapter 'Solidarity' of the Fundamental Rights of the EU the following rights are mentioned:

- Workers' right to information and consultation (Article II-27)
- Right of collective bargaining and action (Article II-28)
- Right of access to free placement services (Article II-29)
- Protection of workers in the event of unjustified dismissal (Article II-30)
- Fair and just working conditions (Article II-31)
- Prohibition of child labour and protection of young people at work (Article II-32)

These rights however, express more of intentions than reality in terms of practice. They are not enforceable, and the influx of migrants – from poorer countries to Europe, and within Europe, from poorer parts to the richer parts – has added further tension to an already highly emotive issue. This has consisted of a variety of population flows, such as Labour migration [seasonal labour, *au pair*, guest labour (Gastarbeiter)]; Asylum seekers; Refugees [civil war refugees, expelled people (Vertriebene)][6]; Foreign experts, Green card; Ethnic mobility ;Immigration[7]; and, Illegal migration, organized crime, drug-trafficking.

3. The challenge of dual citizenship of the European Union

European citizenship is dual: it is in addition to national citizenship of member states and does not replace national citizenship. There is no exclusive European citizenship, only a citizen of a European Member State can become a European citizen and not vice versa. The border line between in and out is clear: only citizens of a member state acquire European citizenship. The question of identity is left to individual legal arrangements.

Summing up the politics of citizenship and migration, there is a tendency to extend the rights of individuals from the economic to the political domain. Also, the EU has gained competences especially in the fields of asylum, border control, refugees, immigration policy, combating terrorism, drug-trafficking, and visas which in the future should – as a consequence of the Schengen agreement - become common European law (asylum and refugees is already in the first pillar). Other fields such as labour migration, foreign experts or ethnic mobility - because of different national situations - belong to national jurisdiction and are mainly dictated by the economic cycle or demographic developments. On the whole, European citizenship gives its citizens more rights than obligations. According to the principle of subsidiarity and as a rule, those policy fields which show national specifics should belong to national jurisdiction, whereas issues that concern the common "space of freedom, security and law" should become community law.

European citizenship is thus derived from national citizenship, coordinated or intermingled trans-nationally. Since the EU is not a state, it cannot have the same quality in passing citizenship to individual members of the European Union. European citizenship is additional to national citizenship and does not replace it. It depends on the political will of the member states to implement the far reaching rights proposed by laws and constitutional principles.

In order to implement a common market *the Treaty Establishing the European Economic Community (EC Treaty) of 1957 states in Article 3 "the abolition, as between Member States, of obstacles to freedom of movement for persons, services and capital" i.e. the abolishment of customs, duties, and quantitative restrictions.*

The Treaty on European Union Treaty (Maastricht, TEU) of 1992, states in the part on **Citizenship of the Union, Article 8**,:

1. Citizenship of the Union is hereby established. Every person holding the nationality of a Member State shall be a citizen of the Union.

2. Citizens of the Union shall enjoy the rights conferred by this Treaty and shall be subject to the duties imposed thereby.

Article 8a:

1. Every citizen of the Union shall have the right to move and reside freely within the territory of the Member States.

Article 8b:

1. Every citizen of the Union residing in a Member State of which he is not a national shall have the right to vote and stand as a candidate at municipal election in the Member State he resides, under the same conditions as nationals of that State.

2. The same right holds for elections of the European Parliament and also the right to petition to the European Parliament and may apply to the Ombudsman.

Article 8c

Every citizen of the Union shall, in the territory of a third country in which the Member State of which he is a national is not represented, be entitled to protection by the diplomatic or consular authorities of any Member State, on the same conditions as the nationals of that State.

Article 8d:

Every citizen of the Union shall have the right to petition the European Parliament in accordance with Article 138d.

Every citizen of the Union may apply to the Ombudsman established in accordance with Article 138e.

Rights of citizens of the Union are further elaborated in subsequent treaties and on policy frameworks.

4. European response: Policy & Legislation

Following are some legislative and policy measures that have been taken to promote social and economic integration in the EU.

Table: 1

Measure	Date of treaty (opening for signature)	Member States who are party to the instrument	Remarks
International Covenant on Economic, Social and Cultural Rights (CESCR)	1966. Entry into force 03.01.1976	All Member States: Austria rat., 1978; Belgium, rat., 1983; Denmark, rat., 1976; Finland, 1976; France rat., 1981; Germany rat 1976; Greece rat., 1985; Ireland rat., 1990; Italy rat., 1978; Luxembourg rat., 1978; Spain rat., 1977; Sweden rat., 1976; UK, rat., 1976 [424]	
European Convention for the Protection of Human Rights and Fundamental Freedom (ECHR) The Secretary-General may request parties to provide explanations on the manner in which their domestic law ensures the effective implementation of the Convention.	1950. Entry into force 03.09.1953	All Member States: Austria into force since 1958; Belgium into force since 1955; Denmark into force since 1953; Finland into force since 1990; France into force since 1974; Germany into force since 1953; Greece into force since 1974; Ireland into force since 1953; Italy into force since 1955; Luxembourg into force 1953; Netherlands into force since 1954; Portugal into force since 1978; Spain into force since 1979 Sweden into force since 1953; UK into force since 1953. [425]	**Austria**: Entire convention is transposed on constitution leve. **Denmark**: Incorporated in law 1992 law, Act no. 285 of 29 April, 1992. **Ireland**: Incorporation into Irish legislation in progress. **Luxembourg**: Approved by a law of 29.08.1953. **UK**: Incorporated into UK Law by the Human Rights Act 1998.
Protocol 12 to the European Convention on Human Rights and Fundamental Freedoms	04.11.2000. Not entered into force yet	(Austria, 2000); (Belgium, 2000), (Finland, 2000); (Germany, 2000); (Greece, 2000); (Ireland, 2000); (Italy, 2000); (Luxembourg, 2000); (Netherlands, 2000); (Portugal, 2000). [426]	**Denmark**: Protocol 12 has not yet been signed. **Ireland**: Protocol 12 has been signed, but not ratified. **Luxembourg**: Protocol 12 has been submitted to Parliament for approval in 2003. **UK**: Protocol 12 has not yet been signed

continued...

International treaties on the protection of migrants/minorities and on discrimination

Measure	Date of treaty (opening for signature)	Member States who are party to the instrument	Remarks
UN-International Convertion on the Elimination of all forms of Racial Discrimination (ICERD) The Convention is monitored and reviewed by a Commitee on the Elimination of all Forms of Racial Discrimination (CERD) comprised of international experts.	1966. Entry into Force: 1969	All Member States: Austria, rat, 1972; Belgium, rat, 1975; Denmark, rat, 1972; Finland, rat, 1970; France, rat 1971; Germany, rat, 1969; Greece, rat, 1970; Ireland, rat, 1978; Netherlands, rat, 1972; Portugal, rat, 1982; Spain, rat, 1969; Sweden, rat, 1972; UK, rat, 1969[420]	**Austria**: Austria; adopted at constitutional level (BGBI. 390) 1973. In February, 2002 the Republic of Austria made a declaration under Art. 14 of ICERD recognising the competence of the Commitee for the Elimination of Racial Discrimination to examine individual complaints. **Denmark**: Act No. 459 of 12 June, 1996 on prohibition of differential treatment in the labour market was adopted as a consequence. **Germany**: Art. 14 signed: 31 August, 2001 **Greece**: Ratified and enacted by law No. 494/1970. **Ireland**: Ratified 19 December, 2000, entered into force on 28 January, 2001. **Italy**: Implemented by law No.654 of 13 October, 1975. Portugal: Enacted by law No. 7/82, April 29, 1982.
Council of Europe's Framework Convention for the protection of National Minorities	1995. Entry into force 01.02.1998	Austria, in force since 1998; Belgium, 2001; Denmark in force since 1998; Finland in force since 1998; Germany in force since 1998; Greece, 1997; Ireland in force since 1999; Italy in force since 1998; Luxembourg, 1995; Netherlands, 1995 Portugal in force since 2002; Spain in force since 1998; Sweden in force since 2000; UK in force since 1998[421].	**Germany**: Took obligation to support the four recognised minorities. **Netherlands** Wet Samen Act (1998) is an implementation of section 2.2 of the ICERD[422] **France**: The Conseil d'Etate considered in its advice to the government of 6th July , 1995, that the Convention was incompatible with the Constitution.
International Covenant on Civil and Political Rights (CCPR)	1966. Entry into force 23.03.1976	All Member Staes: Austria, rat, 1978; ; Belgium, rat 1983; Denmark, rat, 1976; Fnland, rat, 1976; France, rat, 1981; Germany, rat 1976; Greece, rat, 1997; Sweden, rat, 1976; UK, rat, 197[423]	**Greece**: Ratified by law 2462/1997 (FEK 25A/26.2.1997).

continued...

Measure	Date of treaty (opening for signature)	Member States who are party to the instrument	Remarks
ILO Convention 111 on Discrimination (Employment and Occupation)	1958. Entry into force 15.06.1960	All Member States: Austria, rat, 1973; Belgium, rat, 1977; Denmark, rat, 1960; Finland, rat, 1970; France, rat, 1981; Germany, rat, 1961; Greece, rat, 1984; Ireland, rat, 1999; Italy, rat, 1963; Luxembourg, rat, 2001; Netherlands, rat, 1973; Portugal, rat, 1959; Spain, rat, 1967; Sweden, rat, 1962; UK, rat, 1999. [431]	Greece: Ratified by law 1424/1984 (FEK 29A/14-03.1-984).
ILO Convention 117 on Social Policy (Basic Aims and Standards)	1962. Entry into force 23.04.1964	Italy, rat, 1966; Portugal, rat, 1981; Spain, rat 1973 [432]	
ILO Convention 143 on Migrant Workers (Supplementry Provisions)	1975. Entry into force 09.12.1978	Italy, rat, 1981; Portugal, rat, 1978; Sweeden, rat, 1982 [433]	**Italy**: Already covered by laws 943/86 and 286/98.
European Convention on the Legal Status of Migrant Workers. A Consultative Commitee was instituted to examine parties' reports on the application of the Convention. On the basis of these documents the Consultative Commitee draws up reports for the attention of the Commitee of Ministers.	1975. Entry into force 01.05.1983	Belgium, 1978; France, 1983; Germany, 1977; Greece, 1977; Italy, in force since 1995; Luxembourg, 1977; Netherland, in force, since 1983; Portugal in force since 1983; Spain in force 1983; Sweden in force since 1983. 434	

source: http://fra.europa.eu/fraWebsite/material/pub/comparativestudy/CS-Legislation-en.pdf

State of implementation of the Racial Equality Directive

Member State	State of implementation
AT	No: governmental legal initiative to be handled by parliament
BE	Yes, some aspects to be implemented regionally
DK	Yes
FI	Yes, both directives
FR	Partially implemented
DE	No: draft law has to be discussed
EL	No: in progress, to be handled by parliament
IE	In progress (in the form of amendments to existing legislation)
IT	Yes, both directives
LU	No (there are draft legislations for both directives)
NL	No: to be approved by parliament
PT	Partially implemented
ES	Yes, both directives
FI	Yes, both directives
SE	Yes
UK	Yes, amendments to existing legislation

source: http://fra.europa.eu/fraWebsite/material/pub/comparativestudy/CS-Legislation-en.pdf

The following news items in the European press give a preliminary idea of Europe's attempts at coping with the challenge of citizen-making and bringing the economy to order.

"Roma expulsions: EU to start legal action against France"

guardian.co.uk, Wed. 29th Sept., 2010

***„Frankreich gibt im Streit um Roma nach"*[8]**

Sueddeutsche Zeitung onlne. Wednesday 14th, 2010

"Euro zone records strong GDP growth in second quarter. [...]

Germany proved the engine of the euro zone[...] ."

Reuters; Fri, Aug. 13th ,2010

"EU verdreifacht Konjunkturprognose fur Deutschland."[9]

tagesschau; Fri, Oct. 13th ,2010

"Nur in Griechenland schrumpft die Wirtschaft"[10]

FAZ.Net; Wed, May 05th ,2010

Thessaloniki, 2003: European Council adopts the "principle of integration"

as „[...] "*a dynamic, two-way process of mutual accommodation by all immigrants and residents of Member States.*"

source: EUMC, 2006. Muslims in the European Union-Discrimination and Islamophobia.

In this Context, 2005:

"Common Agenda for Integration Framework for the Integration of Third-Country Nationals in the European Union."

source: EUMC, 2006. Muslims in the European Union-*Discrimination and Islamophobia.*

5. Policy challenges and responses of the EU in Indian perception

The perceptual gap between India and the new Europe of the twenty-seven, is epitomised by European reticence regarding the global ambitions of nuclear India, and the Indian perplexity of exactly where to place Europe in a multi-polar world increasingly dominated by the United States and China, is constantly present in the media. The Indian perception is eloquently expressed by analyst C. Raja Mohan:

> Talk of Europe and you get a big yawn in Delhi. India's annual summitry with Europe is always a cold dish amidst the warmth of India's exciting engagement with the United Sates and China. When British Prime Minister Tony Blair arrives here tonight on behalf of the European presidency for the sixth India-EU summit, public interest will be focused on Britain rather than on Europe. Blair's half-a-day visit to Shimla, the old summer capital of the Raj, will surely get more television coverage than the unreadable India-EU declaration. While Indian awareness of Europe as a collective has certainly increased over the years, Euro-pessimism in London, Paris, Rome and elsewhere on the old continent reinforces Delhi's frigidity towards Brussels.[11]

Raja Mohan succinctly expresses the core components of the Indian diagnosis of the European malaise:

> High unemployment, low growth rates, opposition to migration of skilled labour, and the apparent inability to deal with the imperatives of globalisation amidst the rise of India and China have made the European economic future uncertain. Europeans feel trapped between aggressive American capitalism and perceived Asian mercantilism. As America threatens to widen its technological gap with Europe, China takes away manufacturing jobs and India eats into the service sector employment. The stalling of the European project after the French and Dutch rejection of the constitutional treaty, the demographic decline, the challenge of assimilating a restive Islamic minority and the emergence of home-grown terrorism, reinforce the image of Europe on the decline.[12]

Reciprocally, the confusion regarding the identity, profile, and intentions of the new Europe as seen from India are like watching Pirandello many times over. The confusion in the Indian mind about "twenty-seven characters in search of a voice"[13], or, what the "sense of Europe" exactly means, derives not just from the content of policies, values, and identity, but also from its form – one parliament, one executive, one currency, one agricultural policy claiming to speak for a multitude of voices. While one may be aware of Great Britain, and continental countries such as Germany, France, Belgium or Poland, Europe of the twenty-seven, in wake of the eastward expansion, is a novelty. Indian political scientist Rajendra Jain articulates his views on the difficulty of comprehending the new Europe in the following words:

After enlargement, the EU decision-making processes would become even more complex and potentially more difficult for Indian policymakers to interpret and to influence. Indian foreign policy has tended to traditionally concentrate on four large member states of the European Union, viz., France, Germany, the United Kingdom, and Italy, since they are major players in trade, FDI, joint ventures, industrial collaborations, and technology transfer. However, in the "new" Europe, India needs to devote greater political energy and attention to developing closer linkages with some of the new entrants especially Poland (apart from Spain). For many Indians, the enlarged European Union requires a re-profiling of mindsets about a changing European Union in a changing Europe, which in some respects will no longer be what it used to be.[14]

In the opinion of an Indo-European team of authors, the relative vagueness of the "Idea of India" finds its match in the diffuse character of a sense of Europe in terms of the 55% no vote in France to the project of a tighter, binding, European constitution. They explain the diffused character of a "sense of Europe" in the following words.

In contemporary India, a sense of a Europe beyond or above its constituent nations is shadowy at best. Commerce may demand recognition of the European Community, finance, the Euro, and travel, the Schengen. But all these are associated with a Europe of nation states and only vague notions exist of the European Parliament, the European bureaucracy etc, – a situation merely complicated by experience when European institutions require engagement.[15]

6. India and Europe in a multi-polar world

Where does Europe fit within the main framework of post-independence India's foreign policy? Appendix 1 gives salient points in the chronology of this growing relationship. The concerns and conditions that account for this growing relationship are, respectively, the sheer volume of Indo-EU trade, the past pivotal positioning of the EU with regard to Indo-US relations (which India often perceived as biased towards Pakistan and China), Indian apprehensions regarding EU's protectionist agricultural policy, and most saliently, what Arjun Sengupta has called the "natural affinity" of India and the new Europe.

As things stand at the moment, the EU is India's largest trading partner. It is the largest overseas investor in India, much of it in areas of high technology (23 percent of total exports) and investment (25 per cent of the total). Business summits have regularly been held to accompany the political summits. Europe, from the point of view of Indian strategists, provides a much valued chink in the western armour. Thus, Arjun Sengupta holds, "that unlike the US, the EU cannot be considered to be a power that has an interest in dominating another country; it is not possible for the EU to think of pre-emptive strikes or of trying to dominate the policies of other states." In the same vein, I.K. Gujral, a former Prime Minister and foreign policy specialist, holds that Europe is not merely an appendage to American power.[16] Not that there are no disagreements with the EU with regard to its trade policy[17] or attitudes towards India's traditional rivals.[18] Still, in the opinion of hardened observers of the international scene, the policies of EU still represent for India a comparative advantage. One can gather as much from the position taken by Arjun Sengupta.

"... it should not be regarded as an either-or choice but within a system of alliances, some closer than the others. Unlike the US, the EU cannot be considered to be a power that has an interest in dominating another country. It is not possible for the EU to think of pre-emptive strikes. It is not possible for the EU to think of certain states as rogue states and certain states as friendly states. This is simply because the EU as such is not that kind of power which can ensure that all the states within the Union will see eye-to-eye with any of these propositions. I am not saying that they are incapable in intent. The British are equally capable of carrying out a pre-emptive strike if they could or even France at some point of time, but once they are within the EU, the equation changes. India has reached a stage where this kind of power relationship is very important. If you go through the documents of the US foreign policy you can consider how they have set up the whole global map and chosen which country should be more important than another and have built up a whole strategy to deal with that....If we look at the EU, we are not going to be bothered about that. This is a major advantage of our relationship with the EU. If you are familiar with the US conditions for becoming a partner state, whether it is Mexico or Canada or more recently the South Koreans, very categorically there is an undercurrent of conditions that the power dominance of the US has to be accepted. I do not think there is any apprehension regarding a relationship with the EU being constrained by the difficulties of the international power situation."[19]

Sengupta holds that on the contentious Kashmir issue "...the EU's position in general has been much more impartial and helpful [to India] and [not] consistently pro-Pakistan." He warns, nevertheless, that India should not take it for granted that there will be no hostile mention of "human rights violations in Kashmir and there would be protests in the EU, because that is in the nature of their system". Building further on this, he recommends that India needs to become more confident about open markets.

> ...from the Indian point of view, the challenges are much more severe because we have to genuinely believe in open trade. EU is one place where the commodities that are involved are diverse. They have different types of economies, practically at every point they have a face-to-face confrontation. So long as we are not prepared to open up and follow the principles of open trade, I do not consider it is possible for the EU to come forward. If, on the other hand, we are prepared, it is possible for us to plead for a special status. The EU has given special status to other countries outside Europe: not just African countries but also several countries in the Middle East. It started with Israel. In fact, EU-Israel had a special free trade arrangement long before the bilateral treaty arrangements were talked about. If we are prepared to accept the implications of free trade with the EU, this can be a very good way of beginning that.

Finally, the EU, compared to the USA, is seen by Indian analysts as comparatively a 'no-strings-attached business partner', and, India will be well advised to assume the responsibility of an equal partner, rather than pleading for special treatment, as one can only expect from a subaltern.

If we genuinely open up foreign investment and not bother about putting up constraints and bureaucratic hurdles, the EU is another source of investment that will be immensely beneficial to us. There is a big difference between the United States and the EU here. The US can also be a very good source of foreign investment for us, but the US has proved again and again that their foreign investment has to be very closely related to their mainland interest. This is the reason why the US is now telling the Chinese to revalue their currency because they are not importing sufficient products from American MNCs. The EU does not do that; not because they are selfless but because they belong to a particular group where they cannot do something to India which they cannot do to other members of the Union or associate states.[20]

The argument regarding the 'natural affinity' follows from the fact that "this group of countries has experienced the benefits and the prosperity that comes through a Union of a multi- ethnic, multi-religious community, something very similar to our own experience."[21] It took fifty years for the French to recognise the reality of l'Inde as compared to *les Indes*. It might take a while for the sense of Europe to replace an entity that contains but does not quite consist of England-France-Germany-Poland. Ruet, Pal Choudhury, and Vasudevan suggest that Indian diversity finds an echo in the ambiguous identity of Europe.

> Various points of common interest and mutual understanding are evident. An important intra-EU divide exists between the erstwhile colonial and the non-colonial countries. India cuts across the line often and from its own unique perspective, it has a post-colonial understanding of the world. This allows the formal colonial powers and India to arrive at an understanding of major global complexities and it is often that, that counsels the pursuit of global multi-polarity. Inevitably, India's reflective ambivalence globally is a parallel to EU's own. It hesitates

> between rejection and the advocacy of external intervention, and the evolution of EU's external policy is a mirror of India itself. In this respect, it can be said that India needs a dialogue with former colonial powers as another self, even while it strongly desires support for a multi-polar world from the EU.[22]

A comparison of the profiles that Europe and India project in their domestic and foreign policy stances creates an image of a curious reversal of roles. Beset with the problems of slow growth and domestic discontent, Europe, in its international politics chooses to repose her trust in multilateralism, international organisation and rule of law rather than unilateral intervention, much as Nehru's India had done. India, on the other hand, buoyant with robust growth, greater social harmony than the difficult 1980s and 1990s, has learnt to rely on her own military power as the key to her security. India's non-alignment of the 1950s had produced deep scepticism in the western-alliance dominated Europe. Today, with Europe, relatively free of the guiding role of the NATO, projects a profile that closely resembles that of India.

India's current security posture reflects the debates taking place between the four major lobbies in the Indian strategic policy community. The first are the advocates of 'firm India' who argue that India should project itself as a firm, powerful state and be able to use force freely marking dominant strategic theme in Indian policy. This line of thinking, powerfully introduced into Indian politics by Indira Gandhi, continues to be actively represented by those who advocate the bomb as a symbol of national power. They hold that India has evolved a 'will to act' to preserve its vital national interests. With regard to the crisis in Nepal caused by the King's dismissal of multi-party democracy in the backdrop of the Maoist onslaught on the state, India has shown both the capacity and the will to act in concert with other major powers of the world, to restore democracy but simultaneously, preserve the integrity of the state. The second major voice in India's strategic community is the peace mongering "conciliatory India" lobby. These leaders and specialists question the strategies of defence-led economic development, a boastful military profile, and too quick intervention in the affairs of neighbours. They would prefer to deal with Pakistan and China by territorial compromise and negotiation, displaying military power only to supplement diplomacy. The third trend advocates the projection of a "Didactic India", of India as a 'civilisational' state who see India's culture as a resource, a part of her inherent greatness, a valuable diplomatic asset, and that others must become cognisant of the moral quality of Indian foreign and strategic policy. The effort to tie in the Indian diaspora for the promotion of Indian culture abroad is part of this strategy. There is considerable evidence of a large-scale governmental effort to use the American-resident Indian community to advance Indian interests. The process was begun in 1970, when lobbying efforts of both Indians and sympathetic Americans were coordinated from the Embassy in Washington. More recently the Indian government has created a ministry for "persons of Indian origin" (PIOs) and "non-resident Indians" (NRIs). The fourth group combines many of the ideas of all the above lobbies but is pragmatically inclined towards building up a strong relationship with the USA as the means for best ensuring an appropriate security and economic environment for India.

One might believe that the potential for such a development between India and the new Europe, following their natural affinity, based on their countervailing cultural diversity, modern institutions grafted on ancient customs, adherence to multilateralism and belief in orderly rule based on international organisations, must be vast. Free at last of memories of colonial rule, and, at least so far, free from binding military pacts, India and the new Europe must discover their shared world views and, partnership in the new world order.

Is this scenario, as the hard boiled and sceptical neo-realist would argue, a mere throw-back to the heady days of Wilsonian idealism with a touch of Nehruvian nostalgia, indicative more of the penchant for fantasy and wishful thinking that the Orientalists expected from India than rational and strategic calculations? Or, is there, underlying the contemporary juncture of messy multi-polarity, a compelling argument for two converging non-alignments that one has not taken on board merely because of its novelty to the circles of foreign policy-makers, pessimists of the neo-realist school, addicted to short-term calculations?

Starting with its limited objective to document Indian perceptions of Europe, and analyse the gap between perception and reality, the paper has moved in the direction of uncovering the proximity in the profiles of the two, and to explore the potential for a reflexive term of discourse. What evidence might one find in the structure and process of Indian politics and the ontological foundations of her identity to give this quest a sense of reality?

With Manmohan Singh holding forth on the Bandung spirit very much in the Nehruvian mode, and the stream of international visitors calling by, those with long memories of the early years after independence might ask if Indian diplomacy is back to its well worn, noble minded but effete grooves. Such broad similarities between the past and the present are deceptive. Beyond the constants of Indian politics such as familiar faces in high places, and familiar rhetoric, Indian diplomacy has acquired a new pragmatism and a tone of confidence that distinguish it from its earlier avatars. The 1998 tests which brought India opprobrium from all possible quarters, deftly handled in its conceptualisation, implementation, and subsequent damage-limiting-diplomacy have produced an environment conducive to a new sense of realism in Indo-US strategic relations, which, in turn, has become a leading element in similar arrangements with the EU, Russia, China, and Pakistan.

However, laudable as it is, pragmatism on its own does not constitute a doctrine. By keeping one's options always open, riding on a bandwagon when it suits one's convenience and getting off at the slightest sign of trouble (Republican circles in the United States see India's position on Iraq exactly in this light, as indeed they do of France and Germany) can invite the charge of cynical opportunism masquerading as high principle. These reservations continue to hobble transactions such as the purchase of dual use technology[23] or the oil pipeline issue with regard to Iran that could, otherwise, be smooth. In consequence, though there is some recognition of mutual compatibility, US-Indian relations continue to be an uncertain pas-de-deux. This is where the role of EU as a counter balance to too close an identification with the United States is of crucial importance to India.

India's role in world politics is changing in an international context where "rules of international conduct on issues of technology and multilateralism are being re-written,"[24] roles have reversed as superpowers and supplicants of an earlier period reverse roles and a new coalition of major powers is at the forefront of efforts to reorganise the Security Council. Once again, like at the height of the Cold War, fortuitously, Indian policy has gravitated towards placing her interests in the international arena with the right combination of structural realism and national identity. Rather than being self-consciously unique and aloof, this policy is drawing on national identity (culture and ideology), and liberal values of peace and plurality. Perhaps, the time has now come for Indian diplomacy to play a trump card, whose implications they have not yet thought through, in their possession. India is alone among the main powers in the international arena today to not have been a party to the Second World War, and as such, not to have been traumatised by the devastating power of ideologies. That describes the *other face* of Indian pragmatism which gives Indian thinking a *heuristic capacity* to understand ideology – both their own and those of other societies - and the intellectual resources to negotiate across cultures.

Much more than the United States or China, it is with new Europe that India has a natural affinity and can look forward to sharing a reflexive discourse. Democratic, plural, endowed with countervailing interests and identities, and essentially non-aligned, these two entities share a lot of resources on which to build. European pacifism of the 1930s stood for something similar, before the rise of the Third Reich gave ideology a bad name, and conferred on the victorious allies an enduring right to suppress everybody else's ideology except their own, which gradually acquired the aura of an inexorable transition to development, modernity, and democracy. The forces arrayed for and against the America-led invasion of Iraq helped reveal the interests that underpin this unproblematic view of the world. In its second coming, Panchasheela as a *doctrine* should be able to build heuristically on the innate, universal desire for peace, understanding of difference, and respect for the dignity of man. The Indian search for identity can then join the European Union, also engaged in looking for a third way beyond the triumphal self-profiling of the world's only superpower and the effete bickering of those who are opposed to it. But, once again, in making this assertion, one has to be very careful so as not to fall into the trap of wishful thinking, which Nehru's foreign policy could never detach itself from.[25]

Seen from this angle, India and Europe, partners in trade and politics, stand at the threshold of a relationship that remains unconsummated at a deeper level. Raja Mohan, commenting on the unfinished agenda of Indo-European relations, captures the sentiments of Verma:

"While India and Europe say they need each other, they are yet unprepared to pursue the logic to the end. If India needs to rise rapidly and Europe wants to stay relevant, they need to exploit, quickly and intensely, the economic, technological and demographic complementarities. The values of Enlightenment – of scientific reason and individual freedom – that India and Europe share, have re-emerged as the bedrock for constructing any credible world order amidst the challenges of religious extremism and anti-modernism. In order to capture the public imagination in both Europe and India about the prospects of strategic cooperation, they need to send clear political signals and unveil visible mega projects. Europe needs to acknowledge much like the Bush Administration that a stronger India is in the interest of global peace and stability. And in practice, Europe needs to go beyond the legalistic framework of non-proliferation and open the doors for long-term high technology and defence cooperation with India."

7. Conclusion

To conclude, I will quote the Indian novelist Verma again, for to my knowledge, nobody expresses the natural affinity, and reciprocity of India and Europe better than this restless mind, equally at home in both continents, far in advance of his time, and, one might hope, harbinger of the state of things to be. I quote:

> "Two traditions, Indian and European, are still seeking a sort of completion in one another, not through a philosophical discourse or mutual cross-questioning, but by creating a 'common space' within which the voice of the one evokes a responsive echo in the other, feeling the deprivations of one's

own culture through the longings of the other. There are needs, primal and primordial, which may remain submerged or unexplored in a certain tradition for centuries, and like the keys of a piano, they wait for the right moment and just the right pressure of some 'other hand' to be able to discover the notes, strange and mysterious, though always within, us, but never heard before. Such 'listening' is both a discovery and a revelation, a discovery of the other within ourselves and a revelation of ourselves through the other. These utterances have, of course, been made by anthropologists, historians and philosophers on either side; perhaps the time has now come, for both India and Europe, to pause a little and listen to one another in silence – may, indeed, be as 'sound' a method of discourse as any other."[26]

Reference

1. Sources: Total population - National Institute for Statistics and Economic Studies, 2004 figures; Muslim population - French government estimate.
2. Sources: Total population - Federal Statistical Office, 2004 figures; Muslim population - Federal Ministry of the Interior estimate.
3. Sources: Total population - Statistics Netherlands, 2005 figures; Muslim population - Statistics Netherlands, 2004 figures.
4. Sources: Total population - Statistics Denmark, 2004 figures; Muslim population - US State Department.
5. The following arguments are taken from Frank Pfetch, "The Conditionality of European Citizenship: A concept of interrelatedness?", forthcoming in, Citizenship in the Era of Globalization: Structure, Agency, Power, and the Flow of Ideas, Edited by Subrata K. Mitra, Heidelberg.
6. According to the Geneva Convention of 1951 refugees are persons who have to leave their home country because of persecution, out of political, religious, ethnic and other reasons. Refugee politics then is the fight for the causes, regulations and integration.
7. Immigration is state regulation of immigrants from third states as well as the politics of integration (assimilation, acculturation) into a polity.
8. France accomodate on Roma issue.
9. EU Commission triples forcast for German economy.

10. Only Greece' economy is shrinking.
11. C. Rajamohan, "Lessons in chemistry: Why Blair may need to 'sex up' the India-Europe strategic cooperation", in the Indian Express, Tuesday, September 06, 2005. Seen at http://www.indianexpress.com/ 02.11.2005.
12. Ibid.
13. This is reminiscent of Luigi Pirandello's eponymous play – Six Characters in Search of an Author.
14. Rajendra Jain, "India and the New Europe" in I. P. Khosla (ed.), India and the New Europe, New Delh; 2004, p. 84.
15. Joel Ruet, Pramit Pal Chowdhury and Hari Vasudevan, "India's Europe: Cultural Footprints and Conflict Resolution Process", n.14, p. 101.
16. "Our economic relations with Europe are very good, larger than with any other region that I can think of. We look at Europe as a major powerhouse of technology with which we can cooperate and that is a very positive perspective. In addition, our past has revealed that when ever there have been difficulties with America, Europe has generally behaved differently. Therefore, whether it came to sanctions or other issues, we found a different and positive reaction from Europe and it was in our favour." I.K. Gujral, "Europe as seen from India" in Khosla, n.14, p. 13.
17. "We have sharp differences with Europe on agricultural policy. We have been told things are going to change, but they are not changing. Therefore, India is not in a position to really take advantage of globalization when it comes to agriculture." Gujaral, ibid. p. 16.
18. "The EU has a differential approach towards the two major states of Asia, i.e. India and China, in areas of trade and investment. Another power that is emerging on the Asian scene is ASEAN. How does Europe use the emergence of ASEAN as a factor in playing a role in Asia?", Gujaral, ibid, p. 17.
19. Arjun Sengupta, "Future Prospects" in Khosla, n.14, p. 94.
20. Ibid, p.98-99.
21. Ibid, p.100.
22. Joel, n.15, p.107.
23. Bertsch et.al. (Ed.,) Engaging India: US Strategic Relations with the World's Largest Democracy, London;Routledge,1999, p. 264.
24. Ibid, p.269
25. The 1961 integration of Goa by India through military intervention, and India's refusal to conduct a plebiscite in Kashmir as resolved by

the United Nations are often pointed out as examples of India's moral posturing.

26. Raja Mohan's concrete suggestion to move beyond the rhetoric of the 'natural affinity' and into the concrete act deserves careful consideration. He says, "While Europe is desperate to sell nuclear reactors and advanced arms to China, it remains squemish about genuine strategic cooperation with India. If Blair, on behalf of Brussels, recognises India's role in shaping a new, long overdue post-Yalta international system, there will be no reason for him to 'sex up' Europe in his India sojourn. If he can get Brussels to loosen its controls over high technology trade with Delhi, Blair will find it easy to turn India on." Raja Mohan, n.11.
27. Nirmal Verma, India and Europe: Selected Essays, Simla; Centre for the Study of Indian Civilization and Indian Institute of Advanced Study, 2000, p.52.

3

Cultural Diversity and the European Union

Sudarsan Padmanabhan

The European Union has had varied success in achieving consensus in economic, political, and cultural spheres. The economic sphere for its obvious instrumental and developmental benefits has seen the most robust integration. The political cooperation is still directly tethered to the nation-state framework driven by domestic necessities and problems rather than by cosmopolitan ideals. But the most contentious issues have emanated in the cultural sphere. In this paper, the mixed success of the European Union policies in the cultural sphere in negotiating cultural, religious, and ethnic diversity will be discussed. The paper will argue that the European Union's weak record in the cultural sphere could be attributed to the lack of inter-subjective engagement at the individual and social realms in negotiating vexatious issues pertaining to religion, language, culture, and ethnicity.

Introduction

The European Union is a concerted effort to create an integrated economic, social, political, and cultural framework between the countries of the European continent. The integration has been successful at various levels and arguably the utmost success has been in the economic sphere. In an atmosphere where market economy and globalization has been the dominant ideologies, the European nations, small or big, have been involved in the process of market integration. I would argue that the economic integration in a limited sense emanates from the European tradition of economic cosmopolitanism in which the benefits that accrue out of economic liberalization is universalized as a value shared by the world. But, the social, political, and cultural integration has not been very successful because the cosmopolitan ideals have not characterized the interaction between the states of the European Union in the aforementioned spheres of human activity. While the social and political domains are intertwined with the very identity of the nation-state, cultural values have always been restricted to the private sphere without discourse except within the confines of the university walls. In this paper, I would argue that the European Union in spite of establishing transnational and world bodies such as the European Parliament, The Hague, and several other initiatives is not in a position to negotiate racism, islamophobia, and other challenges to its cultural identity because of the neglect of the cosmopolitan ethic that had inspired the European Union originally. A cosmopolitan understanding would be necessary to understand and embrace cultural diversity and hybridity in an increasingly multicultural and globalized world.

Cultural Melting-pot or Multicultural Democracy

The two most dominant theories that deal with cultural diversity in liberal democracies are the cultural melting-pot and multiculturalism. These two theories attempt to define post-colonial liberal democratic experience in negotiating multicultural identities. The cultural melting-pot idea does not encourage assertion of multicultural identities. But the idea of a multicultural society requires free expression of variegated cultural identities openly. Encouraging free expression of cultural identities in a democracy also redefines the relationship between the centre and the margins, the dominant cultural themes, practices and institutions, and the marginalized cultural traditions. Discarding and neglecting alternative cultural traditions introduce discrimination into the social, political, and cultural spheres. This is true even of cultural traditions such as India, which have been traditionally multicultural. When one tradition becomes dominant, it leads to stratification in all spheres of activity. For example, the Indian tradition dealt with cultural differences in the social sphere through stratification even though innumerable cultural practices also evolved simultaneously in hybrid forms. The social stratification was the basis of hierarchy in the political, economic, and cultural spheres as well.[1] Because of the recognition of cultural diversity, there is a reversal of privilege and caste hierarchy, at present. It is interesting to observe that dynamic social interstices challenge cultural stereotypes and hypostatization while a settled procedural democracy is less sensitive to socio-cultural changes and aspirations of the margins. The philosophy of the interstitial that Homi Bhabha advocates could be institutionalized in a procedural democracy, for example, in the form of affirmative action for cultural minorities and, hitherto, oppressed classes. But once the politics of interstices is institutionalized, it ceases to be a philosophy of present.

Without a binding principle or a social commitment at both institutional and individual levels, procedures are ineffectual. The cultural melting pot or multicultural democracy as the ideal of America is a later justification of the idea of America as a symbol of freedom. In any culture, immigrants begin with a distinctive disadvantage of being treated as aliens. In countries like Germany, Britain, and the United States, legal immigrants have more rights and are not discriminated by the state and its institutions. There is a cultivated sensitivity amongst the British, German, and American populace with respect to immigrants. But events such as September 11, 2001 could drastically effect an attitudinal change among a group of people, especially against minorities from the Middle Eastern countries in Europe and North America. It is in this context that Arthur Schlesinger, Jr's observation that there is an obsessive search for the roots amongst the immigrant population of the United States which poses an interesting issue.[2] While Ronald Takaki responds that multiculturalism or multi-ethnicity could be an enriching aspect of the American society, it must be noted that America and the European Union countries that have huge population of immigrants need to have a social, political, and cultural response to multiculturalism. In so far as there is a measured distantiation between various cultures encouraged by the conception of negative or positive liberty rather than a studied engagement with other cultures, a democracy sensitive to cultural diversity would be impossible to achieve irrespective of whether a nation is a cultural melting pot or an advanced liberal democracy that encourages multiculturalism.

Consensus in a Postcolonial World

In the postmodern epoch, the originary or foundational categories have been replaced by the interstitial spaces of the binary oppositional categories such as subject-object, black-white, colonizers-colonized, and capitalist-communist discourse. While globalization has created a common market, post-colonial and post-modern frameworks have created a sense of the present in terms of subjective-identities. The post-colonial and minority groups have started experiencing the presence, while advanced liberal democracies are oriented towards the future. Hence, there is a phase-difference in the conceptualization of ideas such as democracy, religion, economy, justice, and education and what they signify for the developed and developing countries. The tyranny of the universal, which was total in the pre-modern and modern cultures, had camouflaged the interstices, which epitomize difference and instead constructed a canopy of illusion of universality.[3] In this paper, I have argued that a process of consensus cannot avoid cultural differences, conflict of identities, systematic distortions, and a clash of social and individual imaginaries. Conflict between cultural universals and particulars afflict both intra-cultural and extra-cultural discourse. In intra-cultural discourse, a debate on cultural universals and particulars depends on a shared social imaginary within a culture. In an extra-cultural discourse, there is a clash of social imaginaries of different cultures. In the former there is confusion about what constitutes cultural particulars and universals. In the latter, there is a need for conceptual clarification of social imaginaries. In order to facilitate consensus, which aims at partial or limited unanimity, a joint venture in pursuit of agreement, recognition of cultural differences, mutual adjustment of viewpoints, and flexibility in initial and final conceptual positions are necessary. While there is always the danger of panoply of individual identities dissolving into ethical egoism, at the individual level, and cultural conflict, at the social level, celebration of individual identities have immensely contributed to the colourfulness of the world in terms of variegated cultures, languages, customs, and religions. It must be noted that as Cornel West and Bell Hooks averred, historical descriptions of pre-modern, modern, and postmodern epochs have differing significance depending upon social contexts.[4]

Homi Bhabha argues that there is a cultural consciousness of the interstitial and that of the presence that characterizes the postmodern firmament. Bhabha writes as follows:[5]

> It is in the emergence of the interstices – the overlap and displacement of domains of difference – that the intersubjective and collective experiences of *nationness*, community interest, or cultural values are negotiated. How are subjects formed 'in-between', or in excess of, the sum of 'parts' of difference (usually intoned as race/class/gender, etc.)? How do strategies of representation or empowerment come to be formulated in the competing claims communities where, despite shared histories of deprivation and discrimination, the exchange of values, meanings and priorities may not always be collaborative and dialogical, but may be profoundly antagonistic, conflictual and even incommensurable?

While Bhabha's description would encapsulate the Indian post-independence cultural experience to a nicety, it is also true of most advanced countries that are addressing the issue of multiculturalism. Michael Dummett's writings on the plight of economic refugees in European and North American countries have revealed glaring deficiencies in addressing the issues of economic and political asylums.[6] Bhabha refers to an underlying process of cultural hybridization that has cultural difference at the centre. Cultural differences should be recognized and respectfully engaged. According to Bhabha,

"The borderline engagements of cultural difference may often be consensual as well as conflictual; they may confound our definitions of tradition and modernity; realign the customary boundaries between the private and the public, high and low; and challenge normative expectations of development and progress."[7]

Bhabha reiterates constantly that internationalism must be a 'middle passage' that does not totalize individual experience. A lack of recognition of cultural hybridity and the presence of the interstices have had incalculably damaging consequences as witnessed in Sri Lanka, Yugoslavia, Rwanda-Burundi, and Palestine, to name a few. Totalization of particular cultural experiences lead to exclusionary lifeworlds. Bhabha argues that the postcolonial epoch is a celebration of cultural hybridity and interstitial spaces.

The EU Countries and the Post-colonial Question

Riva Kastoryano refers to numerous riots involving North African immigrants in the suburbs of French cities, with the last big riot in November, 2005, that raged on for several days. Kastoryano argues that rioting had become a regular feature of *banlieues* (low income housing) in French cities as they had ceased being public spaces where democratization was encouraged. The outskirts or *banlieues* did not resonate as ghettoes in the imaginary of the French public, which were reserved only for the inner-city black ghettoes in big American cities. The republican-egalitarian polity of France could not tolerate *banlieues* being perceived as discriminatory or segregationist. Kastoryano explains how the lack of vertical mobility and horizontal inequality has fanned structural violence as poverty-stricken, unemployed, non-native, and immigrant population, predominantly Maghrebian, feels completely bottled by the French state. Kastoryano writes: "These places where otherness and poverty go together, where unemployment among youth is far above the national average, are presented as conflict zones between civil society and the forces of order (the police), between generations and cultures, and between national, local, and community institutions."[8] Kastoryano indicates how spatial immobility of the predominantly Maghrebian youth translates into social immobility. The converse is also equally true.

In contrast to the French *banlieues,* the Turkish immigrants in Germany remained in Kreutzberg known as *Kleine Istanbul* even after the gentrification, which provided better access to better facilities and improvement in the quality of life. Unlike the French experience, social mobility was not arrested by spatial immobility, which was voluntary. Kastoryano points out the basic philosophical difference between a republican political system in France and a social democratic political system in Germany, where integration into economy and civil society is ensured. The immigrants have to assume French identity or be excluded as a minority. The French reaction to riots in other countries in Europe such as Britain or the Theo Van Gogh assassination in Holland or the terrorist attack in London was analyzed as the result of weak national identity caused by the fragmentation of a society into various communities vis-à-vis a strong, indivisible, and egalitarian republican conception of a nation-state. Kastoryano also points out with frequent references to various immigrant communities in the French political discourse. These communities, according to Kastoryano, are taken to be in contrast to the national community. The French government encouraged voluntary associations, in this case, the ethnic immigrant organizations. Such voluntary associations lead to the formation of a collective identity, which is once again outside the political sensibilities of the French society.[9]

The pressing question that arises is whether *banlieues* have becomes communities that are territorial in some sense while existing in a sense as non-territories. Because of the local exclusion and social immobility, a non-territorial collective identity is constructed. This identity is inevitably linked to Islam in France. Paradoxically, the French state does not recognize communities and hence is not equipped to debate and negotiate with them. As Kastoryano argues, the French authorities are forced to go back to those religious and community elders from whom they seek to liberate the Maghrebian immigrant community. On the other hand, the protesters and rioters are also claiming their rights as French citizens and not as immigrants. What has been denied to them as French citizens and the discrimination and exclusion perpetrated as a result of alien ethnicity is a double alienation. Nicolas Sarkozy, the former President of France, built his political campaign on the premise of the otherness of immigrants. Sarkozy's campaign was centered on wedge issues such as illegal immigrations, assimilation, and security. All the afore-mentioned issues are directly related to the *banlieues* of the French suburbs.[10] Cesari explains how the distinction between ethnic culture and ethnic belonging is often ignored by social scientists. The double alienation in the younger generation of the immigrant population in France is due to difference and discrimination on one hand and a loss of identity on the other. Cesari calls the younger generation of immigrant North African population as victims of "post-colonial syndrome" in which the "negative imagery built up over decades of colonialism" and "social marginalization are consistently reinforced by cultural inequality."[11]

Ezra Suleiman highlights the yawning chasm between the ideal of republicanism, the one and indivisible French society, and the ground realities of the French political model. An abstract republican understanding of equality and unity has stifled voluntary associations that Tocqueville identified as the hallmark of the American democracy. But the French society and politicians continue to believe that the universalist claims of equality, solidarity, and fraternity are timeless and universal principles. The French elite are proud of their republican heritage vis-à-vis the American democracy. Suleiman argues that republicanism prefers the collective over the individual, the separation of the public – private spheres with strict guidelines for what constitutes public behaviour, with strong emphasis on secularism. The emphasis on the abstract to the neglect of social reality, has pervaded the state funded social sciences. The French state was not served by its own social scientists that were shielded from the reality of the condition of the rioters by their ideological immersion in the timeless nature of the egalitarian French republicanism. When everyone is equal how could a group of French citizens erupt into a volcano with riots spreading far and wide and raging for several weeks? A theoretical construction of equality does not reflect the alienation or social immobility of the affected group. A symbolic expression of frustration against social immobility and exclusion from the mainstream French society manifests in "ritualized attacks on automobiles" that increased exponentially during the November, 2005 riots in France and the ritualized torching of automobiles during the New Year's Eve in Strasbourg.[12]

A community of aggrieved, alienated, and discriminated people are not part of the social imaginary of the French elite because such a community cannot exist politically in the French republic. As a result, the French society and policy makers were not equipped to engage with the rioters since no analysis or hard data about the rioting population was available to the government.[13] Stephanie Dufoix argues that the French republican political model only recognizes private and public spheres, which is not conducive to address the grievance of the protesters from the *banlieues*. Dufoix labels this space after Foucault's heterotopias, which portrayed the status of colonial territories, non-public, non-private spaces governed by laws and institutions of the colonial powers. The French model according to Dufoix is not equipped to address the colonial era crimes or wrongs or of the existence of identity groups that demand group rights within the population.[14] Paul Silverstein and Chantal Tetreault blame the post-colonial urban apartheid epitomized by Jean-Marie Le Pen, Jacques de Villepin, and Nikolas Sarkozy by stigmatizing a section of the immigrant population and responding with more securitization rather than social, political, and economic response and engagement with the alienated groups.[15]

Franck Poupeau, akin to Suleiman, criticizes the failure of French sociologists to engage in rigorous scientific research to understand the reasons behind urban poverty and riots. Poupeau also points out that many neighbourhoods that had an equally high unemployment and poverty rate did not indulge in systematic violence, which was not explained due to the lack of political understanding and paucity of sociological data. Poupeau argues that it was not the poverty per se but the penalization and criminalization of poverty that inflamed the riots. Because of the failure of expert sociologists, claims Poupeau, the political system has continually failed to diagnose the festering wounds and minister to them with specific solutions rather than with general measures like immigration, Islam, internal security, republicanism, and integration into the French society. The depoliticization and desociologization of urban violence and an attitude of axiological neutrality of the experts has skewed the understanding of the social, political, economic, and cultural factors fuelling the riots. Poupeau remarks, "The move to a penal state is all the more surprising in a Europe most believed anchored in the social State."[16]

Islamization or influence of *Tabligh* or *Salafi* ideology is not the major reason for the riots. Olivier Roy indicates the failure of religious leaders to effectively mediate between the rioters and the authorities. Roy also observes that there have been almost no attacks on Synagoues or Churches. So, Roy argues that it would be wrong to attribute the riots to radical Islamization. It is a ghetto youth revolt for Roy.[17] Michel Wieviorka emphasizes the changing character of the immigrants who were earlier mostly from the Maghrebian region. The sub-Saharan descent immigrants have also increased in recent times. The frequent occurrence of suburban riots in French cities is attributed to the decline of the republican political system and the idea of social integration.[18]

Today, France is facing a general challenge, a total crisis where the social, the institutional, the political, and the cultural elements each call for huge changes, and where they don't seem to be conciliated, as was the case when industrial society, State institutions, and the Nation as a collective identity were in direct correspondence. The French model is so deeply damaged that in order to stop the riots, the Government not only relied exclusively on police forces, but also behaved as in times of war, with curfew.

While the social, political, and economic dimensions are strongly emphasized by all social scientists, the complete lack of educational opportunities in *banlieues* is also glaring. All commentators on the French riots have also identified denial.of education and employment opportunities, as the two most important factors in the disgruntlement of the youth of the *banlieues* and the ghettoisation of the French suburbs.[19]

Intersubjectivity and Cultural Hybridization

The approach that characterizes Hans-Georg Gadamer's and Emmanuel Levinas' theories of alterity is the warmth and comfort exuded vis-à-vis the "other." Heidegger grounded the *Dasein* as the dynamic being-in-the-world that straddles the ontic and the ontological level. The ontological level is not an abstraction from the ontic level.[20] But Gadamer and Levinas take the concept of intersubjective relationship to a new level by creating the optimal non-instrumental conditions for mutual interaction between the "I" and the "other." While Gadamer's philosophical hermeneutics desists from a categorical incarceration of the "other," Levinas makes the 'I' completely subservient to the "other." I would characterize Levinas' inversion of the Enlightenment prejudice towards the "I" as the tyranny of the slave. This would probably engender a dread that Sartre perceives in the "other" being the enemy.[21] Levinasian conception of the "other" could also in a remote sense lead to concepts such as reverse colonization, which does not necessarily follow from Levinas' enthronement of the "other" vis-à-vis the "I."[22] On the other hand, Levinas' enthronement of the 'other" to the detriment of the "I" could inflame the fear of the "other". Hegel frequently describes a mediational relationship between the "I" and the "other" in his political writings. Even Hegel's much analyzed master-slave relationship has a reversible moment.[23] What Gandhi characterizes as "cycle of repression" cannot be indiscriminately applied to what Hegel terms as master-slave relationship. On the other hand, structural violence and internal colonization are very much plausible in a state that does not ensure inviolable individual rights. Perhaps, Levinas wants to prevent what is traced to the supremacy of the self, perpetrated by the Enlightenment, by establishing the supremacy of the other.[24]

The failure of the Enlightenment to reconcile reason with reasonableness and to acknowledge the historicity of the theory-practice relation has created conceptual muddles. Bhabha's claim that Goethe's analysis of the unconscious character of progression of history of the peoples necessitates a philosophy of the interstitial cultures and cultural hybridization appears to be both nostalgic and romantic. In some sense, the forces that drive the process of globalization exploit, what Bhabha describes, as the voice of the unhomely, brilliantly. The question that haunts most of the procedural political theorists such as Habermas and Seyla Benhabib is whether a genuine consensus is possible in such an unhomely atmosphere. Seyla Benhabib argues that a discursive consensus is possible in culturally variegated societies and that procedural democracy is amenable to overlapping consensus. Benhabib also qualifies her description by stating that she has the late capitalistic societies under consideration.[25]

In the late capitalistic democratic framework, the relation between market and civil society is very clearly defined. In early capitalistic and developmental economies, the state regulates markets and civil society is dependent upon the state. Moreover, because of globalization the public sphere has undergone a startling metamorphosis. Social categories such as center – margins are under attack. What Habermas considers central to his project of communicative action, the linguistic-communicative competence has to be reevaluated in lieu of the tectonic shift in the center-margin relations. Thus far, liberal political theorists have analyzed the polity only in terms of the corporate-hierarchical and civil society-horizontal (liberal) social formations. What C.K. Prahlad characterizes as the bottom of the pyramid has not been the focus of political theorists because of the yawning theory-praxis chasm.[26]

Existing political theory cannot, because of the politics of liberalism, encourage a drastic rearrangement of social and political sphere in advanced liberal democracies. On the other hand, liberal society has become too fragmented to address issues within a common framework. The emphasis on competition has an osmotic effect on both the market and public sphere. Even Habermas advocates a third alternative to the existing liberal and republican conceptions of politics.[27] So, in order to redress the problems engendered by the estrangement of the public sphere, market, and the private sphere, a more cooperative interpersonal relational framework is necessary. While the distinction between market, civil society, and government stands in a broad sense, structurally the social sphere has been transformed into a clash of alterities and unhomely selves. Even social epistemologists such as Alvin Goldman are trying to grasp the cultural failures in terms of a framework of responsiveness rather than in a deeper sense of cultural particulars versus cultural universals as described by Kwasi Wiredu. It is here that Gadamer's and Levinas' respect for the "other" attains the status of an imperative. Even though Habermas indicates the absence of recognition of advanced moral development in social psychology with respect to the concept of the other, which is theorized on the basis of role formation, significant gestures, and the generalized other because of its neglect of the post-conventional rationalization potential of the human beings, it has great relevance at the level of everyday interaction and in multicultural exchanges.

Conclusion

In a conflict resolution process involving multicultural interlocutors, the ground condition for a dialogue is the recognition of mutual interests. Multicultural dialogue is asymmetric because it involves theoretical, practical, and aesthetic issues, simultaneously. Habermas' stipulation for a successful dialogue aimed at a consensus such as comprehensibility, redeemability, justifiability, and discursivity could be combined with Mead's method of social communication. In multicultural exchanges, the conventional level of social rationalization has greater utility than the postconventional. It is interesting that while Habermas criticizes Hegel for subjectivizing the 'I-Thou' relationship in the analysis of master-slave relation, the post-conventional moral understanding is an abstraction. The post-conventional stage of moral development espoused by Habermas must necessarily encompass the pre-conventional and conventional stages and there must be a vertical movement among the three stages both synchronically and diachronically. At any juncture, each member of the public sphere is at different levels of moral understanding and there is a grid of cooperation and competition that intersects each actor's life in different ways. The post-conventional stage of rationalization of Lawrence Kohlberg, endorsed by Habermas, is not a linear category. It assumes a shared cultural history, egalitarian social environment, motivational factors, and organic development but neglects the vicissitudes of individual experience. In its extreme, the post-conventional stage is fit only for a Buddha, a Jesus, or a Gandhi.

References

1. Romila Thapar, A History of India, London: Penguin Publishers, 1990, pp. 28-49.
2. Ronald Takaki, (ed.) Debating Diversity, Oxford: Oxford University Press, 2002, pp. 23-36. Refer to Arthur Schlesinger, Jr.'s article "The Return to the Melting Pot", pp. 257-260.
3. Homi Bhabha, The Location of Culture, New York: Routledge, 1994. p. 1.
4. Cornel West, "The New Cultural Politics of Difference", Cornel West, (ed.), The Cornel West Reader, New York: Basic Civitas Books, 1999.pp. 119-143; Bell Hooks, "Postmodern Blackness" reprinted from Yearning: Race, Gender, and Cultural Politics, Boston: South End Press, pp. 23-31.
5. Bhabha, n.3, p. 2.
6. Michael Dummett, On Immigration and Refugees, London: Routledge, 2001.

7. Bhabha, n.3, p. 2.
8. Riva Kastoryano, Territories of Identities in France, June 11, 2006. www.ssrc.org
9. Ibid.
10. David Rieff, Battle over the Banlieues,The New York Times, April 14, 2007.
11. Jocelyn Cesari, Ethnicity, Islam and les banlieues: Confusing the Issues. November 30, 2005. http://riotsfrance.ssrc.org/Cesari/
12. Alec. G. Hargreaves, An Emperor with No Clothes? http://riotsfrance.ssrc.org/Hargreaves/,November 28, 2005.
13. Ezra Suleiman, France: One and Indivisible, November 18, 2005. http://riotsfrance.ssrc.org/Suleiman/
14. Stephanie Dufoix, More Than Riots: A Question of Spheres, in Riots in France, http://riotsfrance.ssrc.org/Dufoix/, December 02, 2005.
15. Paul A. Silverstein and Chantal Tetreault,Postcolonial Urban Apartheid, June 11, 2006. http://riotsfrance.ssrc.org/Silverstein_Tetreault/
16. Franck Poupeau, French Sociology Under Fire: A Preliminary Diagnosis of the November 2005 "urban riots", June 11, 2006. http://riotsfrance.ssrc.org/Poupeau/index.html#e2
17. Olivier Roy, The Nature of the French Riots, November 18, 2005. http://riotsfrance.ssrc.org/Roy/
18. Michel Wieviorka,Violence in France, November 18, 2005. http://riotsfrance.ssrc.org/Wieviorka/
19. Catherine Wihtol de Wenden, Reflections "À Chaud" on the French Suburban Crisis, November 28, 2005. http://riotsfrance.ssrc.org/Wihtol_de_Wenden/
20. Hans Georg Gadamer, Truth and Method, Joel Weinsheimer and Donald G. Marshall, Trans., New York: Continuum Publishing Company, 2000; Martin Heidegger, Being and Time, Trans. Joan Stambaugh, New York: SUNY Press, 1996. pp. 77-83.
21. Jean Paul Sartre, Being and Nothingness, Trans. Hazel E. Barnes, New York: Philosophical Library, 1956. Cited from Robert C. Solomon, Introducing Philosophy, New York: HBJ Publishers, 1993. pp. 644-645
22. Levinas, Totality and Infinity, Trans. Alphonso Lingis, Pittsburgh: Duquesne University Press, 1969. Cited from Peter Atterton and Matthew Calarco, On Levinas, Belmont: Thomson-Wadsworth Publishers, 2005.

23. Robert Williams, Hegel's Ethics of Recognition, Berkeley: University of California at Berkeley Press, 2000. pp. 52-59.
24. Bhabha refers to Levinas' ethical love as "the inwardness of the subject ... inhabited by the radical and anarchical reference to the other." Bhabha, n.3, p. 17.
25. Seyla Benhabib, Democracy and Difference, New Jersey: Princeton University Press, 1996, pp. 67-94. Cornel West analyses the process of globalization with respect to the culturally marginalized groups and the problems of redefining their cultural identity vis-à-vis changed social relationships with their erstwhile masters. The cultural politics of difference emphasizes social analysis of binary categories that have historically been unquestioningly accepted.
26. C.K. Prahlad, The Fortune at the Bottom of the Pyramid: Eradicating Poverty through Profits, New Jersey: Wharton School Publishing, 2005. It is ironical that a lack of understanding about the economic status of the poor has been due to the corresponding lacuna in treating them as the 'other,' which has in turn prevented both the markets of the profit as well as the service of the needs of the poor.
27. See, Jurgen Habermas, "Three Normative Models of Democracy", Seyla Benhabib, (ed.), Democracy and Difference, pp. 21-30.

Section-II
Developments in EU

4

Restoring Trust and Confidence in Times of Soaring Public Debts and Deficits: The Case of the Euro

Kurt Huebner

1. Fiscal Conservatism is the Flavour of the Week

Fiscal conservatism has moved to the centre in many parts of the world, in particular in the Euro zone member economies where the Greek debt malaise and the severe austerity response kick-started a serious round of fiscal austerity packages in crisis-prone economies such as Ireland, the UK, Portugal, Spain, France, and the like. Financial crisis contagion spread quickly to fiscal austerity. This paper will analyze the EU and Euro zone members' response to the rise in public debt in the aftermath of the Great Recession and the sovereign debt default crisis in Greece, Ireland, and the economies of the southern core. The paper begins with some general observations on public finances and then turns to a discussion of the European efforts to restore trust and confidence into the Euro by dealing restrictively with public debts. Trust is an essential part of economic transactions, organized by markets as economic actors in order to avoid additional transaction costs, and it is especially relevant for the status of a currency. Any successful mastering of the sovereign debt crises of member economies of the Euro zone will restore the global status of the Euro.

Unlike economic orthodoxy this paper assumes that economic transactions reflect social structures and generally are in dire need of being adequately socially embedded in order to establish regularity.[1] Even though adequate social institutions are supporting trust it is not the case that social institutions automatically *produce* social trust. The production of trust can be better understood as a by-product of social interactions. I follow Fehr with his concept of trust:

An individual…trusts if she voluntarily places resources at the disposal of another party…without any legal commitment from the latter. In addition, the act of trust is associated with an expectation that the act will pay off in terms of the investor's goals. In particular, if the trustee is trustworthy the investor is better off than if trust were not placed, whereas if the trustee is nor trustworthy the investor is worse off then if trust were not placed. [2]

Trust in this sense also plays a central role in the proper working of institutional arrangements such as currency and monetary regimes, and usually is expressed in terms of reliability and calculability. It has been argued that, for example, the Stability and Growth Pact and its rules regarding public deficits and public debts, as well as the associated so-called excessive debt procedure, was meant to build reputation and trust on the side of global financial markets. If those actors were convinced that the Euro will be a safe and stable currency, then economic actors at large will make use of the new currency inside as well as outside of the common currency space.

This paper proposes that the Great Recession and its after-effects have undermined the trust in the common currency in Europe. This is due to the build-up of high levels of public deficits and debts, and the failure of the established institutional mechanisms and procedures that wanted to avoid this 'ugly situation.' Financial markets in particular see the state of public finances in the Euro zone as unsustainable, and politicians respond to this view by strengthening their efforts to restore public finances and thus return trust to the institutional architecture of the Euro. I will make the argument that the multitude of strategic responses from national governments, the EU Commission as well as from the ECB so far has not contributed to building trust in the survival of the Euro and the associated economic and social costs of the selected crisis strategies are high.

2. Public Finances and Sovereign Debt Default

Fiscal conservatism comes either as an inherent economic necessity or as a deep-seated political belief. It goes further without saying that governments like private economic actors are confronted with credit constraints. Even though the limits for state debts and deficits may not be as small as for private actors, they nevertheless exist. However, how those limits look like is no exact science but is up to the financial market community and its pricing of default risks. But a brief glance on state debts in relation to GDP makes it clear that financial markets do not treat all states equal (Graph 1).

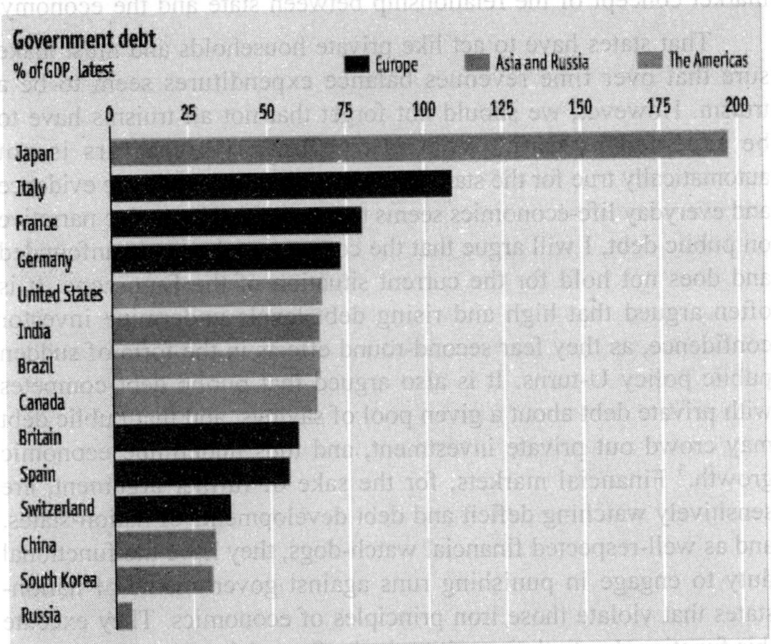

Since the financial crisis has turned into a sovereign debt crisis in Europe the vast majority of experts have acknowledged that the levels of debt are not sustainable and thus fiscal austerity needs to become the action of the day. Indeed, reasons to reduce overstretched fiscal exposure and to return to the virtues of the *Schwaebische Hausfrau*, as German Chancellor Angela Merkel famously has argued, are abundant. The most obvious reason is the existing debt levels that today bind significant portions of tax revenues and burdens future generations with a high load of public debt. It is also argued that debt levels have already been much too high before the financial crisis hit, and would rise even further if politics will not stop the underlying dynamic of public finances. States, so the argument, are using too big a share of the GDP that restricts the functioning of free markets. Not only does the threat of sovereign debt defaults require immediate action to reduce public debts but also a smooth working of private markets requires a much-reduced economic role of the state. In other words, the threat of sovereign debt defaults is used as an argument to move towards a radical market concept of the relationship between state and the economy.

That states have to act like private households and must make sure that over time revenues balance expenditures seem to be a truism. However, we should not forget that not all truisms have to be accepted as truth. What is true for private actors is not automatically true for the state. Even though microeconomic evidence and everyday life-economics seems to trump this alternative narrative on public debt, I will argue that the conventional view is unfounded and does not hold for the current situation of the Euro zone. It is often argued that high and rising debt levels undermine investor confidence, as they fear second-round effects in the form of sudden public policy U-turns. It is also argued that public debt competes with private debt about a given pool of savings, and that public debt may crowd out private investment, and thus undermine economic growth.[3] Financial markets, for the sake of further argument, are sensitively watching deficit and debt developments of nation-states, and as well-respected financial watch-dogs, they have the functional duty to engage in punishing runs against governments of nation-states that violate those iron principles of economics. They execute this function due to their position in the financial markets as liquidity provider and "risk dealers."[4] The events around the financial crisis demonstrated that such a view of financial markets is at its best naïve and in the worst case misleading. Financial markets are not executors of ironclad economic laws but are driven by sentiments, varieties of economic risks models, and interpretations of the 'macroeconomic good' that do not exactly support the scholarly and public functions they are attributed with by the public at large.

In the aftermath of the Great Recession, financial markets in general and rating agencies in particular turned their attention towards sovereign debt risks, and quickly identified critical cases: Greece, Ireland, Spain, Italy, Portugal— the list of usual suspects is well-known, and financial markets have acted accordingly in order to educate politicians and the public at large. This shift in attention can be interpreted as a move towards the emergency brake as financial market actors suddenly seem to have realized that their risk evaluations missed quite a number of critical cases. For quite some time it was the overall understanding under conditions of a common currency, financial markets no longer need to differentiate individual country risk. Sovereign risk premiums were not necessary as it was seen as the job of the Stability and Growth Pact (SGP) to direct member economies back to the accepted level of deviations. This attitude did not change even when in 2003 France and Germany responded to their violation of the SGP with strong efforts to make debt ratio as well as deficit ratios to criteria that can be interpreted by political means. As a matter of fact, during the period of abundant liquidity, financial markets were not at all concerned about debt levels, neither private nor state debts. The widely shared idea that global capitalism has moved into a period of 'Great Moderation' with low and stable inflation rates, low and stable interest rates, high rates of economic growth, and high and increasing levels of liquidity contributed to a rather benign attitude on the side of financial markets.[5] This only changed when the financial crisis hit and it became obvious to all actors that the survival of the capitalist market system needed huge financial injections by governments. Even though it is without question that in many cases pro-cyclical fiscal policies during the period of the 'Great Moderation' prepared underlying forces for increasing public deficits the key factor for the deterioration of public finances was the combined result of fiscal costs of rescues actions for the financial industry, revenue losses due to shrinking GDP, and the fiscal policy expenditure programs in order to revive economic growth. The data in Table 1 underlines that public deficit as part of GDP, went astray with the outbreak of the financial crisis. Starting in 2008, financial markets saw the stabilization costs and its impact on public finances with increasing concern, and thus started to rate country risks for the Euro zone on an individual basis. This change marked the crossover to a regime of sovereign debt default that consequently put the survival of the Euro into question. A paradoxical situation arose in that the socialization of the costs to re-stabilize the financial industry and to effectively deal with the economic crisis, created in the next financial market pressures on member economies, that eventually generated concerns about the survival of the common currency.

Table: 1

Table I.1.1: Budget balances in EU Member States (% of GDP)

	Budget balance					Structural balance					Structural primary balance				
	2007	2008	2009	2010	2011	2007	2008	2009	2010	2011	2007	2008	2009	2010	2011
BE	-0.2	-1.2	-6.0	-5.0	-5.0	-1.3	-2.1	-3.9	-3.8	-4.0	2.5	1.7	-0.3	0.0	-0.2
DE	0.2	0.0	-3.3	-5.0	-4.7	-1.2	-1.1	-1.7	-3.6	-3.5	1.6	1.6	0.9	-1.0	-0.8
IE	0.1	-7.3	-14.3	-11.7	-12.1	-1.6	-7.0	-9.4	-9.3	-10.2	-0.6	-5.7	-7.3	-6.5	-6.7
EL	-5.1	-7.7	-13.6	-9.3	-9.9	-6.8	-8.7	-13.0	-8.5	-8.2	-2.7	-4.2	-8.0	-3.2	-2.4
ES	1.9	-4.1	-11.2	-9.8	-8.8	1.2	-4.1	-8.9	-7.8	-7.0	2.8	-2.5	-7.1	-5.7	-4.4
FR	-2.7	-3.3	-7.5	-8.0	-7.4	-3.8	-3.8	-6.2	-6.2	-6.2	-1.1	-0.9	-3.9	-3.6	-3.3
IT	-1.5	-2.7	-5.3	-5.3	-5.0	-3.2	-3.5	-4.0	-3.7	-3.6	1.8	1.6	0.7	0.9	1.2
LU	3.6	2.9	-0.7	-3.5	-3.9	1.1	2.0	1.2	-1.4	-1.9	1.3	2.3	1.7	-1.0	-1.3
NL	0.2	0.7	-5.3	-6.3	-5.1	-1.0	-0.5	-3.6	-4.9	-4.0	1.2	1.6	-1.4	-2.6	-1.7
AT	-0.4	-0.4	-3.4	-4.7	-4.6	-1.6	-1.7	-2.4	-3.6	-3.6	1.1	0.8	0.3	-0.8	-0.7
PT	-2.6	-2.8	-9.4	-8.5	-7.9	-3.1	-3.8	-8.1	-7.7	-7.0	-0.3	-0.8	-5.2	-4.6	-3.4
SI	0.0	-1.7	-5.5	-6.1	-5.2	-2.9	-4.8	-3.7	-4.4	-3.8	-1.6	-3.7	-2.3	-2.5	-1.8
FI	5.2	4.2	-2.2	-3.8	-2.9	2.6	2.1	0.4	-1.3	-1.0	4.1	3.5	1.6	-0.2	0.2
MT	-2.2	-4.5	-3.8	-4.3	-3.6	-3.1	-5.2	-3.8	-4.0	-3.4	0.2	-1.9	-0.5	-0.7	-0.2
CY	3.4	0.9	-6.1	-7.1	-7.7	2.5	-0.4	-5.8	-6.3	-7.1	5.5	2.4	-3.3	-3.6	-4.2
SK	-1.9	-2.3	-6.8	-6.0	-5.4	-3.7	-4.7	-6.6	-5.4	-4.7	-2.3	-3.5	-5.1	-3.9	-3.2
EA-16	-0.6	-2.0	-6.3	-6.6	-6.1	-1.9	-2.8	-4.7	-5.0	-4.8	1.0	0.2	-1.8	-2.1	-1.6
BG	0.1	1.8	-3.9	-2.8	-2.2	-1.5	0.0	-2.8	-1.1	-0.8	-0.5	0.9	-2.0	-0.3	0.1
CZ	-0.7	-2.7	-5.9	-5.7	-5.7	-2.9	-4.5	-5.4	-4.9	-4.9	-1.7	-3.4	-4.1	-3.2	-2.8
DK	4.8	3.4	-2.7	-5.5	-4.9	3.1	3.3	0.6	-2.7	-3.1	4.7	4.7	2.6	-0.6	-1.0
EE	2.6	-2.7	-1.7	-2.4	-2.4	-1.1	-4.3	-0.6	-2.1	-1.8	-0.9	-4.1	-0.2	-1.6	-1.4
LV	-0.3	-4.1	-9.0	-8.6	-9.9	-4.5	-6.4	-6.9	-6.7	-9.0	-4.2	-5.8	-5.3	-4.3	-6.1
LT	-1.0	-3.3	-8.9	-8.4	-8.5	-3.1	-5.6	-7.1	-6.8	-6.8	-2.4	-5.0	-6.1	-5.2	-4.9
HU	-5.0	-3.8	-4.0	-4.1	-4.0	-5.5	-4.7	-2.2	-2.3	-3.0	-1.4	-0.5	2.6	2.3	1.1
PL	-1.9	-3.7	-7.1	-7.3	-7.0	-2.8	-4.6	-7.2	-6.3	-5.7	-0.5	-2.3	-4.6	-3.5	-2.6
RO	-2.5	-5.4	-8.3	-8.0	-7.4	-4.7	-7.7	-8.3	-7.1	-6.4	-3.9	-7.0	-6.8	-5.2	-4.4
SE	3.8	2.5	-0.5	-2.1	-1.6	1.6	1.1	1.9	-0.2	-0.5	3.3	2.8	2.8	0.7	0.3
UK	-2.8	-4.9	-11.5	-12.0	-10.0	-3.9	-5.2	-9.5	-10.4	-8.7	-1.7	-2.9	-7.5	-7.6	-5.6
EU-27	-0.8	-2.3	-6.8	-7.2	-6.5	-2.1	-3.1	-5.2	-5.6	-5.2	0.6	-0.3	-2.5	-2.8	-2.2

Note: The structural budget balance is calculated on the basis of the commonly agreed production function method (see European Commission (2004)).

Source: Commission services' Spring 2010 European Economic Forecast. The figures for Greece are based on information available prior to the finalisation on 2 May 2010 of the agreement on the conditionality negotiated between the Greek authorities and the Commission, ECB, and IMF.

Five dimensions of this change in attitude require reflection.

(1) Fiscal conservatism is as much a political rhetoric as it is a political attitude towards public finances and the role of the state. The current political anti-state and anti-tax revolt led by the historical Tea Party in the US and kept alive in European countries underline that fiscal conservatism must not be accompanied by insights into economic rationality. On the contrary, the political stance against macroeconomic intervention in order to sustain economic growth and thus create jobs seems willingly to accept rising public deficits. It was well known but less accepted that under certain growth conditions a reduction in public spending triggers a paradox of thrift that takes the form of even smaller growth rates thus shrinking tax revenues further with consequently higher deficits. Those deficits then may trigger a next round of reduction of state expenditure, which may result in a further deterioration of the growth base of an economy (see Annexure). Often enough it is not so much about sound public finance as it is about transforming capitalist regimes into solely market-driven systems that guide austerity programs. In other words, concerns about public deficits and debts can actually be used for transformational political purposes.

(2) Since the Great Recession, it is a well-known fact that financial markets are by no means rational entities. Rather, they are driven by sentiments, greed and irrational expectations. Why then, one ought to ask, should financial actors be seen as financial watchdogs that bark when governments violate opaque rules? A brief glance at the statistics shows (Graph 1) that not all states are born equal. Quite a number of countries with very high (and rising) debt-GDP ratios are treated by financial markets as stable members of the global financial community. If we accept, for the sake of argument, the debt benchmark of the Euro zone, 60% of public debt to GDP, Japan, the US and also emerging market economies like Brazil and India are all serious violators. And even the much praised Canada would not make the mark. However, none of these economies are subject to premiums on the side of financial markets. Obviously, selective discriminators treat similar situations differently.

(3) Absolute debt levels and non-contextualized debt-GDP ratios are not convincing pointers towards an unsustainable situation of

public finances. In empirical terms, Reinhart and Rogoff (2010) showed in a lengthy time series analysis that the relationship between government debt and real GDP growth is weak, at least as long as the debt-GDP ratio is smaller than 90%.[6] Above this threshold, median GDP rates start shrinking by one-percentage point p.a .In other words, public debt is not per se a growth-impeding obstacle. Looking at public deficits, sustainability obviously depends on the level of the underlying interest rate, r, and the growth rate of GDP, g. As long as $r < g$, any budget deficit d (expressed as share to GDP) would result in a debt ratio b, where $b = d/(g-r)$, and b would shrink in relative terms. In the case $r > g$, a growing public deficit automatically results in an increase of b. Deficits can go hand in hand with both rising and declining debt levels.

(4) Projections by the IMF point to an on-going rise in public debt ratios from 60 % of GDP at the end of 2007 to 85 % on average by 2015.[7]The concept of fiscal space has been recently used to generate a point estimate when an economy moves towards or even beyond a sustainable debt ratio. For this purpose, a historically based relationship between the primary balance and thus the fiscal policy of an economy and the development of the public debt ratio is being constructed that eventually leads to the estimation of a public debt limit. The difference between the projected debt ratio for 2015 and the estimated debt limits produces the fiscal space available.[8] The results of this exercise hint that Greece, Italy, Portugal and also Japan have an extremely low probability for additional fiscal space. The situation is slightly better for Iceland, Ireland, and Spain where the probability for additional fiscal space until 2015 is in the range of 50-70 percent. A third group consists of the US and the UK where the probability for remaining fiscal space is estimated between 70 and 80 %. It needs to be stressed that those figures are the outcome of a strongly modelled exercise with strong assumptions, and also uncertainties. Given the sentiment-driven character of financial markets, small events may trigger the perceptions of key actors and kick-start financial stampedes even against the US.

(5) The argument for fiscal austerity hints to the positive effects on trust on the side of global investors. The history of fiscal consolidation episodes undermines this line of argument. On average,

fiscal austerity has a contractionary effect on output; typically a reduction of public deficits of 1 percentage point of GDP reduces GDP by .5 % points within two years and increases unemployment by 0.3 percentage points. In case of an interest rate already close to zero, this effects will get quite larger. Usually, fiscal austerity is accompanied by a depreciation of the currency; typically, a 1-percentage point of fiscal retrenchment is accompanied by a 1.1-percentage point depreciation of the currency. In a monetary union such an effect cannot happen by definition. Instead, fiscal retrenchment may feed its own purpose by increasing the pressure on internal devaluation, in particular on direct and indirect wages (IMF 2010:chapter 3). International investors may interpret fiscal retrenchment as a courageous political strategy whose short term benefits are smaller than its long-term benefits.

High and increasing public debts do not automatically trigger sovereign debt defaults. The probability is high, though, that they eventually trigger or threaten penalties by financial markets that will consequently result in fierce austerity programs by governments. In the following paragraphs I will discuss those general observations more closely.

3. A Closer Look

3.1. Deficits and Financial Markets

I argue that fiscal conservatism is not automatically the most adequate response to high public deficits and debts. It is true though that at first look, the situation in the EU and in particular for Euro zone member states looks dire (see Table 1). In 2009 Ireland, Greece, Spain, France, Portugal, and Cyprus were all poised to violate the 3% hurdle of the Stability and Growth Pact (SGP), and this despite already having strict austerity programs in place.The situation turned from bad to worse in 2010 when all but one member economy of the Euro zone was participating in an excessive deficit procedure.

The list continues with EU member states outside the Euro zone: the UK, Latvia, Lithuania, Poland, and Romania would currently not fulfil the Maastricht criteria of a maximum public debt to GDP of 60%. Given that not all of those economies benefit equally from the low (short-term) interest rate policy of the ECB, and also taking into consideration that long-term rates vary according to risk-evaluations by financial market actors, even economies with positive but decreasing public deficits may end up with an increase of b. Ireland and also Greece are the most prominent cases where despite harsh and rigorous austerity programs, the share of public debt to GDP is increasing, thus confirming the prediction of the paradox of thrift. In other words, austerity programs can go hand in hand with an increase in public debt ratios, and further undermine financial investors' confidence and trust. According to the first assessment of Greece's austerity program, the debt ratio is expected to rise from 130.2 % at present to 143.9 % in August 2014, and this despite a reduction of the public deficit from 13.6 % in 2009 to 2.6 % in 2014 (DG Financial and Economic Affairs, 2010). Similarly Irish public debt to GDP will rise from 65.5 % in 2009 to 112.4 % in 2011 and then to 120.5 % in 2013 before a slight reduction is expected (DG Financial and Economic Affairs, 2011).

High public deficits and debts are attributed to several factors. One reason for the lately observed increase, and in some cases the most important one, is the financial and economic crisis that turned even conservative governments into big-spenders (see Graph 2).

Graph 2

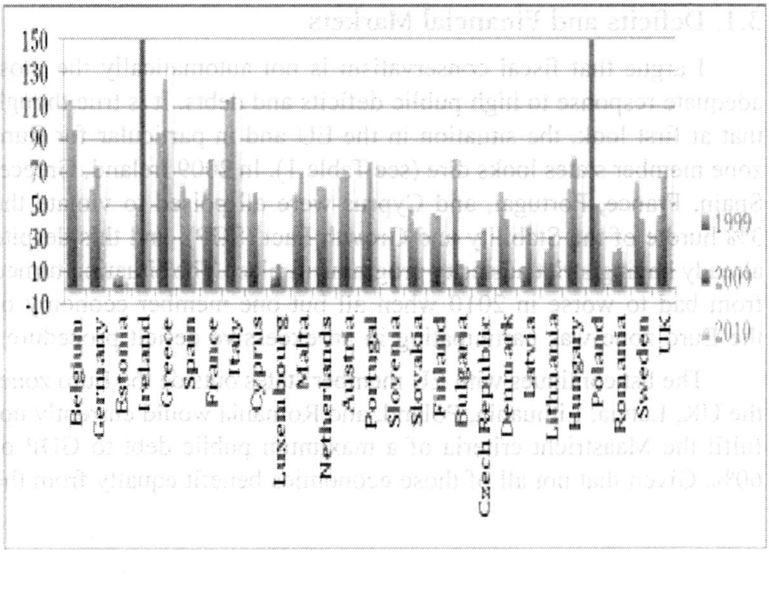

Public deficits in the EU 27-economies started to dive in 2007; and this is reflected in a surge of the public debt ratio. Ireland, for example, managed to come up with public surpluses in the period 2007-2007 for all but one year. Greece, on the other side, was violating the SGP over the whole period of its membership in the Euro zone. Spain belongs to the same category as Ireland, at least in terms of public finances, as the authorities successfully kept public deficits and debts under tight control until the crisis hit. The rise in public debt can be attributed to three dimensions that came with the Great Crisis.

First, governments had to act immediately in order to safeguard the financial industry and its core institutions. Programs and tools differed between the economies but in all cases significant financial rescue funds were spent for this purpose. An extreme response like the one by the Irish government to guarantee the survival of all banks skyrocketed public debt and ate up huge amounts of its GDP (see Table 2).

Table 2: Capital injections to Irish Banks

Anglo Irish Bank ***(Nationalised in January 2009)***	**Total: €29.3bn** (18 1/3 % of GDP), including o €4 bn (June 2009) o €8.3 bn in form of a promissory note (March 2010), increased to 10.3 bn (May 2010). o €8.6 bn through a promissory note (notified June 2010, approved by the Commission on 10 August). o €6.4bn (of which €1.5bn already approved in August 2010) through a promissory note (December 2010),
Allied Irish Bank (AIB)	**Total: €7.2bn** (4½% of GDP), including o €3.5 bn (2¼% of GDP) in preference shares, via the National Pension Reserve Fund (NPRF) (February 2009) (*As part of the capital injection approved by the Commission in December 2010, all preference shares were converted into ordinary shares to increase the equity in the bank*) o €3.7bn cash investment by the NPRF in equity (December 2010)
Bank of Ireland (BoI)	**Total: €3.5 bn** (2¼% of GDP) in preference shares, via the NPRF (February 2009) of which €1.7 billion were converted into equity as part of BoI's capital raise in April 2010
Irish Nationwide Building Society	**Total: €5.4bn** (3½% of GDP), including o €0.1bn through special investment shares (March 2010) o €2.6bn in form of a promissory note (March 2010) o €2.7bn in form of a promissory note (December 2010)
EBS Building Society	**Total: €0.9bn** (½% of GDP) o €0.1bn through special investment shares (March 2010) o €0.25bn in form of a promissory note (June 2010) o €0.525bn in form of special investment shares (December 2010)
TOTAL	**€46.3bn (29% of GDP)**

Note: In addition, covered institutions benefit from the *bank guarantees* granted by the Irish authorities and have *transferred impaired property-related assets* to the bad bank "NAMA".

Source: Commission services

Source: DG Economic and Financial Affairs, 2011, p.13.

In the Irish case the rise in public deficits and debt is the direct consequence of the stabilization action taken by the Irish government. Even though this act of desperation was aimed to regain trust into the country's financial institution, the situation was wobbly enough to pressure Ireland under a stabilization program that was, like in Greece, jointly coordinated by IMF and the EU. Unlike Greece, the Irish government was urged to accept an interest rate for those loans of 5.8% - a rate that put additional pressure on its public finances.

Second, the financial crisis triggered a deep economic crisis with absolute shrinking of GDP in many countries. This implied huge reductions in tax revenues and this resulted in instantaneous increases of debt levels. Third, governments were urged to kick-start their suffering economies in order to avoid a meltdown and to keep unemployment in politically acceptable limit. This resulted in involuntary Keynesian spending programs that put public deficits into red alarm zones. Net lending in the Euro zone as well as in the EU-27 nose-dived deep into negative territory, and public debt as shares of GDP went up.

Net lending (+) net borrowing(-), as % of GDP:

Gross debt (as % of GDP)

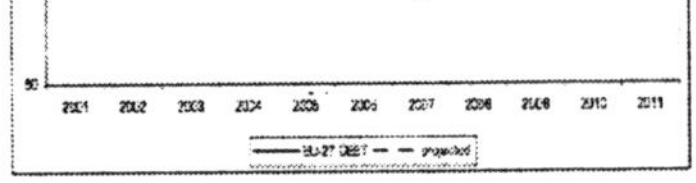

Source: Commission services.

The mostly involuntary Keynesianism was often accompanied by the working of automatic stabilizers that pushed public finances even deeper into the red zone. From a macroeconomic perspective the response of governments was highly adequate as the private sector and private households of most of the Euro zone economies were financially overstretched. In order to get their balance sheets right again, those actors needed de-leveraging, and this was the route taken since 2009 in most of the advanced capitalist market economies. Restoring order in financial accounts is a decisive step towards re-energizing economic growth. However, as the paradox of thrift tells us (see Annexure) it can only work if the reductions of debt level by private actors are accompanied by government efforts to simultaneously *increase* their debt levels[9]. In other words, if all actors de-leverage simultaneously, effective demand and economic growth shrinks, with the consequence of ever higher public deficits. In normal times, higher savings by all actors will increase investment due to the negative interest rate effect of a higher amount of savings. In times where the interest rate is close to zero, an across-the board increase in savings leads directly to a decrease in overall demand and thus in a slow-down of economic growth. Insofar as higher savings lead to lower consumption and investment, and thus to lower production and income, the de-leveraging strategies of the private sector may even fail. The insight of such a perspective is obvious: Not all economic actors can de-leverage at the same time.

Government debt and budget deficits may be seen as unsustainable and yet they are necessary in order to allow a managed and controlled de-leveraging of the private sectors. This general conceptual idea needs some further clarifications, though. The most straightforward explanation for the turn towards fiscal austerity has to do with the state of financial markets as watchdogs. The case of Greece and other European economies made it crystal-clear that financial markets have the power and determination to declare the margins of non-sustainability of public finances. Financial market transactions of all kinds come with regular concerns whether the lender is likely to service and eventually settle the transaction. Information is the critical variable, and it is distributed asymmetrically. In order to fill at least certain parts of the information gap, financial institutions outsourced this task to newly emerging credit rating agencies.[10] The link between credit rating and financial market response is straightforward. Changes in the rating leads to the reassessment of the particular underlying financial product on the side of the lenders. Changes of ratings can also be read as 'new news' for investors and generate a regrouping of investments. Last but not the least, rating changes can kick-start speculation against lenders as it is expected that markets will follow the herd, and being in front of the herd pays off. The massive downgrading of Euro zone economies like Greece and Ireland reflect to some degree concerns about the sustainability of those levels of indebtedness but it seems that it also reflects the growing nervousness in the financial industry to miss another disaster after they missed the build-up of the financial crisis of 2008. Schuknecht, von Hagen, and Wolswijk show in their analysis of government bond yield spreads that the Lehman Brothers default of September, 2008 fundamentally changed the responses of financial markets in the case of high and increasing public deficits.[11] The Greek socialist government's public declaration in late 2009 that it miscalculated Greece's budget deficit is different from Lehman's fall but it surely kick-started an accelerated process of mutual downgrading and punishment of governments by financial markets, as Graph 5 shows (Bank of England, 2010).

Graph 5

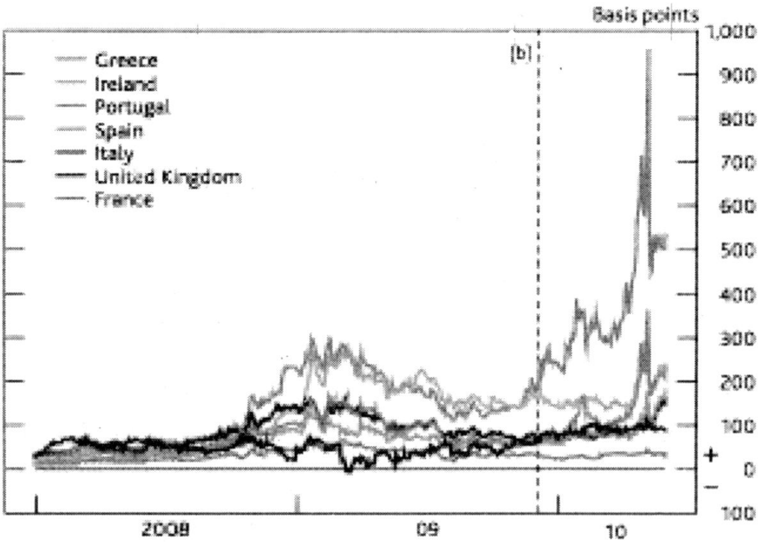

Sources: Thomson Reuters Datastream and Bank calculations

(a) Spread of ten-year government bond yields over German bunds for selected countries. Data to close of business on 10 June.

(b) December 2009 Report.

The high yield spread in the Euro zone reflects the anxiety of global investors about the ability of national governments to successfully return to sound public finances and/or to operate a fiscal austerity program that would reduce the deficit exposure of those economies. Moreover, the increasing spread was interpreted as the inability of the Euro zone to deal with sovereign debt defaults, and this resulted in a strong depreciation of the Euro against the US-Dollar and other currencies. So far, all the governments were able to refinance their bonds, albeit they had to pay much higher interest rates than before. As investors are successful in requesting higher risk premiums, they actually benefit from the downgrading as long as the worst-case of a sovereign debt default or even a haircut is prevented.

In other words, financial markets have the power to 'punish' governments and push them towards austerity programs in order to escape the downgrading of credit agencies. In case of the Euro zone economies they also had the power to kick-start a rally against the Euro and to push the common currency to the brink.

3.2. Policy Responses as Crisis Amplifiers

It was not helpful, to say the least, that the EU and the institutions of the Euro zone were not at all prepared to handle the situation. Responses by governments and the EU were chaotic, un-coordinated, and often unsophisticated. Most of the immediate crisis management was shifted to the European Central Bank, and this created conflicts of its own kind. In order to avoid a flight from the Euro, it was necessary to immediately provide emergency funding for the ailing economies. In 2010, Greece was the first economy receiving a joint EU-IMF rescue package of Euro 110 billion, followed by Ireland. In case of Greece, 80 billion were provided by the member states of the Euro zone, according to the proportionate share in the ECB; the remainder 30 billion Euro came from the IMF. The overall loan comes in tranches and is conditional on the positive passing of IMF-originated economic reform conditionalities.

In May 2010 after lengthy and controversial debates, the national governments launched the European Financial Stability Facility (EFS). This new institution, under enormous financial market pressures was made permanent, and sees the provision of overall 750 billion Euro as emergency funding in case of sovereign debt default crises. It was foreseen that 440 billion (59%) should be provided as credit guarantees by member states, another 60 billion by the EU, and 250 billion by the IMF.[12]

This approach was helpful for a brief time in the sense that the severe speculation against the Euro came to a halt and the currency even started to appreciate against the US-Dollar. The latter may have been supported by the financial markets reception of the outcome of the European Bank Stress Test in the summer of 2010. According to this exercise only six European banks would sink below the 6% threshold of tier 1 capital in case of a sovereign debt default of one of the Euro zone members. It is interesting and alarming at the same time to note that the positive attitude of financial markets was not even disturbed by the news that the facility will provide far less funding then initially planned. For quite some time it seemed as if calm had returned to the markets. This calmness did not last very long, though. In the second half of 2010, financial markets were willing to test the resilience of the crisis management and it was mainly due to the efforts of the ECB that those tests did not result in immediate surrender. In an atmosphere of harsh and serious internal debates that brought the board of the ECB to the brink of an open split the ECB extended its quantitative easing policy by directly buying bonds from stressed countries like Greece, Spain, Portugal, and Ireland. It is estimated that the amount of bad assets stacked at the ECB is up to Euro 80 billion.

While the ECB took the lead in Europe's crisis management the EFS was running into its own problems. In order to get the highest ratings from Moody's, Fitch, and Standards & Poor, the new fund had to agree to an asset backing that took up 20 % of the Euro 440 billion. As not all guaranteeing states enjoy a triple A-rating, the actual amount, which can be guaranteed, will be only around Euro 250 billion.[13] This modification changed the composition of contributions between the three financial supporters. The member states now represented 45 %, as does the IMF; the EU share is 10 %. Only when contagion threatened and financial markets detected Spain and Portugal as potential defaulters the debate flared up as to whether the EFS should be extended beyond 2013 and new money should be poured into this tab. The positions of the EU Commission and national governments as well as between national governments were far apart. When Barosso opted for a financial upgrade of the EFS it was Germany that made it clear that it would not be willing to hand more money to this institution. Luxembourg's Junker came forward with the proposal to issue Euro bonds and to accept haircuts by lenders. Germany's Angela Merkel also was in favour of haircuts but opposed any Euro bonds, not least, as she wanted to avoid any further German shouldering of financial burden, direct or indirect. Germany jointly with France proposed their own version of a European economic government under the label of a *Pact for competitiveness* only to generate a strong opposition from other European partners. In particular the plan to harmonize pension systems, de-index wages from inflation and also to strengthen the budget control beyond the agreement of the so-called European Semester ran into opposition. [14] The European Commission and its 'van Rompuy Task Force' tried hard to navigate through national interests and did come up with its own suggestions by mainly drawing a macroeconomic scoreboard with indicators that go far beyond the criteria included in the SGP.

A case can be made that the *Powell Doctrine* has been a necessary step at the time of strong speculative attacks against the Euro. Today we know that the funds announced are not available, and may even shrink further.[15] The calm of the markets (end-September 2010) should not be read as a sign of regained trust and confidence due to the EFSF. This calmness has more to do with two other factors: (i) The first two quarters of 2010 has shown surprisingly resilient growth in the Euro area, mainly driven by the strong export-led growth dynamic of Germany. This growth spurt impressed markets and resulted in a recovery of the exchange rate of the Euro. (ii) Even more important in calming financial markets was the turn-around of the ECB announcements in May, 2010, to buy government bonds of strongly indebted economies and thus to monetize public debt. Financial markets correctly interpreted this policy change as the end of any no-bail out approach for the ECB.

The first factor has already slipped as growth prospects across the Euro zone start to shrink.[16] The negative effects of de-leveraging of private actors in combination with the turn towards fiscal austerity and the slower growth of the global economy have led to relatively weak recovery. The paradox of thrifts starts to show up big time in some economies of the Euro zone. The decision of the ECB to purchase stressed government bonds definitely helped exposed banks but has also led to deep tensions in the Bank's board, and fed fears of a inflation rate far above the target rate of the ECB. The German head of the Deutsche Bundesbank, Axel Weber, even made his disagreement public. Whether this policy will hold in case of a return to instability and increasing tumult is therefore doubtful.[17]

4. Institution Building and Trust

The EU relies mainly in institution renovation and institution building for its project to restore trust and confidence in the EU and its underlying architecture. Initiatives are abundant, and some steps have already been taken in the last couple of months. At the time of writing, concrete details of the renewed mode of economic governance were not known. The overall direction taken, though, outlined in the Commission's communication from May 12, 2010, and in a second communication from June 30, 2010, as well as by proposals of national governments is clear. (i) Overcoming the patchwork of financial sector regulation and supervision by creating an independent European institution that cooperates with the ECB. The 'European Banking Authority' jointly with a 'European Insurance and Occupational Pensions Authority' and a 'European Securities and Markets Authority' will act as pan-European regulators. The 'European Systemic Risk Board', located in Frankfurt, will provide macro-prudential oversight. (ii) Closer regulation of particular financial products and services, including a tax on financial transactions are in the making. (iii) Launch of a totally renovated version of the preventative arm of the SGP by introducing a so-called European Semester. This exercise will deeply intrude on national public budget preparations and will overall greatly influence the national budgets. The proposed new principle of financial prudence will come with stricter enforcement: "This principle implies that annual expenditure growth will be regulated. Failure to respect keep to the agreed rate of growth of expenditure, in conjunction with the stipulated revenue measures, will make the Member State liable to a warning from the Commission and, if persistent and/or particularly serious, a Council recommendation to take corrective action will be issued under Article 121 of the Treaty. Such a recommendation....would be backed, for the first time and for euro-area countries only, by an enforcement mechanism under Article 136 of the Treaty, in the form of an interest-bearing deposit, amounting to 0.2 % of GDP" (European Commission COM (2010) 526.) (iv) Strengthening the corrective arm of the SGP, mainly via monitoring and supervision and in particular by enforcing higher fines in case of violations. Fines will be of monetary form but may also include strong political fines as temporary loss of voting power and loss of eligibility of EU funds. (v) Stronger emphasis on real-time steps towards reaching the 60 % public debt ceiling and enforcing fines in case of lack of accountable progress. (vi) Possible introduction of national debt brakes as already introduced in Germany through a change in its Constitution. (vii) Enforcing structural reforms in order to overcome gaps in competitiveness and costs by means of a scoreboard.

These plans will result in a fundamentally new economic mode of governance in the Euro zone. It can be safely assumed that the implementation efforts will carefully avoid that this new regime requires a new Treaty. In material terms, this new mode of governance undermines drastically the national base of democratic principles (representation-taxation link), in particular with regards to the planned pre-emptive budget procedures and the European Semester. It also means the end of the current soft mode of governance, in particular of the well-known Open Method of Coordination type. Centralization of power in Brussels is back.

In terms of economic policy, this change gives the wrong answer to establish an adequate new mode of economic governance, as it is a deliberate surrender to the wrong benchmarks set by the global financial markets. First, the announced policies will give the paradox of thrift a visible European face, and thus weaken Europe and the Euro zone as a stabilizing force for the global economy. Greece and Ireland are the most prominent cases where courageous efforts to reduce public deficits resulted in the reduction of economic growth and an increase in the debt ratio. For the short-term, this policy will add to the global growth problems. Second, it will create vicious circles for some Euro zone economies and thus undermine the stability of the zone itself. Greece, in particular will not only suffer socially from the planned programs of fiscal austerity, but will not be able to achieve credible debt ratios in the near future. A haircut decision may be unavoidable. Third, rather than making its mode of governance more flexible by adding discretionary elements, it will add inflexibility and establish a purely rule-based mode of governance.

The EMU is not automatically destined for a doomsday scenario. As long as other parts of the global economy continue to grow, Euro zone economies will benefit, and will be in a position to successfully deal with the default of individual member economies. It needs to be stressed that not all economies are in a position to make use of such a positive scenario. As a matter of fact it seems as if this option increases the polarization inside the Euro zone in particular Germany benefits asymmetrically in the current phase of global growth. However, the situation is filled with uncertainty. By making the reduction or even elimination of public deficits and the shrinking of public debts to central targets of the mode of economic governance, the EU runs the risk of creating, at least in the short-term, more problems than providing solutions. In the current economic situation, the planned turn towards an even stronger fiscal austerity is wrong politics. Indications are already out that this approach does not generate trust and confidence. Rather, it pushes governments into a hare and turtle race where governments are set to loose.

Besides such short-term prospects, the emerging new mode of governance does not pass the social litmus test. The envisaged 'structural' reforms aim to add more flexibility to labour markets and thus shift the labour market power in favour of employers. The possible shrinking of the public sector already generated strikes and social unrest in some European nation-states. Insofar as differences in competitiveness are interpreted by the Commission and national governments as driven mainly by differentials in unit labour costs, the reforms risk kick-starting a wage cost race inside the Euro zone that runs the risk of undermining social compromises. Institution building does not automatically restore trust in the Euro. The proof is in the pudding. In this respect, I fear that the new mode of governance will not deliver what is actually needed.

Annexure

The Paradox of Thrift

The amount of investment depends on the development of economic growth, indexed as GDP. With an increase in GDP, investment increases albeit with a decreasing rate. If the original savings-GDP relation is depicted by S1, and S2 shows an upward shift of savings due to the planned higher savings, this implies at any given level of GDP a fall in the actual amount of savings and investment, and thus of GDP. In other words, planned savings and investment are generating a drop in economic output.

This outcome holds for a closed economy. In an open economy there is always the possibility to overcome the paradox of thrift by achieving an export surplus. In other words, economies with an superiòr international competitiveness position are better sìtuated for severe austerity programs than economies with a weak international competitive position. The option to use the export channel, however, depends on a positive global demand.

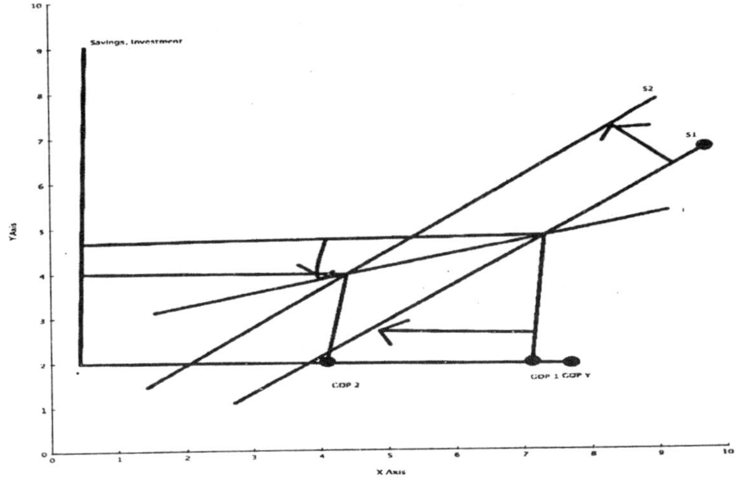

Refrences

1. See Granovetter, M. "Economic action and social structure: the problem of embeddedness",American Journal of Sociology, Vol.91, No.3, 1985, pp. 481-510; Kurt Huebner, Theory of Regulation Critical Reconstruction of a new approach in Political Economy, Berlin, 1989.
2. Fehr, E., "On the economics and biology of trust." Journal of the European Economic Association, vol. 7, Nos.2-3, 2009, pp. 235-266.
3. 'Crowding out', so the summary of Blanchard (2008), "refers to all the things which can go wrong when debt-financed fiscal policy is used to affect output".
4. For a good summary of the operations of financial markets before the Great Recession See, Markus K. Brunnermeier, "Deciphering the Liquidity and Credit Crunch 2007-2008", Journal of Economic Perspectives, Vol. 23, No.1, Winter 2009, pp.77-100.
5. Ben S. Bernanke, "The Great Moderation", www.federalreserve.gov/boarddocs/speeches/2004/20040220/default.htm.
6. Carmen M. Reinhart and Kenneth S. Rogoff, Debt and Growth Revisited", 11 August 2010, www.economics.harvard.edu/faculty/rogoff/files/Debt_and _Growth_Revisited_vox.pdf.
7. Carlo Cottarelli and Andrea Schaechter, "Long Term Trends in Public Finances in the G-7 Economies', IMF Staff Position Note, September 1, 2010, SPN/10/13.
8. Jonathan D. Ostry, et al, Fiscal Space, IMF Staff Position Note, 1 September 2010, SPN/10/11.
9. This result holds for a closed economy. A open economy always has the option to run a trade surplus and thus to escape the paradox of thrift. Given that the tool of currency depreciation is not available for economies like Ireland, Greece, Spain, and Portugal it is up to internal devaluation to deal with the imbalances In this case, though, we are back at the paradox of thrift.
10. Whitegives a good and historically informed overview on credit rating agencies. He also points out that for legal reasons those agencies form 'opinions' rather than'judgments' about the quality of lenders.Lawrence J. White, "Markets The Credit Rating Agencies",Journal of Economic Perspectives, Vol. 24, No. 2, Spring 2010, pp.211-26.
11. Ludger Schuknecht, Jurgen von Hagen and Guido Wolswijk, "Government Bond Risk Premiums in the EU Revisited The Impact of the Financial Crisis", European Central Bank, Working Paper Series, No. 1152/February, 2010,www.ecb.int/.

12. In line with the decisions taken May 9, 2010 within the framework of the Ecofin Council to safeguard financial stability in Europe, Ministers have established the European Financial Stability Facility (EFSF). The EFSF was set up by the 16 countries whose currency is the euro to provide a funding backstop should a euro area Member State find itself in financial difficulties. The EFSF will have the capacity to issue bonds guaranteed by euro area members for up to € 440 billion for on-lending to euro area Member States in difficulty, subject to conditions to be negotiated with the European Commission in liaison with the European Central Bank and International Monetary Fund and to be approved by the Eurogroup.
13. See Frankfurter Allgemeine. FAZ.Net, 21 September 2010: Euro-Rettungsfonds kann nur 250 Milliarden Euro verleihen.
14. The European Semester is meant to strengthen the preventive arm and thus is a crucial element to reform the failed Stability and Growth Pact. The idea is an annual coordination process of national budget planning and public finances with fixed calendar dates. Starting in March each year, the European Council uses the input of the Commission with its Annual Growth Survey as the base to identify economic policy targets and makes first recommendations in order to create convergence. In April, the member states submit their medium-term budgetary strategies to the Commission; the latter prepares a draft proposal for the Council of Ministers. In June and July, the semester ends with country specific recommendations jointly prepared by the European Council and the Council of Ministers.
15. The problem of actual availability was early mentioned by Charles Wyplosz in his piece: "European Stabilisation Mechanism: Promises, realities and principles," VOX 12 May, 2010, http://www.voxeu.org/index.php?q=node/5031.
16. The storm seem to build up again, as the Financial Times reports: "the weak data added to evidence that gloomier global prospects, a strengthening euro, and the crises conditions facing the Greek and Irish economies are taking a toll on eurozone prospects. They did not point to a double-dip recession in continental Europe as a whole– but highlighted the vulnerability of countries still struggling to bring their public finances under control. " "The turn in the world trade cycle has finally reached the eurozone," said Nick Kounis, economist at ABN Amro in Amsterdam.
17. That the EU is no homogenous club with a shared belief in fiscal solidarity was stressed by the vote of Slovakia's parliament in August 2010 not to participate in the conditional loan for Greece.

5

EU-Turkey: The Challenge of Translating Engagement to Membeship

Bhaswati Sarkar

The Turkey – EU engagement started decades back in 1959. Since then there have been a host of enlargements. So what is it that has impeded Turkey's membership and where does Turkey stand today in terms of fulfilling membership criteria? Does Turkey's delayed entry affect only Turkey or does it also affect the EU? What does EU stand to loose if it fails to induct Turkey as a member? This paper focuses on these issues in two sections. To begin with the first section gives a timeline of EU-Turkey accession talks. It focuses on what was required of Turkey to access membership. In other words what are the conditionalities vis-à-vis Turkey. This section also gives a broad overview as to where Turkey stands today so far as these conditionalities are concerned. The second section analyses what delay or non-membership could mean for Europe and Turkey.

Part I

Turkey's attempt at membership began in July of 1959 when it submitted its application to the then EEC. In fact, Turkey and Greece both applied in the same year. Between 1959 to 2010, EU membership increased to 27, the timeline is well known, UK and Ireland in 1973, Greece-1981, Spain and Portugal-1986, 2004- eight Central and Eastern countries and the Mediterranean islands of Malta and Cyprus, 2007- Bulgaria and Romania. Why did Turkey miss the bus? It took 40 years for Turkey to just get a date to start the accession talks. The 2005 Negotiating Framework declares the "shared objective of the negotiations is accession" and further stated "these negotiations are open ended process the outcome of which cannot be guaranteed beforehand."

Membership to the Union is dependent on the fulfilment of a host of conditionalities. Copenhagen criteria 2002 laid new rules for all future accession. EU requires Turkey to commit itself to democracy, constitutional reforms, human rights, abolition of death penalty, reduction of the political role of the army, normalisation of relations with Armenia, and resolution of the Kurdish question and Cyprus and the Aegan.

Constitutional reform –strengthening democracy

Turkey's democratic journey is one of contrasts. Modern Turkey began its journey with the establishment of the Turkish Republic in 1923. The transformation was fundamental and multifaceted – from an Islamic Empire to a national Turkish state, from a medieval theocracy to a constitutional republic, from a bureaucratic feudalism to a modern capitalist economy. This transformation understood as Westernisation was achieved over a long period by successive waves of reformers and radicals. By and large renouncing its Islamic heritage Turkey turned to Europe adopting and applying its way of life to government, society, and culture. Kemal Ataturk's nation state model demanded above all homogeneity in terms of population, territory, history, and language barricaded behind near-sacred frontiers where the military played a prominent role in terms of upholding and pursuing national interest. The Islamic conceptions of identity, authority, and loyalty were replaced. As Lewis puts it, "in the theocratically conceived polity of Islam, God was to be twice replaced: as the source of sovereignty by the people, as the object of worship by the nation." On four occasions in 1960, 1971, 1980, and 1997 when the military found the civil government wanting in upholding the constitution and national interest or wavering towards religiosity, they seized the reins of power through coups. The EU conditionality of civilian control of the military is thus directed against one of the fundamental basis of the Kemalist state. EU has for long been urging Turkey to undertake constitutional reforms. These reforms would paradoxically reduce the role of military which has been a champion of secularism in the democratic polity of Turkey.

Today EU aspiration is the glue that binds together Turkey's key groups – the Muslim democrats, arch-secularists, the armed forces, and business. The centre-right AK party, whose leaders have their roots in Islamic political parties have since their landslide win in November 2000, tried to introduce reforms in line with membership conditionalities. Early reforms aimed at strengthening civil control over the military focused on the MGK(National Security Council), its duties, functioning, and composition. The MGK established by Article 118 of the 1961 Constitution was *de facto* in the hands of the army, headed by a military personnel appointed by the chief of staff and the decisions of the MGK, sometimes secret were not subject to appeal. On 23 July, 2003 the Turkish Grand Assembly passed the 'seventh reform package' to limit the role of the military through reform of the MGK. Firstly it underlined that the MGK is a consultative body, now with a civilian majority. The 7th reform package made it possible to appoint a civilian as Secretary General of the MGK. In August 2004 a civilian appointment was made for the first time. The council has not expanded the executive and monitoring authorities, and does not have the authority, on behalf of the President and the Prime Minister, to follow up on the implementation of the MGK's 'recommendations' any longer. In addition, the MGK does not have unlimited access to all civil institutions and no representative in the Supervision Board of Cinema, Video, and Music. It is, however, still represented in civil institutions such as the High Board for Radio and TV and the Commission for Higher Education, but after criticism in the 2003 European Commission report, this representation was withdrawn from both institutions in 2004.

In September 2010 the much awaited referendum on a package of 26 constitutional amendments was conducted. The amendments addressed the human rights agenda – they expanded the constitutional court and supreme board of judges, strengthened the rights to equality, privacy, collective bargaining and child protection, expanded the jurisdiction of the civilian court over the military, and ended immunity from prosecution to the junta that ruled Turkey after the last coup in 1980. In Turkey, the judges exercise considerable control over the political field. Political parties are frequently banned and candidates declared ineligible. The 1982 Constitution provided that, "no protection will be afforded to ideas and opinion contrary to Turkish national interests, to the principle of indivisibility of the Turkish state and territory, or to Turkish moral and historical values." Based on this limited concept of freedom of thought and speech since 1983, 23 parties were banned by judicial decision for countering constitutional principles. The 2010 reforms won approval by a wide margin with a vote of 58% on a high turnout of 78%. Prime Minister Recep Tayyip Erdogan claimed that his reform package had got popular backing. The European Commission also welcomed the constitutional changes approved by Turkish voters hailing them as a decisive step in the direction towards Europe. "These reforms are a step in the right direction towards fully complying with European Union accession criteria," EU Enlargement Commissioner Stefan Fuele commented. However, opponents of the Prime Minister argue that the result was polarising and claimed that the Erdogan's real purpose is to exert more control over the judiciary himself. By changing the way the top courts are set up, the opposition argues that the ruling AKP aims to bring them under its control.

The European Commission in its 2009 progress report on Turkey's preparedness for membership acknowledges many steps that have been initiated. For instance, Article 301 of the penal code under which scores of writers had been prosecuted for insulting "Turkishness" has been amended; powers of the military courts cut back; a parliamentary committee for women's rights set up, life for non-Muslim religious communities have been made easier; and plans for improving the judiciary and clamping down on black economy have been adopted. However, one of the important and sensitive points in EU-Turkey membership negotiations is the question of Cyprus.

Kurdish minority

The AK party has initiated certain positive steps to deal with Turkey's largest non-Turkish ethnic group – the Kurds, who are concentrated in eleven provinces of the southeast. Regional underdevelopment, denial of cultural rights, human rights abuses by Turkish state security forces, and 25 years of terrorist attacks by the Kurdistan Workers' Party (PKK) sum up the Kurdish problem. The capture of PKK leader Abdullah Ocalan in 1999 was followed by a PKK ceasefire, Ocalan's death sentence was commuted and the brutal repression of all signs of Kurdishness of the 1980s, relaxed. Turkey started accepting international legal oversight and honouring rulings of the European Court of Human Rights. Kurds who had to leave their villages during the government clashes of 1990s received some compensation and retured to their homes. The restrictions on expressions of Kurdish culture were liberalized. Private Kurdish language centres were allowed to operate. In Kurdish areas, use of Kurdish language bumper stickers, music, publications, festive days, radio and television became legal. In January 2009, a Kurdish language 24 hour state television channel was opened. The second report of the Independent Commission on Turkey, of September 2009, observes that these positive developments are not always noted or appreciated in Europe. Some European states on the contrary have been too lenient on the PKK. The Independent Commission was of the view that they should do demonstrably more to prevent PKK fund raising and organisation in their countries.

Alevis

Alevis are a religious, sub-ethnic, and cultural community in Turkey, numbering in the tens of millions. Alevism is considered one of the many sects of Islam. Alevi worship takes place in assembly houses rather than mosques. The ceremony, *cem*, features music and dance which symbolize the main planets revolving around the Sun (with men and women turning in circles), the liberation from ego, and unity with God. Unlike most other Muslim practices, Alevi rituals are conducted mostly in Turkish, and some in Kurdish.

In contrast to Sunni as well as to the Shia Muslim orthodoxy, Anatolian Alevis do not accept shariah, the Islamic judicial system for religious and worldly problems. In addition, Alevis call for a renunciation of violence and equality of women and men in their communities, which differs significantly from the teaching of Sunni Islam in Turkey and Shia Islam in Iran. For years Alevis have had no recognition from the state.

In 2009, the government for the first time begun addressing Alevi leaders' demands for equal citizenship. An early workshop in November was accompanied by a massive rally of 20,000 Alevites in Istanbul's Kadiköy district, calling for "sincerity" from the government. In all, more than 400 people took part in the seven workshops and the report was presented to Prime Minister Erdogan in February 2010. According to the report, all participants agreed that the cemevi had to be granted legal status, although not as places of worship because this could be problematic and even offensive to other Muslims. The report also stated that the majority of the Alevi community called for an abolition of the religious affairs directorate, Diyanet. Instead, they proposed that every religious community pay for its own religious services on a voluntary basis, which they emphasised would contribute to peace between different religions. Regarding compulsory religion courses, all sides agreed that the curriculum should be written down in a neutral language that is acceptable to all segments of the society. Erdogan has promised that the first political steps based on the recommendations of the report will be taken in one to two months. However, concessions will not be easy. They risk being stymied by the Diyanet, the country's powerful religious body that does not recognise anything but Sunni Islam. However, the fact that Turkish citizens can seek redressal from the European court has definitely strengthened communities like the Alevis to be vocal about their demands. Alevis like Hasan Zengin and his daughter Eylem can today file their complaint at the European Court of Human Rights and receive a favourable response. In the context of compulsory religious education in schools, the European Court of Human Rights (ECHR) ruled that the content of these religious classes violated human rights and contradicted the principles of plurality and objectivity. The Cem foundation, a prominent Alevi organisation opened a case against the Prime Ministry in 2005, demanding the community's prayer houses, known as cemevis, be officially categorized as a place of worship like a mosque, church or synagogue. At the same time, the foundation also demanded that Alevi religious leaders be included on the state payroll like Sunni imams. A court later ruled against the foundation's demands, with the Council of State, Turkey's top administrative court, approving the first court's decision, leading the group to ultimately apply to the European court with its requests.

Undoubtedly Turkey with its homogenous national imagery has made encouraging beginnings in dealing with the Kurdish minority and also the Alevis. The prospective membership of EU in initiating these changes cannot be denied. These positive trends can only be sustained by eventually incorporating minority rights in the Constitution.

Islam

In post Ottoman Turkey, Qura'nic schools were closed. In 1926 Kemal replaced sharia as the source of law with an adopted version of the Swiss civil code. In 1928, Islam was abolished as the state religion and in 1937, secularisation was written in the Constitution. However this did not mean a complete break between state and religion. In 1924, Kemal had created the Directorate of Religious Affairs, the Diyanet for regulating and administrating all matters of belief. As Olivier Roy observes, "far from having burned all bridges with religion, the 'secular' state thus continues to be responsible for its organisations and teaching." Turkey's secular state does not mean that Islam is absent from its political and cultural life. On the contrary, the main beneficiaries of Turkey's recent democratisation process have been political groupings, such as the AKP, which believes that Islam should form the country's political choices. This is somewhat ironic, as Turkey's secularists have always seen EU membership as a way of escaping the influence of political Islam and the turmoil of the Middle East. In recent years, Turkey has undoubtedly become a more mature democracy. But culturally Turkey may well become more 'Islamic' as the AKP and other groups try to expand the role of Islam in public life, while respecting the main tenets of Turkey's secular state structure. The AKP's attempt to make the headscarf legal is a case in point. In other words, in Turkey more democracy and more power for Islamic political groups have gone hand in hand.

Cyprus

Cyprus has a long complicated history of Greek and Turkish Cypriots trying to live together after the British withdrawal in 1960.

The constitutional arrangements that provided independent Cyprus non-aligned republic with a Greek Cypriot president and a Turkish Cypriot vice-president and the general executive authority vested in a council of ministers with a ratio of seven Greeks to three Turks, did not last long. Within a short period of time the first disputes started to arise between the two communities. Issues of contention included taxation and the creation of separate municipalities. The legislative veto system, resulted in a lockdown. On December 21, 1963 fighting erupted between the communities in Nicosia. In the days that followed it spread across the rest of the island. The power-sharing government collapsed. How this happened is in itself one of the most contentious issues in modern Cypriot history. The Greek Cypriots argue that the Turkish Cypriots withdrew in order to form their own administration. The Turkish Cypriots maintain that they were forced out. From then on to this day Cyprus continues to be an intractable issue. The invasion of the island by Turkey in 1974 invoking the Treaty of Guarantee, the Turkish Cypriots declaration of independence in 1983, which Turkey is the only country to recognize, the inclusion of Cyprus as EU member in 2004 when the issue of the island was far from settled, all contribute to the present impasse.

Currently, both the Greek and Turkish Cypriots struggle to work out a compromise on the lines of the Annan plan, proposed by the UN Secretary General Kofi Annan in 2002. It proposes a federal United Cyprus republic. One of the most controversial elements of the plan concerned property. During Turkey's military intervention/ invasion in 1974, many Greek Cypriots who owned 90% of the land and property in the north were forced to abandon their homes. Incidentally, a large number of Turkish Cypriots also left their homes. On the Greek Cypriot side, restitution of their property has been a central demand. However, the Turkish Cypriots argue that the complete return of all Greek Cypriot properties to their original owners would be incompatible with the functioning of a bi-zonal, bi-communal federal settlement. To this extent, they have argued that compensation should be offered. The agreement also kept in place the Treaty of Guarantee - an integral part of the 1960 constitution that gave Britain, Greece, and Turkey a right to intervene militarily in the island's affairs. Many Greek Cypriots were concerned that the continuation of the right of intervention would give Turkey too large a say in the future of the island. However, most Turkish Cypriots felt that a continued Turkish military presence was necessary to ensure their security. Another element of the plan that the Greek Cypriots objected to was that it allowed many Turkish citizens who had been brought to the island to remain. While many accepted Greek Cypriot concerns on this matter, there was a widespread feeling that it would be unrealistic to forcibly remove every one of these settlers, especially as many of them had been born and raised on the island.

The Annan plan would only come into force if accepted by the two communities in simultaneous referenda. In the 24 April, 2004 referendum, the Turkish Cypriots endorsed the plan (64.90%). Greek Cypriots resoundingly voted against the plan (75.83%). A week after the referendum, 1 May, 2004 Cyprus joined the EU. Since then there has been no headway. Besides, Cyprus from within the EU has been consistently obstructing Turkey's entry in the Union. The EU has been demanding that Turkey fulfil its Ankara commitment and open its port to Cyprus of which 8 negotiating chapters were blocked in 2006. Cyprus blocked another 6 in 2009 and France has blocked 4 in 2007. Thus 18 of the 35 chapters remain blocked. Egemen Bagis in 2009 agreed that Turkey had promised to open its ports in exchange for ending the isolation of the Turkish Cypriots. If EU countries decided to have direct trade with northern Cyprus, Turkey would be happy to open its ports, he said. On asked whether this would not amount to recognising Northern Cyprus as a state, Bagis said, "they would not be recognising the state. Just like we all trade with Taiwan, but we don't recognise Taiwan diplomatically." He further added that Cyprus talks are important but since Cyprus problem was not a prerequisite for its membership in EU, it should not be a prerequisite in the case of Turkey and "No other candidate country has seen 18 chapters blocked for political reasons."

EU membership of Cyprus reduced its maneuverability in resolving the impasse. In 2004, Greece's threat to block expansion towards Central and Eastern Europe had forced EU to induct Cyprus. As noted earlier while Cyprus was holding negotiations to join the EU, the Annan plan was prepared which aimed at unity. The plan was accepted by a large majority of Turkish Cypriots. The Greek

Cypriot government promised to accept this plan but everything suddenly changed when it became a member of the EU. The EU needs to put pressure on Cyprus in order for the negotiations to restart. It has failed to do so largely because the members are also divided on the issue of Turkish membership.

Armenia

Armenia – Turkey relations are stuck on the former's demand that the 1915 massacre of Armenians be acknowledged as 'genocide.' Turkey's strong reluctance to shoulder any responsibility that the Ottoman empire may have perpetrated during the war has mellowed of late though a final settlement of this sensitive issue is yet to achieved. A European Parliament report in 2000 included the statement that, "The European Parliament calls, therefore, on the Turkish Government and the Turkish Grand National Assembly to give fresh support to the Armenian minority, as an important part of Turkish society, in particular by public recognition of the genocide which the minority suffered before the establishment of the modern state of Turkey." The Turkish-Armenian reconciliation process got serious on the inter-governmental level in 2008. Following Turkish President Abdullah Gül's historic visit to Yerevan, Swiss mediation helped produce Protocols in 2009 that would lead to the establishment of diplomatic relations and the opening of the common border. The Protocols have, however, not been ratified to date. The Turkish government had signed them hoping for some breakthrough in the Armenia – Azerbaijan conflict.

Turkey had originally closed its border with Armenia as a result of the Armenian occupation of the Azerbaijani province of Kelbajar – one of seven districts outside of the Armenian-populated enclave of Nagorno-Karabach, that Armenian forces occupied and ethnically cleansed during the war. For most Turks, some form of progress in the Armenian-Azerbaijani negotiations was a prerequisite for opening the border. De-linking Turkish-Armenian ties from the Armenian-Azerbaijani conflict appears impossible in the Turkish domestic context. Given the close linguistic ties between Turkey and Azerbaijan, the AKP leadership is acutely aware that a single camera crew, filming from Azerbaijani refugee camps to which 800,000 people had been confined by Armenian conquests, could generate a public outcry against the government should it open the border without Armenian concessions. Therefore, much as the West, America, and EU may pressurize Turkey on normalization of relations with Armenia the relations are caught in a bind of a larger context not entirely in Turkey's control.

Part II

Is Turkey on an endless journey to Europe? The stance of leaders of prominent EU states, France and Germany is decidedly negative. Sarkozy and Merkel floated the idea of 'privileged partnership' or 'special relationship' for Turkey. Egemen Bagis, Turkey's chief negotiator said that the term was insulting and French colleagues promised never to use the insulting phrase again as Ankara negotiates full EU membership. There is also a possibility that in Turkey's negotiating mandate EU retains the option of applying permanent safeguards or derogations. For example, a permanent safeguard on the free movement of labour could allow other member-states to keep out Turkish workers even decades after Turkey's accession, if they fear that an influx of such workers may add to existing labour market problems. Such a safeguard would thus deprive Turkey of one of the fundamental 'four freedoms' of the single market. And a derogation of the EU budget may mean that Turkey may never gain full access to EU farm spending and regional subsidies which together make up the bulk of the EU budget. Already the EU has said explicitly that it does not want Turkey to join before 2014. This would mean it will have no say in negotiating the 2014-2021 budget framework.

Membership and European Public Opinion

There is no denying the fact that some EU states and the European public are apprehensive of Turkey's entry. Why this apprehension? Is it true, as some commentators have said, that EU back in the 1960s had accepted the idea of Turkish membership in a fit of absent-mindedness, not as part of a coherent strategy? Many argue that European opposition is largely founded upon a religious/cultural bias. Europeans are wary of opening the EU doors to a country that is 99 per cent Muslim, an attitude aggravated by the arrival of the Justice and Development Party to power in Ankara and the consequent fears of the mounting influence of Islamists. The apprehension to my mind is also the result of EU member states own encounter with Muslim immigrants.

Currently there are some 15 million Muslims in Europe and in some member states such as Denmark, Italy, Germany, Bulgaria, and the Netherlands, Islam is becoming the second or third largest religion in the country. It is often the main religion of some immigrant population. The sense of Islamic identity has recently strengthened. Muslims are also becoming increasingly vocal about their rights in terms of language, education, and representation. The second and third generation Muslims are less guided by the first generation considerations, to fit in. The approach of European states vis-à-vis their Muslim populations vary widely. France for instance, pursued a vigorous policy of assimilation through educational and other institutions guided by the firm belief that the French Revolution ideals of "liberty, equality, fraternity" could be applied to everyone. This policy today stands questioned. In contras, UK adopted a multicultural model. But Britain has also experienced its share of racist riots and terror attacks. Other European countries as Germany, Spain, and Italy have treated minorities as a temporary phenomenon, in the hope that they will eventually leave and were therefore by and large ignored or left to themselves. The Netherlands official policy of multiculturalism suffered a setback following the assassination of Pim Fortuyn and Theo Van Gogh.

The founders of Europe, Konrad Adenauer, Robert Schuman, Jean Monnet were all Christian Democrats. In the course of formulating the Constitutional Treaty many countries, Poland most prominently, lobbied for including 'Christians values' in the draft. Pope John Paul II is also reported to have lobbied European leaders for "a clear reference to God and the Christian faith to be formulated in the European constitution." In 2004, Bolkestein made headlines when he commented that if EU accepted Turkey it would risk becoming 'Islamized' and 'would implode'. Cardinal Joseph Ratzinger, Pope Benedict XVI, called EU negotiations with Turkey "an enormous mistake." Shireen Hunter has argued that a majority of the Muslims have not integrated which she feels is a result of a combination of factors like government inaction, prejudice, legitimate cultural differences, and the desire for segregation among the Muslim themselves.

According to the Eurobarometer, January 2007 Report on Discrimination, 44 percent of Europeans feel that discrimination on grounds of religion or belief is currently widespread in Europe, and 64 percent perceive racial discrimination as a fairly common problem. Earlier in 2000, the Runneymede Trust Report in UK pointed out the pervasive negative image of Muslims in Britain. Using wide documentary evidence, the report highlighted strong anti-Muslim tendency across Britain. Muslims suffered discrimination due to factors of 'colour, class, culture and creed.' In the 2007 EU report on racism in Europe, Germany again came in for criticism for discrimination against foreigners in the job market and housing and for violent crimes against them. Plans to build new mosques in major European cities like Rotterdam, Amsterdam, Copenhagen, Munich, Cologne, Berlin, Strasbourg, Athens, and Granada have been highly controversial and met with strong local resistance. In Rotterdam, where one of Europe's largest mosques is being built, the Deputy Mayor Marcos Pastors described the Oriental-style domed mosques as an 'ugly marble thing.'Officials throughout Europe are also pushing hard to influence the appearance of mosques and discouraging them to be built in the traditional architecture of their native lands. In Amsterdam, the Turkish Islamic community to avoid protracted conflict with Dutch authorities, calls its mosques Westermoskee and has designed it to integrate the building with its environs.

Since the 2001 transatlantic terror strikes and subsequent ones in Madrid and London, the Muslim population/community across Europe has gained heightened visibility. All eyes are trained on how the community has reacted to this act of violence, have they spoken loudly and clearly against them. Questions like "do you consider yourself European Muslim or a Muslim in Europe" have been hurled at Muslim community leaders which is not the best way to engage in inter-cultural dialogue. Overall, it is evident that the EU member states experience with Muslim immigrants has been far from trouble free. A number of EU surveys and studies indicate the growing Islamophobia in EU member states. There is thus a real apprehension in the public mind about Turkey's membership. Contrasting and conflicting position of EU leaders and their hesitancy feeds into this public apprehension instead of countering it. When the European people voted resoundly against the Constitution Treaty, there was great disappointment among the European elite but they worked towards circumventing it and Lisbon became a reality in 2009. In the case of Turkish membership the leaders instead of shaping public opinion conveniently chose to follow it. Austria's decision in 2008 to put the issue to referendum is a case in point.

Enlargement Adjustments

Apart from that, the size and population of Turkey will definitively have implications on EU's institutional structure. By 2015, Turkey is projected to overtake Germany in population. If allowed into the EU, it would surpass Germany in the number of its representatives to the EU parliament and, thereby its voting power. Taken together with the fact that the EU spends the majority of its money on agriculture and aid to poverty stricken areas in its member countries and Turkey desperately needs both the outlays, this it is argued would severely tax the EU budget.

"Negotiations area humiliating process," observes one of Poland's former chief negotiators. "The EU makes it very clear that you are joining them, not the other way round." Turks like others before them will find that very term 'negotiations' a misleading way of describing the accession talks. The EU is not just a club based on a shared identity, but also a huge set of rules and regulations. Its day-to-day business is not about values but about fire safety in shops and hygiene standards in dairies. European integration reaches deep into a country's policies and institutions. It affects not just high politics but daily life: how animals are slaughtered, how sewage is treated, and what products can be advertised on billboards. The EU covers foreign and security policies too, many of which are very sensitive in Turkey.

The deepening of Turkey's democratisation took place largely because of the 'golden carrot' of EU membership. It is true, as Turkish leaders often stress, that the reforms were necessary in themselves. In fact, given the current deadlock over blocked chapters, they have decided to harmonize anyway. But harmonisation in the short run will be painful. The costs of complying with EU rules will make it harder for many Turkish businesses to compete. Turkish industry will have to invest in new machinery and technology to comply with the EU's stricter health and safety provisions. Already, some interest groups in Turkey are resisting EU demands. The pharmaceuticals industry dislikes EU rules on the free movement of goods. Local authorities are bridling at EU's demands for allowing all businesses, including foreign ones, to compete for lucrative public contracts. Foreign companies in Turkey are not happy about the EU asking the government to eliminate tax breaks for foreign investors and special economic zones. All this could quickly turn against Erdogan if the EU was seen as unwelcoming and disingenuous. There are reactionary forces in the army, the state administration, and in the politics that oppose EU accession because of the radical reforms it requires. These forces would seize on any EU foot-dragging as proof of the Union's bad faith. The uneasy alliance favouring reform would quickly dissolve. The EU's decision to lift visa restrictions with several Balkan states that have not even begun membership talks while refusing to do so in the case of Turkey for instance, is difficult for ruling Turkish elite to comprehend or defend.

While it is all right to argue that the incumbent member is undoubtedly fundamentally transformed before gaining access to EU, every single enlargement has also been a process of mutual adjustment. Turkey's accession is unlikely to be an exception to this rule. It is time that European leaders seriously debate on the consequences of Turkey's possible accession to the EU's institutions, budget, and policies. The prospect of Turkish membership also begs a number of larger questions, such as: What kind of club should the EU be? And: where are the borders of Europe? If Turkey moves towards membership, should Ukraine and others have a chance to join too? And if enlargement continues, would an inner core of EU countries committed to deeper integration, be necessary and desirable?

Sceptical EU leaders need to realise that while negotiations are open ended they cannot, for any practical purpose, be endless. Turkish premier Recep Tayyip Erdogan, recently said, "Our patience has worn thin." The EU needs to state its position on Turkey's accession clearly and unequivocally. "Don't keep us waiting," is a new phrase in the Turkish political lexicon in its bid for EU membership. Turkey on its part would do well to keep its cool, for nothing would suit EU better than Turkey itself giving up on its membership agenda. Turkey should on the contrary embark on serious public relation exercise and bring to the focus of European public its strong secular legacy and Western orientation, its strengthening democracy in terms of institutional reforms and minority rights and they need to meet criticism not with prickliness and nationalist rhetoric, but with moderation and coolness.

Turkey's Assertive Foreign Policy and EU

In the past few years, however, Turkish foreign policy has changed profoundly. Turkey has made its EU membership aspirations the central tenet in its foreign policy. Its pro-US stance remains solid, but is less automatic. In March 2003, the Turkish parliament dared to say No to letting US troops pass through Turkey to open a second front against Iraq. But the prospect of EU membership has also affected Turkey's regional strategy. For example, Ankara has moderated its position on the touchstone issue of Cyprus. Turkish Foreign Minister Davutoðlu's policy is founded on three main pillars: maintaining 'zero problem' relations with the neighbours, pursuing a proactive and multilateral foreign policy in Turkey's wide neighbourhood, and utilising the Ottoman heritage as a foreign policy asset. It is building stronger ties with the countries around its borders – Iraq, Iran, Syria, Russia, even Armenia. Ankara has also taken the diplomatic initiative to manage or mediate long-standing conflicts in the region. It has also brokered talks between Damascus and Tel Aviv while proving itself a champion of the Palestinian cause. Since the second half of 2009, Turkey established high-level strategic council meetings with Iraq, Syria, Greece, and Russia. These are joint cabinet meetings where bilateral political, economic, and security issues are discussed in detail. Turkey abolished visa requirements with a host of countries Syria, Tajikistan, Albania, Lebanon, Jordan, Libya, and Russia. Ankara's mediating capacities, enhanced by its ability to go where no European power could go independently, should logically work in Ankara's favour in its EU membership application. Trade and business links between Turkey and its neighbours have been flourishing. Turkey says it wants, and is able, to spread stability and prosperity across its borders.

Does this mean Turkey has become more attractive to the EU? Turkish politicians and intellectuals argue that they will be more useful to their allies if they are also on good terms with their allies enemies. But appealing both to the East and West will not be an easy balance to strike. It might be read as too Muslim and Middle Eastern for the Europeans, and too secular and Western for Middle Easterners. Erdogan and his colleagues would have to be more careful about making statements that appear to set Turkish foreign policy apart from western objectives. Today's Turkey enjoys credibility in the Muslim world. Professions of friendship with Ahmedinejad or a seeming defence of al-Bashir appear unnecessary and counterproductive. Moreover, Turkey would have to supply some evidence that it uses its growing ties with neighbouring countries to pass on tough messages from time to time and stand up for western values. For example, instead of rushing to congratulate Ahmedinejad on his victory in the rigged election of June 2009, Turkey should have insisted that democratic rules be upheld.

EU in turn needs to realise that a Turkey committed to reform in lieu of membership in the Union reflects its own success. The EU wielding its "soft power" has been able to reshape countries and influence regions by attraction rather than coercion. The EU has successfully changed critical aspects of Turkey's political and legal systems in a way that the US, despite having a long and intimate relationship with Ankara, never managed to do. Some scholars have gone so far as to argue that the style of Turkish diplomacy have become more European. As two shrewd observers note: "While in the past Turkish foreign policy has focussed on the importance of military security and balance-of-power politics, it now increasingly appreciates the value of civilian instruments of law, economics and diplomacy, as well as multilateral settings in which to pursue its aims."

The Energy Card

Turkish politicians stress the role their country is naturally poised to play in EU's energy security by acting as a bridge to the resource-rich regions in its neighbourhood. Turkey's development as a European energy hub looks natural, given its lucky location between countries that harbour 70 per cent of the world's oil and gas reserve to its east, north and south, and one of the world's biggest energy markets in the west.

The 2007 energy policy package published by the European Commission had diversification of sources of energy supply right at the top of the priority list. The Caspian and Central Asian regions are central to the Commission's diversification plans. Until now, Europe has only been able to import gas from Central Asia and the Caspian via Russian territory (the Turkey-Greece interconnector breaks this monopoly, but the quantities are small so far). But the project that could make a bigger difference to Europe's energy security, and to Turkey's role as an energy hub, is Nabucco. This 3,300 kilometre pipeline would run from eastern Turkey via Bulgaria, Romania, and Hungary into Austria. Once it reaches full capacity, it could transport 31 billion cubic metres of gas to the EU every year. Critics say that this would be insignificant compared with the EU's overall gas needs, and with the amounts that it is still likely to buy from Russia. But for John Roberts, an energy expert at Platts, the doubters are missing a point. He argues that the mere existence of an alternative supply route would strengthen the EU's hand in negotiations with Russia, and thus force Gazprom to sell gas on a more competitive basis. The future of Nabucco is today uncertain as Turkey threatens to withdraw from the project if the energy chapter continues to be blocked by EU.

Conclusion

Summing up the developments in EU-Turkey engagement one could argue that the membership is poised precariously. The frustration in Turkey is palpable, especially when the leaders hear ideas of less than a full membership being floated in European capitals. Turkey is a NATO member and its linkages to other European bodies are well established. It is a member of the Council of Europe (1949), European Court of Human Rights, OSCE, and even the European football league. It appears that Turkey is at once both European and not so, if we heed what some of the opinion makers have to say.

Non-membership or delayed membership will not leave EU repercussion free. Psychologically Turkey appears better placed in terms of dealing with both membership and non-membership. EU is still divided, indecisive, and apprehensive about Turkey's entry. If Turkey's entry as many leaders and public despair has the potential of fundamentally affecting EU in terms of its identity, personality and institutions, turning Turkey away would also have internal and external impact. The 15 million odd Muslims in the EU are closely watching how the membership story unfolds. It could serve as fodder for radical groups which question Western standards and domination. Externally the loss of credibility would negatively affect its external policy especially in the immediate neighbourhood. The prospect of membership has been the EU's single most effective foreign policy tool. In their desire to join the Union, countries across the European continent have consolidated democracy, opened up their economies, strengthened their public administrations, and improved relations with their neighbours. The accession process has worked wonders in Central and Eastern Europe, helping these countries to move from chaotic post-communism to orderly EU membership in a decade and a half. The EU could do the same for Turkey, provided it stops dragging its feet. Turkey has been trying to move closer to the EU for 40 years. If EU leaders make these talks unnecessarily difficult, they could undermine the usefulness of accession as a foreign policy tool. If the EU cannot offer a credible timetable for accession to a key partner like Turkey, it will lose its leverage, not just in Turkey but also in many other countries aspiring to join the EU. EU's other agenda of countering clash of civilizations with a dialogue of civilization is also then likely to become a difficult exercise.

The EU while pressing for compliance to membership rules needs to acknowledge how far Turkey has already come. This is a country that experienced four military coups in the last half-century, but is now pursuing previously unthinkable reforms. The current government has shown not only a firm commitment to making Turkey fit for EU membership, but also the capacity to do so. After years of espousing Westernisation a Turkey rejected would most likely move towards Russia and its immediate neighbours. As pointed out its recent foreign policy posturing already indicates this and internally it could experience democratic reversal and an Islamic backlash .Thus a slow or sudden death is likely to impact both significantly.

References

1. Esra La Gro and Knud Erik Jorgensen (eds.,) *Turkey and the European Union: Prospects for a Difficult Encounter,* New York: Palgrave Macmillan, 2007.
2. Olivier Roy(ed.), T*urkey Today: A European Country,* London: Anthem Press, 2005.
3. Joseph S. Joseph (ed.), *Turkey and the European Union: Internal Dynamics and External Challenges,* London: Palgrave Macmillan, 2006.
4. Mehmet Ugur, *The European Union and Turkey: An anchor/ Credibility Dilemma,* England: Ashgate, 1999.
5. Second report of the Independent Commission on Turkey, *Turkey in Europe: Breaking the Vicious Circle,* September 2009.
6. Katinka Barysch, Turkey's role in European energy security, http://www.cer.org.uk/pdf/essay_turkey_energy_12dec07.pdf.
7. Katinka Barysch, Should the Nabucco pipeline project be shelved? http://www.cer.org.uk/pdf/pb_Nabucco_5may10.pdf.
8. David Hannay, Cyprus: The Costs of Failure, http://www.cer.org.uk/pdf/bn_cyprus_1sept09.pdf.
9. "The EU and Turkey: drifting apart? Key conclusions of the 4 Bosphorus conference," organised by the British Council, Turkish Economic and Social Studies Foundation (TESEV) and the Centre for European Reform Istanbul, October 5-6, 2007. http://www.europeum.org/ess2010/doc/Turkey.pdf.
10. Katinka Barysch, *Can Turkey combine EU accession and regional leadership?* http://www.cer.org.uk/pdf/pb_barysch_turkey_25jan10.pdf.
11. David Barchard, *Turkey and the European Union,* http://www.cer.org.uk/pdf/p093_turkey.pdf.
12. Sinan Ulgen, *Turkish politics and the fading magic of EU enlargement,* http://www.cer.org.uk/pdf/pb_ulgen_turkey_8sept10.pdf.

Section-III
EU and the World

6

European Union's External Relations: Nature, Priorities & Issues

Hartmul Elsenhans

1. A European foreign policy as a manifestation and an instrument of European integration, prototype of a new type of power in a new global system

The most remarkable aspect about the European Union in the world seems to lie in the fact that the dimensions under which this topic should be dealt with are at the very centre of the problem. Do we deal with a new "power" for which the characteristics of a full member of the international system, a state apply? Do we deal with a new type of power and how does it fit into the layers of the existing or emerging international system? How does it fit into an "international" system which itself undergoes deep transformations which we may only see in their very first manifestations but which will become the structuring traits of the global system in which we live? The European Union has its representations in the international arena, which enjoy some of the attributes of diplomatic representations although they are not headed by real ambassadors.[1] They are on the list of diplomatic representations but not integrated in the alphabetical order in the list of the embassies of states; but headed by diplomats who had mostly been ambassadors, who are advised by their central administration in Brussels not to insist on this title in their actual positions.[2] They negotiate important agreements, especially in the domain of trade relations, which according to the Lisbon Treaty are a Union competence. In other spheres of international intercourse there are parallel competencies shared with the member states: This is the case of development assistance where Union programs coexist with national programmes of the member states.[3] And there are strictly national foreign policies in the realm of security[4] although there is also the European Union Common Foreign and Security Policy (CFSP) and the European Security and Defence Policy (ESDP) with extended mechanisms of coordination, especially the Political and Security Committee (PSC) as the central institution of these CFSP and ESDP. Both, however, do not really deal with the most important issues of any foreign policy, the relation of the Union with the other major powers, USA, China, and also Russia (although there is a common strategy in relation to Russia).[5]

A closer look into the institutions of the PSC will reveal that most of the institutions are related to the relations of the Union with partners in relatively uncontroversial policy fields like Eastern Europe or the Mediterranean, where European Union institutions prevail over national ones, however, only as long as there are no serious problems in the region, as shown by the European Union behaviour during the Tunisian and Egyptian revolutions of 2011.

From a realist point of view, the European Union is not considered as a state which can engage all the resources available on its territory for organising the affirmation of its rank and influence in rivalry with other states even by mobilising military power, although the European Union has military means at its disposal.[6] From an institutional or a constructivist point of view the European Union is a major power which through the concerted action of its Union level institutions and its member states participates in the construction of a new global system where the rule of law matters more than the power of the states because military power is less and less useful for preserving security, and where security can no longer be defined in the traditional ways inherited from the Westphalian inter-state system which prevailed until the middle of the 20th century.[7]

Globalisation requires a new concept of security including security from environmental dangers, chances for economic development, and political structures in all participating states that allow the development of the Kantian vision of a peaceful global system which is based in the interests of humanity escaping the fate of disaster through violence.[8]

The European Union appears as a composite actor where Union level institutions cooperate with national decision makers based on member states within a European security community.[9] This community is not as unified as a nation but cohesive because member nations are no longer assumed to follow their national goals at least without restraint. Hence, the European Union appears as a new type of participant in a global system which is just in the making, where the new characteristics of this actor are particularly appropriate to manage peaceful change at the global level. It can be argued that the fact that the European Union is not a nation state as other powers claim to be, should not be considered as a deficit in its quality as an actor at the global level but as characteristics which demonstrate its fundamental modernity in a new global world to which other powers are called to adapt by changing themselves, their internal structures, and their external behaviours. The emerging global system may be expected to be composed by actors with similar characteristics

Such a focus seems more appropriate for viewing the role of the European Union than the description of its economic importance or military power. Certainly, the European Union is a major economy with a share in world trade of 16.2%, the highest share of any major economic block in world trade. The position as a source of foreign direct investment is similarly important,[10] with Great Britain, Germany, and France sharing the major part of the total.[11] Its role as a finance centre stands second only to the United States.[12] Its share in world industry is still above its share in world population. It has experienced de-industrialisation less than the other highly industrialised regions of the West. Although its share in high technology products and exports is lower than its share in world industrial exports and production,[13] it has kept up in modernising its production. Its share in military potential is obviously far below the United States,[14] but the European Union is, after the United States the only unit of the global system capable of projecting military resources abroad and even outside its near neighbourhood.[15] Even if the European Union is a military dwarf in comparison to its economic potential, its low profile in this area is not the consequence of a lack of resources but the result of preferences of its member states and the Union as whole. These preferences are usually described as priority for the role as a civilian power with clear priorities for a liberal, state-free world economy with peaceful conflict management.[16]

In both, economic and security matters close cooperation with the United States is hoped for, with a clearly subordinate role of the Union outside Europe's near neighbourhood and a more independent role in close cooperation with the US in areas of geographical proximity to Europe (Eastern Europe, Mediterranean, and the still sub-Saharan Africa). At the economic level, there is a priority for environmental concerns where there is tension not only with environmentally less conscious and economically catching up economies of the South, as well as with the US. At the political level, the European Union pretends to be more committed than all other powers to the defence of human rights and democracy promotion following the predictions of the theory of democratic peace.

These orientations of the European Union are the result of its own structures. These structures in turn result from an attempt to overcome the nation state in its present form which was inherited by the 19th century modification of the Westphalian system. Under the impact of mass mobilisation subsequent to the transition from "traditional" society with their priority of local communities only superficially overarched by large-scale territorial powers, to modernity with masses becoming disposable for new forms of social and economic integration, the Westphalian state invented the concept of nation as a community of destiny,[17] which attempted to place all other solidarities to the second level. In its form of ethnic definition this concept of a nation state in Europe has failed to provide peace and security. By engaging in the process of European integration, Europe is trying to find a post-ethnic new order often called constitutional patriotism.[18] This post-national perspective will also guide new emerging powers in a new multipolar world system.

2. A common foreign policy as an instrument of identity formation in the process of a deepening of European integration

The process of European integration can be viewed as a unique social experiment that tries to overcome the existing identities by a new set of identities, which allows in turn to build a new state structure. This new state structure of continental Europe was projected to be based on new ties of solidarity beyond the collectivities on which the European state system had been built till 1945. This process is not new with respect to the formation of translocal communities but with respect to the conditions under which it occurs.

The formation of nations in Europe since the 16th century and in an intensified form since the 18th century had been just such a process like the processes of nation building which occurred in the other continents later on. The basic challenge of such processes consists in the invention of identities beyond the local communities of tribe and religion, which characterise pre-capitalist structures of which smaller ones are usually called communitarian modes of production (with often a clear pattern of social stratification)[19] and larger ones called tributary modes of production with clearly distinguishable ruling classes which rule over relatively fragmented, exploited, predominantly rural classes of producers who have a relatively loose link with the ruling classes and remain separated from each other with relatively limited perceptions of their solidarities.[20]

Under the impact of the emergence of capitalism with its intensified division of labour, the necessity to remain competitive that was imposed on those with access to economic surplus, triggered off the mobility of labour. Those in control of the economic surplus tried to have access to ever cheaper labour. In the search for cheap labour to be employed in the manufacture of new products to be produced increasingly in larger units, in larger quantities, and for larger markets, labour had to move, by the pull or push effects, to new production sites and establish a new pattern of socialisation in order to create some social cohesion. The need to communicate with strangers with whom there were no ties of kin or family made common language an outstanding element of feeling at least somewhat close. In most cases, a shared language became a criterion for creating new "invented" communities.[21] In Europe, this process was slow and allowed established regional languages to become link languages that dominated closely kindred languages, so that from the attempts of the European tributary structures of the composite monarchies of European feudalism national languages emerged which superseded local languages and pushed them to the role of mere dialects.[22] These national languages had to be adopted by the ruling "elites" which often were much more cosmopolitan in outlook, a point already made by Engels in 1884.[23] The units that emerged were not the result of natural processes. Therefore there were political struggles linked to the attempts of ruling groups with more or less territorial clout to enlarge, unify, and homogenise the territories under their control. Linguistically, large parts of Western Germany were originally closer to Dutch than to the "high" upper German language which finally prevailed. In southern France, languages were spoken with clear affinities to Northern Italian or South Eastern Spanish vernaculars.

In Europe, this process of the emergence of political unity was characterised by the emergence of a distribution of power where imbalances between states became dangerous. A major part of the economic core region from South Western England via the Rhine axis and the Swiss Alp passes to Northern Italy, the blue banana of Eurostat,[24] was claimed by Germany as being part of her. This made Germany a disproportionately powerful region if she pretended to be politically united. Westphalia (1648) attempted to limit this power and to disperse. The Vienna system (1815) maintained these goals and complemented the arrangement by taking account of this entity of a nation. It balanced its cultural unity through political diversity, but failed through German unification after 1866-1870, which proved to be disastrous as Germany, after Bismarck, attempted to become hegemonic. After 1945, the two major rival powers, Britain (under the initiative of Churchill)[25] and especially France[26] took the initiative of solving this structural challenge of a Germany too powerful to be left without control and not powerful enough to exercise itself hegemony by integrating Germany as an equal partner into an institutional structure where equality and not power mattered.[27] Potential German power was tamed by Germany's equal but as one member among many other ones minor position in more or less supranational institutions. These institutions became more comprehensive during the intensification of the process of European integration, in order to attract more support in the form of the expectedly slow emergence of a European body politic. European integration drives the constitution with its own social and political basis because the elites want it without being "committed" because not yet Europeanized social bases permit it and follow without playing itself a very active role. In order to accelerate this process, a large variety of seemingly heterogeneous mechanisms was and is applied.

The basic structure of the elite-driven process of European integration consists in the following: There is an overarching consensus, among European (initially West European) elites on never putting into question the priority of the formation of a European body politic. Within this framework, more and more areas of policies are put together in order to make the European societies dependent on the community level decision-making processes so that the output of the European political and economic system can create new loyalties and by this means complement the national identities with a new European identity. Until the goal is achieved, the interests articulated in these European societies are to be absorbed by the mechanisms of compromise within the national political systems so that Anti-European forces at these national levels never can enter into an open conflict with the European Union even if they are still powerful. For managing this permanent compromise, the member state governments had and still have to remain in the driver seat. The decisive role of the member state governments is not an obstacle to integration, but the very condition for avoiding the constitution of anti-European fronts in the still "national" political bodies. This contradictory simultaneity of an overarching interest of elites in European unity and the necessity of blocking nationally powerful interests from using the national institutions in an uncompromising manner for achieving their interests explains the multiple balances between supranationality and intergovernmental decision-making within the Union. Because the factually intergovernmental process of most European Union decision making aims at allowing the national interests to become increasingly Union-level oriented, the opposition between the constructivist institutional and the intergovernmental interpretations only relates to the forms in which agreements are achieved but not their intrinsical quality.[28] The decision-making process is admittedly intergovernmental. It is, however, embedded in an intentionally organised process of changes of perceptions in the body politic, where Union-level impulses and national orientations interact and lead to, a still ongoing and uneven process of identity formation. This simultaneous presence of drives from both levels, makes the distinction between the two approaches concerns essentially a level of analysis problem. With respect to its dynamics, this distinction is artificial.

The main vehicles of this process are the emergence of common economic interests through the intensification of economic integration and the steering of this process in order to limit negative fallouts on potentially affected groups by a multitude of compensatory policies, the avoidance of possible clashes and the use of the still existing national frameworks for promoting convergence in business management, state-business relations, labour relations and cultural attitudes. A favourite field for intergovernmental efforts for identity creation is foreign policy. The process of European integration has benefited from two foreign policy aspects: The fear of a renewal of nationalism and the fear of the Soviet Union.

As the wars of the 20th century have been very disastrous, no foreign policy issue between the members is important enough to justify open conflict. France generously accepted the return of Saar to Germany in 1955. Italy's German-speaking minority in Alto Adige saw its rights to cultural identity recognised within the framework of the Italian state. No country could accede to the European Union that had territorial claims on its neighbours. Belgian unity was preserved. No irredenta movement was acceptable. No boundary established by the settlements following World War II (which basically confirmed the settlements of 1919, with the exception of the Polish-German boundary) was modified.

Initially the incipient European unification process was aimed at strengthening Western Europe against the threat of the further expansion of the Soviet Union. Two of the three major forces which emerged from the victory over Nazism in continental Europe were the Christian Democrats, whose role in European unification had been decisive from the beginning, and the Social Democrats who rejected proposals of neutralism and of a Third Way between the two new superpowers (at least in their majorities), and opted for a close alliance with the US which saved Europe from fascism, German hegemony, and through the Marshall plan from economic chaos in the wake of which the communists may have hoped for a political takeover.

This foreign policy consensus about the equality of all European nations on the basis of the 1945 territorial settlement under the ultimate protection of the US within the framework of the US economic strategy already defined in 1935, of liberalising the world economy in order to make the world "safe for democracy"[29] was never questioned despite controversies over details such as whether Europe should be more European or more Atlanticist. There was a largely shared consensus about the anchorage of Europe in a larger Atlantic community under the leadership of the US. This also determined the relation between Europe and the rest of the world (such as in the case of decolonisation). Because of this unanimity behind US leadership, the foreign policy appeared as an ideally appropriate field of identity creation by putting together decision-making in a non-controversial policy field, which could serve as a symbol for common interests, even if the foreign policy was still the main attribute of the governments of the member states.

Foreign policy became the main area for exercising intra-Union intergovernmental cooperation so that the foreign policy remains largely under the control of member governments. But at the same time it became a major field of identification for Union level institutions to emerge and become visible. This explains the existence and the limits of CFSP and ESDP.[30] Its main areas concern non-West-European issues, mainly issues where identity of perceptions and dependence on US leadership are of the highest. The close links of the European Union with the US and the latter's interest in avoiding a politically independent European "superpower" explains these de facto limitations to areas of minor interest in the "great" game between the powers.

The process of constitution, i.e. "construction" of a European identity, which overrides the hitherto relevant and historically predominant "ethnically" determined identities in Europe occurred within a framework where serious challenges for Europe from outside and inside were absent. After the fall of the Berlin Wall, Europe was no longer threatened by the Soviet Union. The threat from the countries on the Southern shore of the Mediterranean was not yet important. Such a change of identity is not compelling. There is no external colonial power in Europe comparable to the British raj in India or the Japanese occupation (and the threat of other powers) of China which would trigger off a feeling of commonness which was at the origin of Indian nationalism and the mobilisation of the Chinese peasantry behind the modernised "literati" of the Chinese Communist party.[31] This process is therefore slower and more complex in the case of Europe. It can however be, considered as irreversible. It implies a concentration on those visible aspects of European foreign policy behaviour, which command high support in most member countries. European foreign policy therefore privileges issues closely related to the values, which are at the basis of the European integration process.

The European process of creating supra-local identities (i.e. national ones) was characterised during the 16th - 19th centuries by the absence of non-European threats. Therefore, today Europe is behind the emerging powers of Asia, China, and India, in developing less parochial cultural elements of common identity than language. China and India have succeeded in this because of the necessity of the struggle against colonial alienation and exploitation. Nevertheless, European integration is a quite similar process. It occurs under conditions of low-intensity immediate external threat, so that the mass public follows only slowly. In the elite perceptions of the long-term perspectives of Europe, however, such threats are quite present and often mentioned.

European integration aims at creating a united Europe through a democratic process, instead of the hegemony of one power, on the basis of the long-term interests of all Europeans in maintaining cohesiveness in a world where individual European states can no longer command much influence if they remain isolated from each other. European Union anticipates in some sense the real danger of a decisive demise of Europe comparable to the demise of the older Asian empires in the late 18th century. In order to avoid the experience of dependency, Europe has to be constructed without any visible and materialised danger of dependency. For this, the necessary changes in behaviour and feelings of identity have to be established before the large masses experience the consequences of external dependency. It is assumed that by multiplying experiences of commonness wherever possible, such changes in behaviour can be "constructed". In the European Union studies, there is the importance of "constructivism" far in excess of the real nature of observable behaviour changes and their isolation from emerging realities. In the area of practical foreign policy behaviour, there is also a focus on the moralistic dimensions which can serve for the internal purpose of creating a European "identity" in the body politic. European ideology serves quite realistic purposes.

3. A world civil power against realist power politics

One aspect of the external behaviour of the European Union that especially provokes criticism and a lack of understanding outside the North Atlantic area is the European claim to behaving as a civilian power that does not follow realistic principles of power politics.[32] Especially from the comments of analysts from newly emerging powers in Asia who see this behaviour as a sign of Europe not sticking to the rules of the game of international relations.[33] With newly emerging powers this creates uneasiness, as the behaviour of European Union and its member states seems to be unpredictable, unreasonable or untrustworthy. The European Union appears to be an unreliable partner.

This aspect of the European foreign policy is, however, the direct result of the power configurations and internal structures on which the process of European integration is based. This implies the possibility of a realist explanation provided that one leaves the exclusive focus on the state and follows sociological realism. To paraphrase Raja Mohan's quote, the option for a civilian power role is not the result of a rejection of realist principles in foreign policy but the consequence of instrumentalising foreign policy for a realist strategy of international alliance building in order to get audience and visibility for a pro-integration "transnational" European wide coalition.[34] This behaviour therefore implies that the European Union follows interests, but that, as any other power, it defines its interests in a way which allows it to mobilise internal support.

The European Union does not emerge as a state, which promises its citizens international standing by the projection of power to the outside world on the basis of which the citizens feel powerful and identify with it. Instead of the national grandeur of the old foci for reference, the nation states have proved to be a source of disaster for Europe. Because of the history of Europe, power, especially military power, is fundamentally suspect. International relations should follow the rule of law and be oriented to finding a compromise as the exclusive form of conflict resolution. All nationalists' feelings comprise of rancour against an external power. In Europe, because of its history the targets of this rancour feeling is Germany, and in Eastern Europe Russia, albeit to a lesser degree (even in Poland). A national resentment in the member states on the basis of these memories therefore would be divisive. The alternative is a Europe based on the rejection of the glorification of the power status of the collectivity with which one has to identify.

Any large social movement such as nationalism or the movement for a European integration, has a unifying myth. In the case of nationalism, this had been initially the feeling of the "Third Estate" to be as valuable as the legally privileged nobles. Nationalism invented the "citoyen" as an independent producer with equal rights on the markets against privilege and monopoly of the lords and the trading companies and equal right of participation in the control and production of public goods through political structures.[35] When economic equality was not produced by the market, the working people invented class solidarity. The only means by which the privileged (not only the new ones but also the remnants of the "*Ancien Regime*") could counter this new myth of solidarity was a reformulation of the nation as an ethnic group against the foreigners with well-known results.[36] A movement to counter this feeling had to overcome this ethnicised identity.

Two factors implied that such a counter-movement to ethnical solidarity could rely only on the values of the bourgeois revolution. On the one hand, the citizens identified their relations with the collective unit on the basis of the rule of law, property rights, and the right to formal participation, ultimately the patriotism for the values of a democratic constitution. On the other hand, labour had been attached to the collectivity on the basis of the welfare state. The welfare state had developed in all European countries in a path-dependent way with a multitude of country specific regulations despite a high degree of international coordination.[37] Unifying those systems through European integration proved to be extremely difficult.[38] Each group wanted to maintain all its advantages so that harmonisation implied convergence to the highest level. The case of German unification has shown that the integration of another system into an existing one implies costly improvements for all especially for the less comprehensive ones without any savings in the more comprehensive ones.[39] The alternative was negative integration, i.e. the slow removal of many privileges and the convergence to those standards that were common to all.[40] So labour criticised the social "cold" of the European Union.[41]

Invariably the polls show that identification with the European Union is highest if the respondents are better off, better educated, ultimately members of the new middle classes.[42] These new middle classes are predominantly consumerist, without identification with nationalist values and have developed in the last four decades post-materialist orientations.[43] Any foreign policy, which increases their identification with the European integration, has to reflect these orientations.

This set of values, which a common foreign policy can address, fits nicely into the set of resources a common European foreign policy can mobilise. The Union level is still too weak to impose on its citizens sacrifices such as conscription, which always was based on the national law before it was abrogated in many European countries. The mobilisation of draftees for military purposes abroad is the task of national governments. In all Western industrialised countries, the mobilisation of draftees for other purposes other than for the strict defence of their own sanctuary is extremely difficult as shown by the latest events, the wars of decolonisation.[44]

Because the European Union does not dispose of the identification of a traditional national state, it had to act as a civilian power in its dealings with the external world. Since the Maastricht

Treaty, the European Union follows an active policy of intervention in external regions, especially the Balkans and also sub-Saharan Africa where it privileges civilian instruments of capacity building.[45] Because of the crisis of state-centred development, as shown by the demise of rent-based state classes in the South and of really existing socialism in the East,[46] the European Union finds in all the respective areas, partners. These partners basically want to prosper on the basis of new contacts with the West, especially access to the markets of the European Union. Just as in the case of "informal colonialism" of the first three quarters of the 19th century,[47] there are always powerful "bridgeheads" for the West who can fulfil the task of locally stabilising the existing order. They are able to maintain the rule of law as their local power positions depend on property rights in local assets (most visibly in the case of the privatisations in Eastern Europe) which are protected under conditions of the establishment of bourgeois democratic structures with liberal economic systems.[48] Due to the weakness of labour, which normally cannot impose secondary income redistribution on a large scale, and due to market imperfections, the rents, which are appropriated in such systems, do not openly appear as politically appropriated rents and hence go easily with such a liberal economic order.[49]

In prioritising civil methods of intervention with limited military resources that are meant to maintain order and hence also the existing structure of property rights, the European Union can associate NGOs to its efforts to build social bridgeheads for avoiding precarious social situations which through severe crisis could lead to disorder and popular resistance.[50] These NGO-supported civilian tutelary regimes have taken over large parts of sub-Saharan Africa where European influence is still important.[51] In development strategies, they use development assistance for basically a market oriented growth strategy, where capacity to export is the motor of growth, and social assistance measures mildly contribute to avert the severest consequences of the limits of such strategies.[52]

The methods of European Union foreign policies in areas of its specific interests, the strengthening of civil society, "formal" democracy, rejection of ethnic nationalism and identitarian "fundamentalist" moments, the rule of law, the strengthening of police forces (and not military forces),[53] correspond to the resources available to the Union for the projection of influence abroad, towards the goal of making external power politics compatible with internal support bases for the foreign policy of the Union (and its member states), for pooling European resources in case the interests of a member state have to be defended with the support of other members (sub-Saharan Africa), etc. As long as these strategies work, because "troublemakers" in the regions concerned have no viable alternative model of developing economic resources for their own project without access to Western markets, there is no reason to change this profile, even if it appears as non-rational in the eyes of realist analysts of international relations.

It should be noted that these strategies do not work in relation to powers with an independent power base, such as the emerging powers of Asia. These powers, however, are no target of an independent posture of the European Union but of quite traditional national foreign policy strategies followed by member state governments in close cooperation with the US. Probably a major reason for support of such a civil power profile is the differences in capabilities of power projection by major powers of the European Union. Any open realist defence of interest by projection of military power will render the vulnerability of Germany to moral critique because of her past. On the other hand, focus on the civil power profile enables Germany (unlike Britain and France) to conceal its intents and achieve one of her major post World War II aims - the recovery of equality with other middle powers in the international arena, a very "realist power politics" goal. The differences over Libya have laid open this dilemma. Hence, it is clear that there is an affinity between this civilian power (limited to specific regions) and the global economic strategy of the European Union, which the Europeans Union and member states follow also in relation to major powers.[54]

4. The commitment to a liberal economic world order

The European Union was born also as an attempt to marry growth promotion by the state and (increasing) market relations. Such a combination was favoured especially by those member countries which felt less competitive on the world market. It was meant to allow war-torn, economically destroyed, but also backward (in relation to the United States) economies to re-enter the world market.[55] France and Italy had engaged in modernisation by comprehensive state planning and the creation of publicly financed and even state owned enterprises in high technology sectors (chemistry, oil, mining, car production, and computers).[56] Since the start of the European integration process one of the points of contention between the industrially advanced Benelux and Western Germany on one side, and France and Italy on the other had been concerning the role of the state in economic modernisation.[57]

This divergence has been decided in favour of the predominance of the market due to the success of European integration. The realisation of a single market (1993) implied the end of older forms of government to business partnerships as they implied distortions in competition.[58] The Maastricht Treaty established a Union competence in industrial policy but the Union efforts to promote high technology have been nearly absent whereas the US substitute of a Department of Defence does not exist at the Union level because of the essentially national character of the military procurement policies, although case-by-case programs exist.[59]

In the French decolonisation process there had been some beginnings of a government-to-government cooperation in which the more developed "metropolis" accepted privileged cooperation on the basis of concessions on raw material, rents in favour of less developed economies in exchange for privileged access to their markets for high technology products, especially equipment.[60] The French position in this regards, called at the time 'co-development', found their clearest expression in the French Algerian gas agreement in 1982,[61] but had already lost at the Union level in 1975 when German Chancellor Schmidt imposed a European position, also on France, which was in line with the US position during the Paris Conference on International Economic Cooperation which OPEC had imposed on the West.[62]

The logic of European integration via the market combined with compensation in favour of the losers of the emerging patterns of specialisation in the form of improvements in their infrastructures (widely applied in order to promote the economies of the southern member states) implied the removal of all distortions in competition, especially the so-called hidden distortions. Government procurement and quality requirements had to treat all Union enterprises alike. The opening of the telecom sector and in the Cassis de Dijon judgement of the European Union, Court of Justice decisions were milestones in the policies of deep integration and reform of rules "behind" the boundaries.[63] The European experience had shown, that harmonisation through positive adjustment of standards is more difficult than removal of standards.

Those in favour of liberàlisation pursued the programme, which was more easy to apply than those who wanted a standardisation of rules which limited the freedom of business. This explains why the process of economic convergence was characterised by so-called negative integration. This made integration more attractive to the most modern segments of the business sector. Its role became visible in the "European Round Table of Industrialists" as an advocacy group that promoted the agenda of the single market. This same logic applies to the removal of regulations on the financial sectors.[64]

In following the logic of the creation of a single market and a unified capital market as well as as a result of the incapacity of the member states to replace national by Union-wide commonly agreed regulations, the European Union could not avoid becoming also at the world level the protagonist of deregulation (with one exception, the establishment of environmental safety standards). Forces opposing deregulation had no viable alternative not only because agreeing to Union-level rules was difficult at the level of the decision-making process, but also because coalition building at the Union level was relatively easy for the most dynamic sectors of business, but difficult for the "counterweight" in welfare capitalism, labour. Capital follows universal rules as it removes most rules and operates in principle only in the sphere of economic exchange.[65] Labour has to exercise its role within the framework of politically constructed institutions. Not only the precise rules to manage capitalism by labour but also the political forces to impose their implementation emerge in capitalism, in a path-dependent manner.[66]

They take varied forms depending on the various configurations at the time of their emergence (power relations and preferences which dominated in that period) and are carried over in the process of institutional change. The difference between labour organisations in the European Union is presented in the most visible example with powerful and relatively concentrated unions in Germany where by strikes occur rarely, and weak unions in France with "anarchical" tendencies and a limited potential to impose their demands by means of "class collaboration." [67] Attempts to coordinate labour at the Union level have occurred, however, without much practical relevance for the struggle between labour and business at the local levels.[68] European integration has therefore weakened labour, a result that is welcomed by businesses. As a result, the neoliberal "*pensée unique*" made further ground. Here higher wages are but a cost element which limits growth "per se" because it reduces investable surplus and, in addition, growth in relation to competitors as it increases relative costs.

This has important implications: in order to maintain competitiveness of any single "nation", the Union should not become a transfer community, although it has been conceived as a transfer community. The Common Agricultural Policy implied that economically less advanced partners with higher shares of agriculture in national incomes, received transfers through subsidised agricultural prices.[69] No new transfers for weaker economies were, however, introduced with enhanced integration through the introduction of the Euro. Especially, there were no provisions on how to deal with the consequences of the end of protection through exchange rate adjustments for technically less dynamic economies of the type of compensatory financing between state budgets which characterises federal states.

One result is, that attempts to modernise the application of Keynesian principles of demand management under conditions of the crisis and the neoliberal onslaught in the wake of Thatcherism and Reaganomics, becomes further complicated through the intensification of European integration. National attempts and the implementation of such principles (in Germany "concerted action") were never transposed to the Union level especially also because the national competition of production sites was always considered as an instrument for enabling technically less advanced members of the

Union to catch up on the basis of lower production costs, hence also lower real wages.[70] Attempts to create a "social Europe" explicitly excluded "harmonisation" of wage levels; as such, harmonisation would have implied massive intra-European Union labour migration as usually occurs within a national economy.

The mechanism of union-wide wage increase for increasing employment by means of enlarging the final demand is never mentioned in the programs for a social Europe. These programs, such as the Luxembourg process started in 1997 on the so-called job summit in order to implement the employment title of the Amsterdam treaty and the Cardiff process (1998) which continued it,[71] insist on the possibilities of labour to organise freely (including the right of trade unions to organise and mobilise in the work- place) and measures to enhance the negotiating power of labour by improving the levels of employment. These programs therefore have the capacity of improving employment possibilities through improving the skills of workers.[72]

The requirement of raising real wages in order to make consumptive potential meet the productive potential has after being taboo for a long period at the Union level (especially after the Mitterrand experience of 1983), only recently surfaced, when the French finance minister correctly diagnosed that the debt problems of Germany's major partners in the European Union were also due to the very restrictive German wage policy.[73]

In the now dominating neoliberal world, the only means to improve demand consists in increasing balance of trade surpluses. Those who could achieve a balance of trade surplus imitated Germany as best they could, and those who could not limit their balance of trade deficits, when the instrument of devaluation had been excluded through the introduction of the Euro could not avoid the attempt to cheat the public on the increase of their indebtedness.[74]

This orientation has German base: the most powerful trade union in Germany which largely determines the outlook of German labour, has its basis in metal working. During the recent crisis Germany adopted a system of state-supported part-time work which allowed to maintain employment quite in line with the insights of endogenous growth theory on technical progress which is seen as dependent on the interplay of human capital within long standing teams. It is from this sector of German industry where Germany receives most of its export surplus. This sector has since long been export oriented with German shares of more than 25% in world equipment exports.[75]

Early on, this sector had been identified as the core of the German neo-corporatist structures which is at the heart of what is commonly called Rhenish capitalism.[76]Germany as the main source of Union export earnings never developed an understanding of the relevance of low exchange rates for promoting exports because in this industrial sector quality and much less, price is paramount for success.[77] German interests overlap here with the interests of Britain, which compensated deindustrialisation by the growth of its financial "industry", a branch that is normally loath of currency devaluations: higher international prices of its currency increase the purchasing power of locally created "artificial" money, artificial because it is based on speculation. This interest is shared by the European financial sector that has become more important as a result of the 'financialisation' of the European economies. Technical monopoly (in investment goods production) and organisational monopoly (in the financial sector) explain the European preference for talking about free markets without insisting on the precondition of the Smithonian operation of free markets, i.e. perfect competition.

The European Union as a beneficiary of such invisible and apparently inexistent barriers to competition promotes the removal of many other more administratively imposed barriers which cannot be explained as being due only to superior efficiency. This is called the deep trade agenda, which the emerging Asian countries reject, as in the case of the Singapore agenda.[78] The European Union is also more indifferent than the United States to the implications of devaluation-driven export-oriented manufacturing growth as followed not only by China, but by most of the emerging economies. The European Union is therefore a tactical partner for the emerging economies of the macro policies at the global level, especially exchange rate policies, despite many frictions with these countries and a traditional but limited contribution to export led growth for these emerging economies.[79] One can argue that the European Union with its orientation on environmental issues has found a more elegant means of protecting its industries.

5. A leader in the world environmental movement

The low profile of the European Union in the macro-political conflict on globalisation and management of the world economy is compensated by its avant-garde role in environmental issues. In the public opinion the political oppositions which are provoked by the dominance of neoliberal principles, are "silenced" in Europe by the often vociferous critique of the irresponsibility of the United States and China on the climate issue and other environmental affairs.

Visibility on this issue in Europe is due to three mechanisms: among the industrialised blocks of North America and Europe, Europe is much more densely populated so that environmental resources in the form of unpopulated areas are limited. Europe has neither forests nor depressions, which can be expected to contribute to the regeneration of the endangered atmosphere. Europe has exhausted most of its raw material bases. Since the 1890s, European industry was searching for raw materials in the non-yet industrialised world more than the American industry. Also the strong position of US companies in raw materials production in the Third World is not so much the result of scarcities encountered in supplying the US market. The US companies had early on participated in the supply of European markets with raw materials. When cheaper sources were discovered in the continents of the South, they had to maintain position in the supply of Europe and partially Japan by participating in the exploitation of the newly discovered low-cost raw materials from cheap production sites in Latin America, Asia, and Africa.[80] Based on their inherited position on North American raw material production, such non-European companies were eager to participate in the differential rents these production sites outside the industrialised world allowed to generate. Also through losses in assets in non-European countries during and subsequent to the world wars of the 20th century, Europe's position is low in raw material production so Europe is especially raw material conscious despite or because its limited profile in world raw materials production.

The shift in all industrial countries to post-materialist values in Europe is especially relevant. The ecologist movement has become the main movement along with the reforms within the capitalist system. Given the turn of the labour movement mostly in favour of those who are still employed and not the marginalised ones, with a clear aspect of neo-corporatism in favour of relatively privileged parts of the great mass of the population, the green movement exercises considerable influence not only in its own constituency, but also on all labour parties and on the Christian Democratic parties. It is particularly strong in Germany, the Benelux, and also now in France. In the economically most advanced area of Germany, the South West, it has bypassed the Social Democratic Party. Green issues are attractive especially to those parts of the electorate, which are particularly supportive of European integration, and the development of a European identity. They are shared by all those non-governmental organisations that ally with the European Union in promoting democratisation and strengthening of the civil society in the South.[81]

Environmental issues are not only an item for international conferences where the European Union can (mildly) oppose the United States, but also criticise the reckless methods of industrialisation in the newly competitive nations of the South. Green issues can be connected to issues of developmental assistance and be brought into menu, which comprise of democracy promotion and support for civil society organisations, so that they become the link for the cooperation between European Union institutions, national development agencies, and non-governmental organisations.[82] This obviously leads to the integration of such issues in the presentation of these organisations in European public opinion.

Environmental issues, perhaps unintended by their promoters, have secondary effects on European coalition building. Due to the importance given to environmental issues on the European product market, environmental industries provide an increasing number of jobs and knowhow, which is used in the production of products that meet European environmental standards. This confers on them a competitive advantage in the European market alongside other quality characteristics. Meeting high environmental standards implies that those who have to respect them, enjoy comparative cost advantage in relation to producers who in their home markets, face less demanding standards for their mass production, also in expanding low income markets in other regions of Asia, Africa or Latin America, to which they export increasingly.

High environmental standards together with humanitarian labour standards can play the same role as non-tariff barriers against low-cost producers from low-labour-cost economies, and hence are supported by both labour and business in high-cost economies. Imposing high environmental standards in environmentally less advanced economies increases the export opportunities of the European producers, as they have acquired a leading worldwide position in environmental industries and technologies that can also be sold abroad. Government expenditures for this purpose in the form of development assistance are less criticised than spending on the support of "corrupt" regimes or for other purposes. Such expenditures increase the leverage of European agencies, private and public, national and Union-wide ones, for clientele building in the South. This favours the growth of organisations in this policy field and creates possibilities for professional advancement. Imposing environmental standards requires similar arrangements such as monitoring fair labour standards, the interdiction of child labour, and opening up new employment possibilities for non-governmental organisations that recruit mainly from the new post-materialist middle classes in Europe.

6. Persistent alignment with the United States

The focus on the environment as a distinguishing characteristic in comparison to the United States is the exception in the European foreign policy. The greater insistence on democracy promotion together with a clear preference for civilian conflict resolution is a complement to the US strategy, not a substitute. Alignment with the United States and some divergences with them are both compatible with maintaining the solidarity within the Western camp. The European Union has never attempted to be a rival power, which challenges the supremacy of the United States.

The United States has consistently promoted European integration.[83] European integration was born as an element of the

US strategy to impose its form of hegemony through cooperative allies. Because of their internal structures, the preferences of their ruling elites and also because of public opinion, these allies supported the American way of managing international affairs since 1945. There were divergences within the member states of the European Union on the orientation of the Union elites relations with the United States. The controversy over an Atlanticist versus a "European" united Europe in the 1960s led to a heated debate between France and other member states, as well as within many member states. [84]

However, the Gaullist attempt to strongly affirm France's global role was never meant to break the Atlantic alliance. France asked for a greater hearing within the alliance by proposing a directory of the three NATO powers with a permanent seat in the Security Council of the United Nations.[85] De Gaulle's strategy of enhancing the "*rayonnement*" of France in the world by assuming the role of a speaker for the Third World within the Western alliance failed.[86] But from the very beginning, this role was always meant to be exercised within the Western alliance. The establishment of an independent nuclear force was conceived precisely on the basis of the assumption that France ultimately would enjoy the nuclear cover of the US. The so-called strategy of "*tout-azimout,*" a concept of nuclear defence against all other powers, was meant as an instrument to enable France to impose the shift to nuclear war by itself, even if her allies would refrain from doing on the ground that the issue at stake was not worth of engaging the escalation process, considering that only France was in danger.[87] I add for the admirers of the independent stance of France in emerging powers of Asia, that the famous appeal of June 18, 1940 explicitly referred to France's chances of victory because of the support of the US, which was considered as inevitable in the long run.

Britain attempted and attempts a similar goal of voice in the US decision-making process on long-term global behaviour of the West by playing the card of special relationship, which the US is normally ready to accept.[88] Britain and France continuously refurbished their independence in foreign policy because this gives them a higher stance in relation to other major powers inside Europe, especially Germany. Britain behaves as the successful daughter of whom the mother is proud, and France is the naughty daughter in the difficult age, which protests in order to be loved. In these games, Germany has always privileged her relations with the United States as only the United States was able to protect West Germany against the Soviet threat. The German peace movement may have cherished the idea that the fall of the Iron Curtain would allow it to downplay the role of NATO in the management of European security issues.[89] The greater salience of economic issues in the wake of the decline of the Soviet military threat after the fall of the Berlin Wall has allowed for the intensifying of economic cooperation with successor states of the Soviet Union. There was, however, never a German attempt to replace the strategic dependency on the US by an explicit or implicit German-Russian alliance.[90] For the German foreign policy elite, membership of united Germany in NATO was considered as vital even after the demise of the Soviet Union. This membership did not only mean protection from threats from more powerful countries outside NATO, but especially security from the threat of the formation of a coalition of European states which would aim at protection from a new German threat and diplomatically isolate Germany within Europe.

Europe continues to be traumatised by the two attempts at hegemony since the establishment of the Vienna order in continental Europe against the emerging bourgeois-liberal political order: Germany's claim to rule Europe in the first half of the 19th century (not only under fascism) and the Soviet attempt to spread the world revolution of a dictatorial bureaucratic order. From the three tasks of NATO, only the second (to keep the Russians out) has disappeared. The third, to keep the Germans down remains, and therefore the first, i.e. to keep the Americans in, continues to need to be fulfilled

The Eastern enlargement of the Union has strengthened the interest in maintaining the leading role of the US in European security matters. Not only Britain and, in a more complicated manner, France never questioned this role seriously. For Germany, it is the ultimate guarantee of conjuring up apprehensions of its European allies so that its economic predominance, on which German prosperity is partly based, becomes acceptable, without the political counter strategies of its neighbours.

Because of these traumatic experiences, any European foreign policy, which is not ultimately endorsed by the US, would create apprehensions and divide Europe creating distrust between European Union member states and in their public opinions. Good relations with the US in all strategically important issues are a basic condition for European unity. As long as there is no European body politic, hence a European Union nation, European Union will follow the same principle as the emerging US foreign policy of the early 19th century: avoid entangling alliances, in the European case of today with non-Atlantic powers.

7. A European Union in an emerging multi-polar world of new emerging powers

The described overarching structure emerges with an independent profile in other less critical fields of foreign policy where the European Union can keep the West flexible in relation to the rest of the world by being more accommodative. If this leads to intensified cooperation with the rest of the world at levels where the European Union and its member states excel, i.e. economic matters and democracy promotion and finally, the strengthening of the civilian aspect of transnational relations, better for the overall strategy of the US which aims at establishing hegemony by "acceptance," even "invitation" from the side of competing powers.[91]

This role however, seems difficult to realise for the European Union because of the profile of the civil societies that really emerge in the South outside the building of clientelistic networks by the European civil actors in the South. These civil societies do not match with the profiles of civil society, which dominate the European Union. This results in permanent misunderstandings. The state classes in the South that emerged after decolonisation on the basis of political centralisation of economic rents to be used for state-led industrial diversification under the leadership of secular nationalists, which followed more or less pronounced strategies of social restructuring, some claiming to be socialists, have declined politically.[92] Nevertheless, secular nationalists have not disappeared. They have to share power in many countries where state-led industrialisation ran into the well-known contradictions of inefficiency and even incapacity to generate the resources for the continuation of this process of industrialisation. The challengers with whom they have to share, are the cultural nationalists in Asia, parts of Africa, and neo-populist forces in Latin America where the need of defending a non-Western culture is not plausible enough to serve as a rallying motto.[93]

The cultural nationalists follow pragmatic economic policies not only in Islamic countries[94] but also elsewhere, labelled "moral" economy which apparently suits the West without fulfilling its demands for total liberalisation as shown by the universal rejection of the Singapore agenda.[95] Those state classes which were successful in integrating the mass of the population into the growth process, especially by radical agricultural reforms, have been able to maintain most of their power and continue nationalist courses with few exceptions, whether they had been communists as in the People's Republic of China or nationalists in South Korea.

Economic liberalisation with government control.of the strategic heights, which today are constituted by the national innovation systems, are pursued by regimes under the strong influence of cultural nationalists and by regimes still under the control of secular nationalists and populists.[96] Only where the development efforts were so unsuccessful that there was no perspective of dynamising the local economy by extending local, especially rural mass markets, local elites pursue diligently the agenda of the West, such as in most countries of sub-Saharan Africa.[97]

The secular forces maintain their nationalism but lose influence. The social democratic forces in the West, which remain relatively strong in European Union countries, lose their partners. The cultural nationalists are in most cases on their way into the middle of their societies and become moderate forces especially when the economic forces connected to the non-monopolistic small and medium scale businesses are able to replace ideological "entrepreneurs" as leaders of these movements.[98] The process is not dissimilar to the rise of the populist mass parties in Europe in the late 19th century, which was often inspired by Catholic social teachings. In some cases, these forces became the backbone of fascism, not too dissimilar from extremist versions of cultural nationalists in the South. In both cases, cultural nationalists have become influential either through fascism or, after 1945, through the Christian Democratic political movement in Europe, because the influence of secular forces was too weak to be capable of implementing social reforms so that the secular forces lost the support of more or less important sectors of the masses, especially those who were less integrated in employment and mass organisations which could defend them in the labour market.[99]

The path towards moderation of the cultural nationalists and the emergence of democratic currents among them could lead to new alliances between the West and the South which would fit into the global project of American hegemony, whatever the foreign policy orientation of these moderate movements. Although these cultural nationalists, especially in their moderate tendencies, largely admire the US,[100] the corresponding forces in the US, such as the religious right, do not show an understanding of the type of moral economy the cultural nationalists in the South deem necessary in order to compensate the negative effects of the market, especially an absence of its capacity to provide welfare for the still marginalised masses and reliable growth opportunities for small and medium-scale industry without government protection.

The Christian Democrats in continental Europe do marry an admittedly limited understanding for moral economy often under the label of social market economy (because of the greater capacity to achieve welfare and self-steering of the market in comparison to developing economies) but do not perceive the cultural nationalists in the South as partners force an equivalent role of their own respective societies.[101]

The West's interface with the South increasingly passes through non-governmental organisations.[102] It seems fair to observe that they are without contact with the real civil societies of the South, secular and cultural nationalists, because of their "postmodern" outlook, which tends to deny the legitimacy of nationalism in the South.[103] Beyond tiny bridgeheads, which depend on the influx of resources through project activities, the Western NGO "scene"[104] seems to be isolated and often manipulated by their own local bridgeheads. These bridgeheads try to instrumentalise them, as is the case of declining middle-class secular nationalists who give up nationalism and

Marxism for the sake of appearances, in order to defend their positions against the rising cultural nationalists.[105]

The bridgehead formed by the truly cosmopolitan property-owning groups in the South is in a comparable relation for two reasons: it is politically isolated from the masses and economically often dependent on exploiting growth opportunities provided by the West by means of rent seeking and market imperfections.[106]

Hence the European Union appears as a progressive actor with a modern agenda in search of strengthening civil society dimensions in its relations with the South, from which the supporters of this image expect a qualitative change in the international system. This appears as a laudable enterprise as it opens up new opportunities for cooperation and conflict management. At the same time, the reliable part of the civil societies in the South to which this pattern of the European Union foreign policy profile relates, is tiny. There is a certain blindness of this "beacon" of qualitatively new international relations (in the eyes of the Western cosmopolitan community) vis-a-vis the really mattering civil society forces in the South, where secular and cultural nationalism are the two most influential forces.

The European Union is becoming post-national and opens up for these forces new possibilities, but does not transform them really. Both tendencies of nationalism in the non-Western world subscribe to projects of using the state in order to catch up to the most modern technologies. They will not give up their national control over their local innovation systems. They will therefore reject "deep" trade liberalisation, as far as they can remain independent from favours that the European Union provides, and this is the case of most of the larger countries of the South, which comprise of most of the population of the South.

States under the decisive influence of these nationalisms, be they cultural or secular, will not give up the attributes of sovereignty, whatever their ideological cultural values, because there is a basic politico-economic mechanisms of rent appropriation, which works even under conditions of export-oriented catching-up industrialisation and therefore economic liberalisation.[107] Those economies, which were successful in benefiting from increasing manufactured exports, were not the ones with the lowest real wages, not even poverty-ridden sub-Saharan Africa, but East and South East Asia. Even the World Bank had to admit that they were characterised by shared growth.[108] They had low labour costs because they could devalue below purchasing power parity.[109] Devaluation below purchasing power parity implies that the workers, including additional export sector workers, can buy locally with their local currency income more than this income could provide, if used in the world market for additional imports.[110] The difference has to be supplied by local production, especially local agriculture and the local small and medium scale industries, the so-called informal sector, whose share in the consumption of low income households is high. Devaluation supplies additional jobs through exports on the basis of subsidy from the local production, ultimately the mobilisation of a rent.[111]

Devaluation is costly and therefore the support for new industries in order to make them competitive at moderate levels of devaluation is reasonable. South Korea and Taiwan have shown the way of state intervention in order to diversify their industries, so that technically more demanding industries can be launched.[112] This is a process of mobilisation of rent, economically not so different from launching an industrial diversification programme by an oil country, but administratively more feasible because the usual strategy consists in using already created local knowledge and expertise for "climbing up (and down)" the value chain (the famous French "*remonter les filières*").[113] This strategy requires state accompanying of export orientation as shown in the recent positive evaluation of rent by South East Asian economists.[114] This process is more easy for larger countries with larger markets quite in line with Hilferding's analysis of the catch up also of the late 19th century Germany.[115]

The South is characterised by the emergence of continental states (China, India, Brazil perhaps also South Africa) which develop a regional role. These states will not forego their possibilities of mobilising rents for upgrading their position in the international division of labour. (Some of these powers, and soon all of them, are major powers, as no other power can impose on them their will.) The Iraqi war has shown that even the major superpower, the US, is unable to prevail if the issue cannot be dealt with nuclear weapons, an experience the decolonising powers of the European Union had already undergone.[116]

We are heading for a multi-polar international system with three to perhaps nine superpowers which strive to bring the regional neighbourhoods under their decisive influence, where they are able to project their power and create synergies.[117] These powers are forced to respect the other powers' regional interests and cooperate in a way not too different from the one intended by the Vienna system of the 19th century with norms of legitimacy of the participants and norms of conduct drawn from a realist interpretation of the rules of the interstate game. These powers are basically defensive, as they are multi-ethnic with dominant groups which limit the role of the myth of the nation as a community of destiny. They normally do not have irredenta territories. Where such territories exist, they deal with these issues in a cautious manner. For them there is no incentive to erect supranational structures, which apply abstract rules. They prefer contact with each other for finding mutually acceptable solutions by negotiation on the basis of broadly but legally non binding rules which they can interpret in a concerted manner. This will be a civilised world society, but not a world society under the rule of law.

Smaller states will maintain their sovereignty as majority of the votes for coalitions of small states are useless in order to impose the smaller states' will against major powers,[118] so that any single small state sees a stronger guarantee for its interests in the attributes of sovereignty, instead of in the overarching role of international organisations with law making and law enforcement capacities.

The European Union with its national character and it being bound together by the long-term interests of its members, which constitute a security community, but not a nation in the traditional sense, is not different from other continental powers and fits well into such a basically a-national system of multi-polarity where major powers normally act with restraint. In that sense, the described profile of the European Union foreign policy is the future of the international system with often observed discrepancy between the European Union's global principles and its simultaneous pursuit of its own much more parochial interests.

References

1. Hazel Smith, European Foreign Policy. What It Is and What It Does, Pluto, London, 2002, p.110.
2. Michael Bruter, "Diplomacy Without a State: The External Delegations of the European Commission,"Journal of European Public Policy, Vol.6, No.2, 1999, pp.185.
3. In 2007 EU supplied $ 61.54 bn., 58.8% of all DAC development assistance (44.4% of total development assistance). The EU was the second largest European donor with $ 11.63 bn., slightly less than Germany ($ 12.3 bn.) and slightly more than France ($ 9.9 bn.), calculated from OECD data, http://stats.oecd.org, download 12th February, 2011.
4. Giovanna Bono, "The Perils of Conceiving EU Foreign Policy as a 'Civilizing' Force," Internationale Politik und Gesellschaft, No. 1, 2006, p.151.
5. Barbara Lippert, The Discussion on EU Neighbourhood Policy- Concepts, Reform Proposals and National Positions. International Policy Analysis, Friedrich-Ebert-Stiftung, Berlin, July 2007, p.3.
6. Stanley Hoffman, "Towards a Common European Foreign and Security Policy?," Journal of Common Market Studies, Vol. 38, No.2, 2000, p. 197; Chevènement, Jean-Pierre, "In den Nationen liegt die Zukunft Europas: Zur Herausbildung einer europäischen Souveränität braucht es die Zustimmung der Völker," in Frankfurter Allgemeine Zeitung; Deutschland Radio Berlin; Centrum für angewandte Politikforschung (ed.) Fazit: Nation, Frankfurter Allgemeine Zeitung, Frankfurt am Main 1998, p. 19.
7. James A. Caporaso, "The European Union and Forms of State: Westphalian, Regulatory or Post-Modern," Journal of Common Market Studies, Vol.34, No.1, May 1996, p.46; Thomas Risse-Kappen, "Exploring the Nature of the Beast: International Relations Theory and Comparative Policy Analysis Meet the European Union,"Journal of Common Market Studies, Vol.34, No.1, May 1996, esp.p. 74; Philippe C. Schmitter, "Some Alternative Futures for the European Polity and Their Implications for European Public Policy," in Yves Mény Muller, Pierre and Jean-Louis Quermonne (eds.) Adjusting to Europe. The Impact of the European Union on National Institutions and Policies, Routledge, London, New York, 1996, pp. 26-27.
8. Dennis Pirages, Globalization: States, Markets and Global Public Goods, International Studies Association, New Orleans, March 2002. p.6; John Gray, "Global Utopias and Clashing Civilizations:

Misunderstanding the Present," International Affairs, Vol.74, No.1, 1998, pp. 149-163.

9. Deutsch, Karl W., The Analysis of International Relations, Prentice-Hall, Englewood Cliffs, N.J., 1968, pp.183-88.
10. In 2008 47. 43 %, UNCTAD: World Development Report 2010, http://www.unctad.org/sections/dite_dir/docs/ wir2010_anxtab_4.pdf.
11. In 2008 47.6 of the EU total flow of foreign investment came from Great Britain, France and Germany, http://www.unctad.org/sections/dite_dir/docs/wir2010_anxtab_4.pdf, 52,6% of total stock was in the hands of EU members, of which 47.8% in the hands of these three countries, http://www.unctad.org/sections/ dite_dir/docs/wir2010_anxtab_4.pdf.
12. On the basis of the 100 largest stock exchanges of the world, the share of New York is 38%, the share of EU 20,7% (without Zurich), http://www.loansandcredit.com/worlds-largest-stock-exchanges/.
13. Share of EU in world exports of machinery and transport equipment (2009)40.7%, share of EU in office and telecommunication equipment 24.8%, share in world manufacturing exports 43.5%. http://www.stat.wto.org.
14. World military spending by (in US $ bn.) US- 663.3, UK - 69.3, France - 67.3, Germany - 48.0, Italy - 37.4 Spain - 19. 4, Netherlands -12.6, Poland - 10.9, Sweden - 6.1, and Belgium - 5.7, http://www.sipri.org/yearbook/2009/05.
15. Hans-Georg Ehrhart, "Die EU als zivil-militärischer Krisenmanager: zwischen Anspruch und Wirklichkeit," Integration, Vol.28, No.3, July 2005, pp. 219; Gustav Lindstrom, Enter the EU Battlegroups. Chaillot Paper 97, Institute for Security Studies, Paris, February 2007, pp.10-12; Claudia Major, EU-UN Cooperation in Military Crisis Management: The Experience of EUFOR RD Congo in 2006. Occasional Paper 72, European Union Institute for Security Studies, Paris, September 2008, p.9 ff; Radek Khol, "Civil-Military Co-ordination in EU Crisis Management," in Agnieszk Nowak, (ed.,) Civilian Crisis Management: The EU Way. Chaillot Paper No 90, European Union Institute for Security Studies, Paris, 2006, pp. 123-138.
16. Smith, n.1, p.271; Klaus Scharioth, "Die neuen sicherheitspolitischen Herausforderungen und die internationale Rolle Europas," Integration, Vol.28, No.3, July 2005, pp. 249.
17. Often in the interest of the economically less powerful; See, Robert G. Hall, "A United People?: Leaders and Followers in a Chartist Locality, 1838-1848," Journal of Social History, Vol.8, No.1, Autumn

2004, p.185; Elías José Palti, "The Nation as a Problem: Historians and the National Question," History and Theory, vol.40, No.3, October 2001, p.332; Craig Calhoun, "'New Social Movement' of the Early Nineteenth Century," Social Science History, Vol.17, No.3 Autumn 1993, pp. 387-94

18. Following Jürgen Habermas Cf. Thomas Meyer, "The Challenge of Today: The Politics of Cultural Identity. Cultural Difference, Citizenship and Global Cooperation," Dialogue and Cooperation, No.9, 2004, pp. 72-80; Christoph Dorau, Die Verfassungsfrage der Europäischen Union. Möglichkeiten und Grenzen der europäischen Verfassungsentwicklung nach Nizza, Nomos, Baden-Baden 2001, p.106.

19. Christian Mährdel, "Zur Entstehung des Feudalismus in Ostafrika," Wissenschaftliche Zeitschrift der Karl-Marx Universität Leipzig, Vol.7, No.1/2, 1957, pp. 130-131; Jack Goody, "Feudalism in Africa," Journal of African History, Vol.4, No.1, 1963, pp. 1-18; Louis E. Wilson, "The Evolution of Paramount Chiefs among the Adangme to the End of the Nineteenth Century: the Case of the Krobo (Ghana)," Genève-Afrique, Vol.24, No.2, 1986, pp. 73-100.

20. Laura Hostetler, "Qing Connections to the Early Modern World: Ethnography and Cartography in Eighteenth-Century China,"Modern Asian Studies, Vol.34, No.3, July 2000, pp. 626; Y. Subbarayalu, "The Côla State," Studies in History, Vol.4, No.2, 1982, pp. 293.

21. T. K. Oommen, "Insiders and Outsiders in India: Primordial Collectivism and Cultural Pluralism in Nation-Building," International Sociology, Vol.1, No.1, 1986, pp. 63.

22. Gilles Boulard, "L'ordonnance de Villers-Cotterêts: le temps de la clarté et la stratégie du temps (1539-1992)," 123, No.609, 1999, pp. 47

23. Friedrich Engels, "Über den Verfall des Feudalismus und das Aufkommen der Bourgeoisie [1884]," in Karl Marx and Friedrich Engels, Marx Engels Werke. Vol. 21, Dietz, Berlin 1972, pp. 395

24. Gert-Jan Hospers, "Beyond the Blue Banana? Structural Change in Europe´s Geo-economy," Intereconomics, Vol.38, No.2, March/April 2003, pp. 77-78; Karen E. Smith, European Union Foreign Policy in a Changing World, Polity, Cambridge, Mass.; Oxford 2008, p.43

25. Wilfried Loth, "Vor 60 Jahren: der Haager Europa-Kongress," Integration, Vol.31, No. 2, April 2008, pp. 179-190.

26. Frank Roy Willis,, France, Germany, and the New Europe (1945-1963), Stanford University Press, Stanford, Cal., 1965, p.80; Edmund Dell,, The Schuman Plan and the British Abdication of Leadership in Europe, Oxford University Press, Cambridge, Mass.; London; New Delhi; Oxford 1995, p.11.

27. Cf. also the analysis in Le Populaire July 1943, Edition for the southern zone: "There is only one procedure: the incorporation of the German nation in an international community which is powerful enough for re-educating, disciplining and, if necessary, dominating Germany" (translation H. E.), quoted in Henri Michel and Boris Mirkine-Guetzévitch: Les idées politiques et sociales de la Résistance, Presses Universitaires de France, Paris1954, p. 381. On such ideas in the French resistance, See, Smith, n.1, p. 35.
28. Craig Parsons, "Showing Ideas as Causes: The Origins of the European Union," International Organization, vol.56, no.1, 2002, p.49; Andrew Moravcsik, "Constructivism and European Integration: A Critique," in Thomas Christiansen, Kund Erik Jorgensen and Antje Wiener, (eds.): The Social Construction of Europe, Sage, London 2001, pp. 177-78; Thomas Risse, "Social Constructivism and European Integration," in Antje Wiener and Thomas Diez (eds.): European Integration Theory, Oxford University Press, Oxford 2004, pp. 159-176.
29. Arthur W. Schatz, "The Anglo-American Trade Agreement and Cordell Hull's Search for Peace 1936-1938," Journal of American History, Vol.57, No.1, June 1967, p.89; Micheal J. Hiscox, "The Magic Bullet? The RTAA, Institutional Reform, and Trade Liberalization," International Organization, 53, 4, Autumn 1999, p.671.
30. Melanie Morisse-Schilbach,Diplomacy and CFSP - Insights from Historical Institutionalism, Dresdner Arbeitspapiere Internationale Beziehungen, Technische Universität Dresden 2002, esp. p.7; Douglas Hurd, "Developing the Common Foreign and Security Policy," International Affairs, Vol.70, No.3, July 1994, pp. 421-428; Álvaro de Vasconcelos, A Strategy for EU Foreign Policy. Report 7, Institute for Security Studies, Paris, June 2010.
31. Partha Nath Mukherji, "Do Challenges to Nation Building Ever End,"Kerala Sociologist, Vol.37, No.2, December 2009, p.7ff.; Oommen, n.21, p.63.
32. Christian Freres, "The European Union as a Global 'Civilian Power': Development Cooperation in EU-Latin American Relations," Journal of Interamerican Studies and World Affairs, Vol.42, No.2, Summer 2000, p.66; Hanns W. Maull, "Zivilmacht Bundesrepublik Deutschland. Vierzehn Thesen für eine neue deutsche Außenpolitik," Europa-Archiv, Vol.47, No.10, 1992, pp. 269-278.
33. "The idea that Europe has overcome the Machtpolitik has become a dominant theme in European thinking about international affairs. The Europeans ... now believe that the old Continent has consciously and deliberately left behind what German Foreign Minister Joschka

Fischer calls the 'old system of balance with its continued national orientation, constraints of coalition, traditional interest-led politic sandthepermanent danger of nationalist ideologies and confrontations'. While Americans and Indians might describe this as simplistic idealism, the belief has struck deep roots in Europe. The Europeans have also come to believe that their transcendence of power holds lessons for others, and that they have a civilizing mission in the modern and pre-modern states. Americans are dismissive of the European miracle of collective security and the German lion lying down with the French lamb and their lessons for the rest of the world." C. Raja Mohan, Crossing the Rubicon: the Shaping of India's New Foreign Policy, Viking; New Delhi, 2003, p.75

34. Gnesotto writes: "Depuis 1999, l'invention et la mise en œuvre de la PESD ont permis à l'Union européenne de se positionner comme un acteur stratégique majeur sur la scène internationale:avec plus de 7.000 hommes aujourd'hui déployés en Bosnie-Herzégovine, ...". Nicole Gnesotto, "Préface," in Agnieszka Nowak, (ed.) Civilian Crisis Management: The EU Way. Chaillot Paper No 90, European Union Institute for Security Studies, Paris 2006, pp. 7-8; Cf. also Anne Faber, "Europäische Nachbarschaftspolitik und externe Demokratieförderung durch die EU im Spiegel der Forschung," Integration, vol.31, no.1, January 2008, p. 92; Michael Merlingen, Rasa Ostraukaite, , "Power/Knowledge in International Peacebuilding: The Case of the EU Police Mission in Bosnia, Alternatives: Global, Local, Political, vol.30, no.3, 2005, pp. 297-323; Hans-Georg Ehrhart, "EU-Krisenmanagement in Afrika: die Operation EUFOR Tchad/ RCA," Integration, vol.31, no.2, April 2008, pp. 145-158.

35. Robert G. Hall, "A United People? Leaders and Followers in a Chartist Locality, 1838-1848," Journal of Social History, Vol.38, No.1, Autumn 2004, p.185; Guy Hermet, "Populisme et nationalisme," Vingtième siècle. Revue d'histoire, No.56, October-December 1997, p. 34

36. Nancy Fitch, "Mass Culture, Mass Parliamentary Politics and Modern Antisemitism: The Dreyfus Affair in Rural France," American Historical Review, Vol.97, No.1, February 1992, pp. 55-95.

37. Alexander Hicks, Joya Misra, Tang Nah Ng, "The Programmatic Emergence of the Social Security State," American Sociological Review, Vol. 60, No.3, June 1995, pp. 329-349; Christoph Sachße, "Der Wohlfahrtsstaat in historischer und vergleichender Perspektive," Geschichte und Gesellschaft, Vol.16, No.4, 1990, pp. 479-490; Gerald Friedman, "Strike Success and Union Ideology: The United States and France 1880-1914," Journal of Economic History, vol.48, no.1, March 1988, p.23; Michael Huberman and Christopher Meissner,

"Riding the Wave of Trade: The Rise of Labor Regulations in the Golden Age of Globalisation," Journal of Economic History, vol.70, no.3, September 2010, pp. 678-681.

38. Fritz W. Scharpf,, "The European Social Model," Journal of Common Market Studies, vol.40, no.4, November 2002, esp. 658; Pierre-Alain Muet and Henri Sterdyniak, "Faut-il une Europe sociale?," Revue d'économie politique, Vol.115, No.6, November-December 2005, pp. 673-676.

39. Gerhard Lehmbruch, "Die improvisierte Vereinigung: Die Dritte deutsche Republik," Leviathan, Vol.18, No.4, 1990, pp. 462-486.

40. Cf. Beate Kohler-Koch, The Commission White Paper and the Improvement of European Governance. Jean Monnet Paper 6/01, Symposium: The Commission White Paper on Governance, New York School of Law, New York 2001, p.12; Fritz W. Scharpf, Notes Toward a Theory of Multilevel Governing in Europe. Discussion Paper 00/5 Max-Planck-Institut für Gesellschaftsforschung, Köln 2000, pp.16-18; Roland Bieber, et al., 1992: One European Market. A Critical Analysis of the Commission's Internal Market Strategy, Nomos, Baden-Baden 1988, p.313.

41. Martin Rhodes, "The Future of the 'Social Dimension': Labour Market Regulations in Post-1992 Europe," Journal of Common Market Studies, Vol.30, No.1, March 1992, p.25.

42. Hans Rattinger, "Einstellungen zur europäischen Integration in der Bundessrepublik: Ein Kausalmodell," Zeitschrift für Internationale Beziehungen, Vol.3, No.1, June 1996, p. 45; Michael Bruter, "Diplomacy without a State: The External Delegations of the European Commission," Journal of European Public Policy, Vol.6, No.2, 1999, pp. 183-205; Matthew J. Gabel, "Economic Integration and Mass Politics: Market Liberalization and Public Attitudes in the European Union," American Journal of Political Science, Vol.42, No.3, July 1998, pp. 936-953; Joachim Schild, "Ein Sieg der Angst – das gescheiterte französische Verfassungsreferendum," Integration, Vol.28, No.3, July 2005, p. 196.

43.RonaldInglehart, "Post-Materialism in an Environment of Insecurity,"American Political Science Review, Vol. 75, 1981, pp. 880-885.

44. Jean Baechler, "Revolutionary and Counter-Revolutionary War: Some Political and Strategic Lessons from the First Indochinese War," Journal of International Affairs, Vol.25, No.1, Summer 1971, p.77; Andrew Mack, "Why Big Nations Lose Small Wars: The Politics of Asymmetric Conflict," World Politics, vol.27, no.2, January 1975,

pp. 184-86; Jason Lyall, "Do Democracies Make Inferior Counterinsurgents? Reassessing Democracy's Impact on War Outcomes and Duration," International Organization, Vol.64, No.1, Winter 2010, p. 167.

45. Smith, n.24, p.135.

46. Hartmut Elsenhans, "The Rise and Fall of Really Existing Socialism,"Journal of Social Studies (Dhaka), No.87, January-March 2000, pp. 1-16.

47. John Gallagher and Ronald Robinson, "The Imperialism of Free Trade,"Economic History Review, Vol.6, No.3, 1953, pp. 1-15.

48. Diane Ethier, "Is Democracy Promotion Effective? Comparing Conditionality and Incentives," Democratization, Vol.10, No.1, Spring 2003, p. 99; Erzsébet Szalai, "Postsocialisme et mondialisation en Hongrie," Homme et la société, No.145, July-October 2002, pp. 121ff; Bernard Hours and Monique Selim, "De l'apprentissage de la démocratie à son interdiction: Les ONG en Ouzbékistan," Tiers Monde, vol. 49, no.193, January-March 2008, p.127.

49. Cf. Mária Huber, "Demokratieexport nach Osteuropa: US-Strategien in der Ukraine," Blätter für deutsche und internationale Politik, Vol.50, No.12, December 2005, pp. 1463-1472; John A. Gould and Carl Sickner, "Making Market Democracies? The Contingent Loyalties of Post-Privatization Elites in Azerbaijan, Georgia and Serbia," Review of International Political Economy, Vol.15, No.5, December 2008, p.740; Anna Grzymala-Busse and Pauline Jones Luong, "Reconceptualizing the State: Lessons from Post-Communism," Politics and Society, Vol.30, No.4, December 2002, p.545.

50. Cf. Matthias Dembinski and Jutta Joachim, "Die GASP als Regierungssystem: Plädoyer für einen Perspektivwechsel in der GASP-Forschung am Beispiel des EU-Kodexes zu Rüstungsexporten," Integration, vol.31, no.4, October 2008, pp. 371ff.; P. H. Liotta and Owen Taylor, Europe Takes on Human Security. INEF Report 80, Institut für Entwicklung und Frieden, Duisburg 2006, pp.75ff; Mathias Mogge and Birgit Dederichs-Bain, "Cotonou – eine Zwischenbilanz. Ein Blick auf die zivilgesellschaftliche Realität," Zivilgesellschaft & Entwicklung, Winter 2005, p. 32.

51. John M. Makumbe, "Is There a Civil Society in Africa?", International Affairs, vol.74, no.2, 1998, p.314; Julius O. Ihonvbere, "On the Threshold of Another False Start? A Critical Evaluation of Prodemocracy Movements in Africa," Journal of Asian and African Studies (Leiden), Vol.31, No.1/2, 1996, p.128; Issa G. Shivji, "The Silences in the NGO Discourse: The Role and Future of NGOs in

Africa," Africa Development, Vol.31, No.4, 2006, pp. 22-51; Mike Powell and David Seddon, "NGOs and the Development Industry," Review of African Political Economy, Vol.24, No.71, March 1997, p. 9.

52. James Petras, "Imperialism and the NGOs in Latin America," Monthly Review, Vol.49, No.7, December 1997, p.12; Tina Wallace, "NGO Dilemmas: Trojan Horses for Global Neoliberalism," Socialist Register, Vol.40, 2004, pp. 202-219; Henrik Secher Marcussen, "NGOs, the State and Civil Society," Review of African Political Economy, Vol.24, No.69, 1996, p. 420.

53. Ruby Gropas, "What Role for Human Rights in the European Security Strategy?," in Tobias Debiel and Sascha Werthes, (eds.): Human Security on Foreign Policy Agendas. Changes, Concepts and Cases. INEF Report 80, Institut für Entwicklung und Frieden, Duisburg 2006, p.56; Michael Merlingen and Rasa Ostraukaite, , "Power/Knowledge in International Peacebuilding: The Case of the EU Police Mission in Bosnia, Alternatives: Global, Local, Political, Vol.30, No.3, 2005, p.297; Hans-Georg Ehrhart, "EU-Krisenmanagement in Afrika: die Operation EUFOR Tchad/RCA," Integration, Vol.31, No.2, April 2008, pp. 145-146.

54. The instrumentalisation of this area of foreign policy for coalition building within the Union becomes visible in the surprise shown with respect to the positive role of the army and the negative image of the police in the Egyptian revolution. The openness of the army was a result of the demise of the centre of a state class to which a less compromised segment, the officer corps wanted not to be linked to, quite likely to the opposition of the more idealistically minded segments of state classes which are always observed in such state-class and rent-dominated structures whereas in 19th century Europe, with its class-structured societies the army was just another stronghold of the powers in place, which comprised of more resources than the police, even if the police became after 1945, the privileged element of counterinsurgency also in the West. Hartmut Elsenhans,State, Class and Development, Radiant, New Delhi 1996, pp.296-308; Hartmut Elsenhans, La guerre d'Algérie 1954–1962. La transition d'une France à une autre. Le passage de la IV à la Ve République, Publisud, Paris 2000, pp.475ff.

55. Alan S. Milward, The European Rescue of the Nation-State, Routledge, London, New York 1992, p.126 ff.; Jacques Pelkmans, "Economic Theories of Integration Revisited," Journal of Common Market Studies, Vol.18, No.4, June 1980, p.335

56. Alan R. Posner, "Italy: Dependence and Political Fragmentation," International Organization, Vol.31, No.4, Autumn 1977, p.821; John Zysman, Political Strategies for Industrial Order. State, Market, and Industry in France, University of California Press, Berkeley, Cal.; Los Angeles 1977, p.197

57. Werner Bührer, "Die Spitzenverbände der westdeutschen Industrie und die europäische Integration seit 1945: Motive, Konzepte, Politik," Jahrbuch für Wirtschaftsgeschichte, Vol.2, 2008, pp. 53-72; Jürgen Elvert, "Weichenstellungen für die Römischen Verträge – Akteure und Überlegungen der Bundesregierung 1955," Integration, Vol.30, No.3, July 2007, pp. 302-312; Wilfried Loth, "Der Weg nach Rom – Entstehung und Bedeutung der Römischen Verträge," Integration, vol.30, no.1, February 2007, p.42.

58. Vivien A. Schmidt, "Loosening the Ties that Bind: The Impact of European Integration on French Government and its Relationship with Business," Journal of Common Market Studies, Vol.34, No.2, June 1996, pp. 223-253; Colin Hay, Matthew Watson, and Daniel Wincott, Globalisation, European Integration and the Persistence of European Social Models, POLSIS University of Birmingham, Birmingham, March 1999; Shigéyasuk Osabe, "Le marché unique européen et la transformation de la politique industrielle," Economies et Sociétés, H.-S. vol.34, October 1998, pp. 111-124.

59. Daniel Keohane, et al., Lessons Learned from European Defence Equipment Programmes. Occasional Paper 69, Institute for Security Studies, Paris 2007, p.18; Erkki Aalto, "Interpretations of Article 296," in Daniel Keohane, (ed.): Towards a European Defence Market. Chaillot Paper 113, Institute for Security Studies, Paris, November 2008, pp. 13-15.

60. Alexander J. Yeats, "Do African Countries Pay More for Imports? Yes," World Bank Economic Review, Vol.4, No.1, January 1990, pp. 1-20; Hildegard Lingnau, Die Entwicklungspolitik der Sozialistischen Partei Frankreichs (PS). Programmatischer Anspruch und praktische Ausführung, Diploma Thesis, Berlin, August 1988, p.52; Gérard Fuchs, "La politique française de coopération: Un contrepoids vis-à-vis des Grands?," Vierteljahresberichte der FES – Probleme der internationalen Zusammenarbeit, no.100, June 1985, p.161.

61. Philippe Messine, "Nord-Sud: la gauche, an I," Critiques de l'économie politique, July-September 1982, p.17; Belaid Abdesselam, Le gaz algérien. Stratégies et enjeux, Bouchène, Algier 1990, p.335.

62. Maryse Fahri, "Dialogue Nord-Sud: l'impasse," L'économiste du Tiers Monde, July-August 1977, p. 9; Anne-Marie Mureau, L'Europe

communautaire dans la négociation Nord-Sud. Ambitions, intérêts et réalités, Presses Universitaires de France, Paris 1984, esp.p.275.

63. Maria Green Cowles, "Setting the Agenda for a New Europe: The ERT and EC 1992," Journal of Common Market Studies, vol.33, no.4, 1995, p.513; John Peterson and Elizabeth Bomberg, Decision-Making in the European Union, Macmillan, Basingstoke 1999, p.221; Justin Greenwood, "Electricity Liberalization," in Robin H. Pedler, (ed.): European Union Lobbying: Changes in the Arena, Palgrave Macmillan, Houndsmill 2002, p.291; Dennis Swann, "The Single Market and Beyond - An Overview", in Dennis Swann, (ed.): The Single European Market and Beyond. A Study of the Wider Implications of the Single European Act, Routledge, London, New York 1992, p.20; Alasdair R Young and John Peterson, "The EU and the New Trade Politics," Journal of European Public Policy, vol.13, no.6, 2006, pp. 795-814.

64. Manuela Spindler, Regionalism and the Role of Ideas: The EU and APEC Compared, ISA/ECPR, Vienna 1998; Eric Helleiner, "Explaining the Globalization of Financial Markets: Bringing States Back in,"Review of International Political Economy, vol.2, no.2, 1995, p.328.

65. Ferdinand Tönnies, Gemeinschaft und Gesellschaft: Grund begriffe der reinen Soziologie, Curtius, Berlin 1935, esp.p.43-44.

66. Alan Booth, Joseph Melling and Christoph Dartmann, "Institutions and Economic Growth: The Politics of Productivity in West Germany, Sweden, and the United Kingdom, 1945-1955," Journal of Economic History, vol.57, no.2, June 1997, p.433; Gerhard A. Ritter, "Staat und Arbeiterschaft in Deutschland von der Revolution 1848/49 bis zur nationalsozialistischen Machtergreifung," Historische Zeitschrift, vol.231, no.2, October 1980, p.358; Christiane Eisenberg, "The Comparative View in Labour History – Old and New Interpretations of the English and German Labour Movements Before 1914," International Review of Social History, Vol.34, No.3, 1989, pp. 403-432.

67. Bruce Weston, "Unionization and Labour Market Institutions and Advanced Capitalism, 1950-1985," American Journal of Sociology, Vol.99, No.5, May 1994, p.26ff.

68. Torsten Müller, Hans-Wolfgang Platzer and Stefan Rüb, "Die europäischen Gewerkschaftsverbände. Zur Entwicklung ihrer Organisation und Politik seit den 1990er Jahren," Integration, Vol.33, No.1, January 2010, p.63; Patrick Pasture, "Trade Unions as a Transnational Movement in the European Space 1955-65. Falling Short of Ambitions?", in Wolfram Kaiser, Peter Starie, (eds.,) Transnational uropean Union: Towards a Common Political Space, Routledge, London, New York 2005, pp. 121-23.

69.Gisela Hendriks, Germany and European Integration: The Common Agricultural Policy: An Area of Conflict, Berg Publishers, New York, Oxford 1991, p.48; Horst Ungerer, A Concise History of European Monetary Integration. From EPU to EMU, Quorum, New York 1997, p.63.

70.Lisbet Hooghe, , "EU Cohesion Policy and Competing Models of European Capitalism," Journal of Common Market Studies, Vol.36, No.4, December 1998, p.473; Grandomenico Majone, "The European Community between Social Policy and Social Regulation," Journal of Common Market Studies, Vol.31, No.2, June 1993, pp. 159-161.

71. Arne Heise, "Der Kölner Prozess – Theoretische Grundlagen und erste Erfahrungen mit dem EU-Makrodialog," Integration, Vol.24, No.4, October 2001, p. 390; Arne Heise, "The 'Cologne Process': A Neglected Aspect of European Employment Policy," Internationale Politik und Gesellschaft, 2002, pp. 88-102; Ashiagbor Diamond "EMU and the Shift in the European Labour Law Agenda: From 'Social Policy' to 'Employment Policy'," European Law Journal, vol.7, no.3, September 2001, p.327; Ulrich Schröder, "Wirtschaftspolitik", in Werner Weidenfels and Wolfgang Wessels (eds.): Europa von A bis Z, Europa-Union-Verlag, Bonn 2002, p.372.

72. Stephan Klecha, Europas Sozialpolitik als schwieriger Aushandlungsprozess. Akteure und Handlongsoptionen unter besonderer Berücksichtigung der Arbeitszeitpolitik, Friedrich-Ebert-Stiftung, Bonn-Bad-Godesberg, October 2007, p.8.

73. Marc Lombard, "A Re-examination of the Reasons for the Failure of Keynesian Expansionary Politics in France, 1981-1983," Cambridge Journal of Economics, Vol.19, No.3, April 1995, pp. 359-372; Annicet LePors, "La contrainte extérieure - parlons en," Economie et politique, no.302, September 1979, p.41; Wolfgang Münchau, Letzter Ausweg gemeinsame Anpassung- die Eurozone zwischen Depression und Spaltung. WISO direkt: Analysen und Konzepte zur Wirtschafts- und Sozialpolitik, Friedrich-Ebert-Stiftung, Bonn-Bad-Godesberg, June 2010, p.4; Thomas Fricke, "Nach dem Griechenland-Desaster: Die Währungsunion braucht grundlegende Reformen," in Friedrich-Ebert-Stiftung (ed.,) Euroland auf dem Prüfstand. ist die Währungsunion noch zu retten? Friedrich-Ebert-Stiftung, Berlin 2010, p.4.

74. Klaus Busch, Umbruch in Europa. Die ökonomischen, ökologischen und sozialen Perspektiven des einheitlichen Binnenmarktes, Bund, Köln 1992, p.282; Klaus Busch, Gewerkschaftliche Tarifpolitik in Europa– Handlungsbedingungen und -möglichkeiten in alternativen Integrationsszenarien. Expertise im Auftrage der Hans-Böckler-Stiftung, Ms., Osnabrück 1993, pp.32ff.

75.Jonathan Eaton and Samuel Kortum, "Trade in Capital Goods," European Economic Review, vol.45, no. 4-7, March 2001, p.1203; Unido: World Non-electrical Machinery. An Empirical Study of the Machine-Tool Industry, United Nations, New York 1984, p.8076 Michel Albert, Capitalisme contre capitalisme, Editions du Seuil, Paris 1991.

77. Alfred Boss and Jörg Döpke, "Bundesrepublik Deutschland: DM-Aufwertung dämpft Konjunktur nur wenig – Aufschwungstempo 1996 dennoch gering," Weltwirtschaft, vol.46, no.2, 1995, pp. 144-166.

78. Alasdair R Young and John Peterson, "The EU and the New Trade Politics," Journal of European Public Policy, vol.13, no.6, 2006, p.796; C. Satapathy, "Trade Facilitation. Commencing Negotiations at WTO,"Economic and Political Weekly, vol.39, no.32, 7th August, 2004, p.3578.

79. Exports of East Asia, Latin America, and South Asia to the USA were in 2009 still 15 % higher than the corresponding exports to all European economies, own calculations from http://unstats.un.org/unsd/trade/imts/analyticaltradetables.htm; Harry G. Johnson, "US Economic Policy Toward the Developing Countries," Economic Development and Cultural Change, vol.16, no.3, April 1968, p.366.

80. Charles Harvey and Jon Press, "Overseas Investment and the Professional Advance of British Mining Engineers, 1851-1914," Economic History Review, vol.42, no.1, 1989, pp. 64-89; Christopher J. Schmitz, "The Rise of Big Business in the World Copper Industry 1870-1930," Economic History Review, vol.39, no.3, 1986, pp. 392-410.

81.Adriaan Schout and Andrew Jordan, "Coordinated European Governance: Self-Organizing or Centrally Steered?," Public Administration, vol.83, no.1, 2005, pp. 218-20; Álvaro de Vasconcelos, A Strategy for EU Foreign Policy. Report 7, Institute for Security Studies, Paris, June 2010, pp.31-33.

82.Christoph Knill, "Private Governance across Multiple Arenas: European Associations as Interface Actors," Journal of European Public Policy, vol.8, no.2, April 2001, p.236; Michael Zürn, Gregor Walter, Sabine Dreher and Marianne Beisheim, "Postnationale Politik? Über den politischen Umgang mit den Denationalisierungs-Herausforderungen Internet, Klimawandel und Migration," Zeitschrift für Internationale Beziehungen, Vol.7, No.2, 2000, pp.313ff; Helmut Breitmeier and Volker Rittberger, Environmental NGOs in an Emerging Global Civil Society. Tübinger Arbeitspapiere zur Internationalen Politik und Friedensforschung 32, Abteilung Internationale Beziehungen, Tübingen 1998.

83.Leo Panitch and Sam Gindin, "Global Capitalism and American Empire,"Socialist Register, Vol.40, 2004, p.19; Charles S. Meier, "The Foundations of Productivity: Foundations of American International Economic Policy after World War II," International Organization, Vol.31, No.4, Autumn 1977, pp. 613-15.

84.Georges-Henri Soutou, "Les problèmes de sécurité dans les rapport franco-allemands de 1956 à 1963," Relations internationales, Vol.58, No.4, Winter 1989, pp. 227-251; Klaus Hildebrand, "Der provisorische Staat und das ewige Frankreich: Die deutsch-französischen Beziehungen 1963-1969," Historische Zeitschrift, Vol.240, No.2, April 1985, pp. 283-311; Arnulf Baring, Unser neuer Größenwahn. Deutschland zwischen Ost und West, Deutsche Verlagsanstalt, Stuttgart 1988, pp.169-75; Alfred Grosser, La politique extérieure de la Ve République, Seuil, Paris 1965, p.137ff.

85. "Un des buts essentiels de la politique extérieure du Général de Gaulle, c'est cette contrainte exercée sur les Américans pour les obliger à consulter", Alfred Grosser, La politique extérieure de la Ve République, Seuil, Paris 1965, p.143.

86.Hartmut Elsenhans,"La décolonisation dans la gloire. La guerre d'Algérie et le rôle mondial de la France," in Pierre Robert Baduel, (ed.): Chantiers et défis de la recherche sur le Maghreb contemporain, IRMC, Tunis 2009, p. 482.

87. Hartmut Elsenhans, La guerre d'Algérie 1954–1962. La transition d'une France à une autre. Le passage de la IV à la Ve République, Publisud, Paris 2000, p. 368ff.

88. Dianne Kirby, "Divinely Sanctioned, "The Anglo-American Cold War Alliance and the Defence of Western Civilization and Christianity, 1945-48," Journal of Contemporary History, Vol.35, No.3, September 2000, pp. 389-96; George C Herring and Richard H. Immerman, "Eisenhower, Dulles, and Dienbienphu: 'The Day We Didn't Go to War' Revisited," Journal of American History, vol.71, no.2, September 1984, p.363.

89. Ernst-Otto Czempiel, "Foreign Policy Strategy of the Federal Republic of Germany and the Relevance of Central and Central Eastern Europe and the Southern Mediterranean to It," in Hartmut Elsenhans, (ed.,)A Balanced European Architecture. Enlargement of the European Union to Central Europe and the Mediterranean. Une architecture européenne équilibrée. L'ouverture de l'Union Européenne vers l'Europe centrale et la Méditerranée, Publisud, Paris 1999, pp. 22-23.90 David N. Gibbs, "Washington's New Interventionism: US Hegemony and Inter-Imperialist Rivalries," Monthly Review, vol. 53, no.4,

September 2001, pp. 29-34; Peter Gowan, "Making Sense of NATO`s War on Yugoslavia," Socialist Register, 36, 2000, p. 275.

91.Leo Panitch and Sam Gindin , "Global Capitalism and American Empire," Socialist Register, 40, 2004, p. 4; Geir Lundestad, "Empire by Invitation? The United States," Journal of Peace Research, vol.23, no.3, August 1986, pp. 263-277; Geir Lundestad, "'Empire by Invitation' in the American Century," Diplomatic History, vol.23, no.2, Spring 1999, pp. 189-217.

92. Hartmut Elsenhans, State, Class and Development, Radiant, New Delhi; 1996; Hartmut Elsenhans, "Decolonisation: From the Failure of the Colonial Export Economies to the Decline of Westernised State Classes," Maghreb Review, vol.19, no.1/2, 1994, pp. 95-122.

93.Hartmut Elsenhans, "Fundamentalismus in der Dritten Welt als Herausforderung an das internationale System des 21.Jahrhunderts: Kultursoziologie oder Politökonomie als Therapie," Comparativ. Leipziger Beiträge zur Universalgeschichte und vergleichenden Gesellschaftsforschung, vol.4, no.6, 1994, pp. 9-20; Hartmut Elsenhans, "The Rise of New Cultural Identitarian Movements in Africa and Asia in the Emerging Multipolar System," Comparative Studies of South Asia, Africa and the Middle East, vol.32, no.3, forthcoming; Aníbal Viguera, "'Populismo' y 'neopopulismo' en América Latina," Revista Mexicana de Sociología, vol.55, no.2, July-September 1993, p.64; Kurt Weyland, "Clarifying a Contested Concept. Populism in the Study of Latin American Politics," Comparative Politics, vol.34, no.1, October 2001, pp. 18ff; Manochehr Dorraj and Michael Dodgson, "Neo-populism in Comparative Perspective: Iran and Venezuela," Comparative Studies of South Asia, Africa and the Middle East, vol.29, no.1, 2009, pp. 149-51.

94.Cf. Among many: Herta Müller, Marktwirtschaft und Islam: Ökonomische Entwicklungskonzepte in der islamischen Welt unter besonderer Berücksichtigung Algeriens und Ägyptens, Nomos, Baden-Baden 2002; Rachid Ouaissa, "Aufstieg und Mäßigung des politischen Islam in Algerien", in Holger Albrecht and Kevin Köhler (eds.,) Politischer Islam im Nahen und Mittleren Osten: Zwischen Sozialbewegung, Opposition und Widerstand, Nomos, Baden-Baden 2008, p.149; Christopher Alexander, "Opportunities, Organizations, and Ideas: Islamism and Workers in Tunisia and Algeria," International Journal of Middle East Studies, vol.32, no.4, November 2000, p.484; Sorab Behdad and Farhad Nomani, "What a Revolution! Thirty Years of Social Class Reshuffling in Iran," Comparative Studies of South Asia, Africa and the Middle East, vol.29, no.1, 2009, p.103; Abd al-Monein Said Aly and Manfred W. Wenner, "Modern Islamic

Reform Movements: The Muslim Brotherhood in Contemporary Egypt," Middle East Journal, vol.36, no. 3, Summer 1982, p. 351; Yildiz Atasoy, "The Islamic Ethic and the Spirit of Turkish Capitalism Today," Socialist Register, vol.44, 2008, p.135.

95. Gérard Heuzé, "Les nationalistes hindous aux prises avec le développement : De l'homme nouveau au consommateur frustré," Tiers Monde, vol.40, no.160, 1999, p.732; Sanjay Kumar, "Impact of Economic Reforms on Indian Electorate," Economic and Political Weekly, vol.39, no.16, April, 17th, 2004, pp. 1624; Herta Müller, "Mullahs twixt Might and Markets," German Research, 1999, p.39; Salwa Ismail, "The Popular Movement Dimensions of Contemporary Militant Islamism: Socio-Spatial Determinants in the Cairo Urban Setting," Comparative Studies in Society and History, vol.42, no. 2, 2000, p. 370; Hartmut Elsenhans, "The WTO, Globalisation and New Political Movements of the South", in Hartmut Elsenhans and Rajendra Kumar Jain (eds.,) India, the European Union and the WTO, Radiant Publishers, New Delhi 2006, pp. 72-74.

96. Cf. among many, Alberto Olvera and Avritzer, Leonardo, "El concepto de sociedad civil y el estudio de la transición democrática," Revista Mexicana de Sociología, vol54, no.4, October-December 1992, p.243; José M. Vadi, "Economic Globalization, Class Struggle and the Mexican State," Latin American Perspectives, vol.28, no.119, Summer 2001, p.131; Raymond A. Hinnebusch, "Syria, the Politics of Economic Liberalisation," Third World Quarterly, vol.18, no.2, June 1997, p.263; Henry Bienen and John Waterbury, "The Political Economy of Privatisation in Developing Countries," World Development, vol.17, no.5, May 1989, p.623.

97. Hartmut Elsenhans, "External and Internal Factors of the Crisis in Africa," African Development Perspectives Yearbook, vol.15, 2011, pp. 59-88.

98. Sebastian Schwecke, New Cultural Identitarian Political Movements: The Bharatiya Janata Party Between Cultural Identity and Middle Class Interests, Routledge, London, New York 2011, pp.149ff; Pradeep K.. Chhibber, "State Policy, Rent Seeking, and the Electoral Success of a Religious Party in Algeria," Journal of Politics, vol.58, no.1, 1996, pp.144ff; Marsha Pripstein Posusney, "Enduring Authoritarianism. Middle East Lessons for Comparative Theory," Comparative Politics, Vol.36, No.2, January 2004, p.129; Carrie Rosefsky Wickham, "The Path to Moderation. Strategy and Learning in the Formation of Egypt's Wasat Party," Comparative Politics, Vol.36, No.2, January 2004, p.207.

99. Dick Geary, "Working-Class Identities in Europe, 1850s-1930s," Australian Journal of Politics and History, Vol.45, No.1, March 1999, p.31; Theodor Geiger, Die soziale Schichtung des deutschen Volkes. Soziographischer Versuch auf statischer Grundlage, Ferdinand Enke, Stuttgart 1932, esp. p.32.
100. In the Muslim world with a mixture of admiration and hatred because of the Palestine issue, Verghese Koithara, "India-US Defence Cooperation. Expectations and Prospects," Economic and Political Weekly, Vol.40, No.32, 6th August 2005, p. 3585; Pankaj Mishra, "The Other Face Of Fanaticism," New York Times Magazine, February, 2nd, 2003, pp. 1-5; Patrice Claude, "Les islamistes égyptiens sensibles au discours de M. Obama," Le Monde, June, 11th, 2009, p. 6.
101. The parallelism between the Christian Democratic formula of social market economy and the concept of moral economy of the Islamists is made explicitly by Müller; See, Müller, n.94, p.9.
102. Yasemin Topçu, Humanitarian NGO-Networks: Identifying Powerful Political Actors in an International Policy-field. Paper 99-302, Wissenschaftszentrum Berlin für Sozialforschung, Berlin 1999, pp.23-27; Sarah Lister, "Power in Partnership? An Analysis of an NGO's Relationships with its Partners," Journal of International Development, Vol.12, No.2, March 2000, pp. 227-239; Andrew Natsios, "NGOs and the UN System in Complex Humanitarian Emergencies," Third World Quarterly, Vol.16, No.3, 1995, pp. 407-409; Jude Howell, "Civil Society in China: Chipping Away at the Edges," Development - Journal of the Society for International Development, Vol.50, No.3, September 2007, p.22.
103. Lucy Earle, "Community Development, 'Tradition' and the Civil Society Strengthening Agenda in Central Asia," Central Asian Survey, Vol.24, No.3, September 2005, pp. 251; D. Rajasekhar, "The Interface between Gram Panchayats and NGOs: Issues, Strategies, and Ways Forward," Journal of Karnataka Studies, Vol.1, No.2, April-October 2004, p.75; Susantha Goonatilake, Recolonisation: Foreign Funded NGOs in Sri Lanka, Sage, Beverly Hills, Cal.; London; New Delhi 2006, p.279.
104. Very pejorative expression used in Mali, reported in the interview by the author with a Professor of Political Science in Bamako, Mali in 2009.
105. Nazmul Ahsan Kalimullah, "Government-NGO Relations in Bangladesh: Prospect and Retrospect," Journal of Social Studies, No.87, January-March 2000, p.72; S. Akbar Zaidi, "NGO Failure and the Need to Bring Back the State," Journal of International

Development, Vol.11, No.2, March/April 1999, p.267; Sara Gordon R.,"La cultura política de las organizaciones No gubernamentales enMéxico," Revista Mexicana de Sociología, Vol.59, No.1, January-March 1997, p. 60; Ian Gary, "Confrontation, Co-operation or Co-optation: NGOs and the Ghanaian State During Structural Adjustment," Review of African Political Economy, Vol.24, No.68, 1996, p. 163.

106. William Graf, "The State in the Third World," Socialist Register, Vol.31, 1995, p.154; Catherine Newbury, "Introduction: Paradoxes of Democratization in Africa," African Studies Review, Vol.37, No.1, April 1994, p.2.

107.Hartmut Elsenhans, "Renten in der exportorientierten Industrialisierung: Zur notwendigen und widerspruchsvollen Rolle des Staats," in Peter Gärtner, (ed.,) Staatlichkeit im Epochenbruch? Antworten aus der Perspektive des Südens und Ostens, Hamburgisches Welt-Wirtschafts-Archiv, Hamburg 2001, esp.pp.261-66.

108. John Page, et al., The East Asian Miracle. Economic Growth and Public Policy, World Bank, Washington 1993, pp.29ff

109. Hartmut Elsenhans, "Globalisation in a Labourist Keynesian Approach," Journal of Social Studies (Dhaka), no..89, July-September 2000, pp. 24-31; Hartmut Elsenhans, "Macroeconomics in Globalization: Productivity, Wages, Profits, and Exchange Rates in an Era of Globalization," Brazilian Journal of Political Economy, Vol.22, No.85, January-March 2002, p.69; Hartmut Elsenhans, "Globalization, 'New' Trade Theory, and a Keynesian Reformist Project," in Mary Ann Tétreault, et al (eds.,) Rethinking International Political Economy: Emerging Issues, Unfolding Odysseys, Routledge, London, New York 2003, pp. 165-194.

110.Haichun Chen, M. J. Gordon and Yan Zhiming, "The Real Income and Consumption of an Urban Chinese Family," Journal of Development Studies, Vol.31, No.1, October 1994, pp. 201-213.

111.Hartmut Elsenhans, "A Benign Globalization vs. a Doomsday Scenario: How to Make Globalization in a Capital and Welfare Perspective," Review of Global Politics (Taipeh), no.10, April 2005, pp. 36-39.

112.Wilfried Holtgrave, Industrialisierung in Singapur. Chancen und Risiken industrieorientierter Spezialisierung, Campus, Frankfurt am Main, New York 1987, pp. 59-81; Lynn Krieger Mytelka, "The Transfer of Technology: Myth or Reality?," in Carol Cosgrove and J. Jamar, (eds.,) The European Community's Development Policy: The Strategies Ahead. Conference organised at the College of Europe,

Bruges, 4-6 July 1985, De Tempel, Bruges 1986, p. 258; Stephan Mark Haggard, Pathways from the Periphery: The Newly Industrializing Countries in the International System, Dissertation, Berkeley, Cal., 1983, p.283.

113. Abelkader Sid Ahmed, Un projet pour l'Algérie: Eléments pour un réel partenariat Euro-Méditerranéen, Publisud, Paris 1995, pp.77-78; Jacques Ould Aoudia, "Les enjeux économiques de la nouvelle politique méditérranéenne de l'Europe," Maghreb-Machrek/Monde Arabe, no.153, July-September 1996, p.35.

114. Mushtaq H. Khan and Kwame Sundaram Jomo, "Introduction," in Mushtaq H. Khan and Kwame Sundaram Jomo (eds.,) Rents, Rent-Seeking and Economic Development. Theory and Evidence in Asia Cambridge University Press, Cambridge et al. 2000, pp. 1-20.

115. Rudolf Hilferding, Das Finanzkapital. Eine Studie über die jüngste Entwicklung des Kapitalismus [1909], Europäische Verlagsanstalt, Frankfurt am Main 1968, p.451.

116. Hartmut Elsenhans, "Les manifestations de décembre 1960 et la reconnaissance de la révolution algérienne," in Daho Djerbal (ed.,) Décembre 1960. Le Dien Bien Phu politique de la guerre d'Algérie, Naqd, Algiers 2010, pp. 27-62; Hartmut Elsenhans, "Was uns Algerien lehrt," WeltTrends, Vol.18, No.75, November-December 2010, pp. 39-47.

117. Hartmut Elsenhans, "State, Economy, Power and the Future of the International System," Strategic Digest (New Delhi), Vol24, No.4, April 1994, pp. 552; Hartmut Elsenhans, On the Political Economy of the Status-quo International System and the Defeat of National Liberation Movements and Social Democracy at the Global Level in the Twentieth Century. Contribution to the 45th Annual Convention of the International Studies Association, Montreal, Canada, March 2004.

118. As shown by the dispute settlement mechanism of the WTO, if the conflicting parties are a major economic power and a small economy. B. S. Chimni, "WTO and Environment: Legitimisation of Unilateral Trade Sanctions," Economic and Political Weekly, Vol.37, No.2, January, 12th, 2002, p.138; Robert Z. Lawrence, The United States and the WTO Dispute Settlement System. Council Special Report. The Bernard and Irene Schwartz Series on American Competitiveness Council of Foreign Relations, New York, March 2007, p.7.

7

EU and India, China Relations

Rajendra K. Jain

China and India are both important for the European Union because of their demography, large domestic markets of a billion plus each, large consumers of energy, and because they are vital for dealing with regional problems and global issues. However, Beijing has been and continues to be more central to European interests than New Delhi because of its political clout, its economic potential, the substantially higher economic stakes, and trade. As a result, there is a variable engagement of the Union towards the two rising Asian powers and a qualitative difference in the attention and focus given by the European Union to China than India.

This chapter is divided into four sections. The first section begins with a discussion of how the EU perceives India and China. The second section discusses Indian perceptions of the EU-China relations. The third one highlights some similarities in the Chinese and Indian approaches towards the EU. The concluding section outlines several lessons that India can learn from China's engagement of the EU.

EU Perceptions of China and India

There are differences between how the European Union perceives India and China. EU policy-makers and think-tankers have for many years argued that China takes the European Union far more seriously. Most people in Brussels have generally tended to feel that

Indian policy-makers appeared to need convincing that the EU is "a player that matters."[1] President Romano Prodi complained that India was "too focused" on the United States in its foreign and economic policy, which "came at the expense of the EU."[2] Europeans often have often urged India to shed its so-called narrow "prism of Pakistan" once and for all and develop a wider "world-view like that of China" in order to create a more meaningful partnership.

Europeans argue that China has made greater efforts at understanding EU institutions than India. Some of them conclude that the Chinese perhaps understand Europe better than even the Europeans themselves. The EU, many Indians feel, does not make things easy given the complexity of its institutions, proliferating regulations, and rotating presidency. A major reason for this is that the Indian elite's perceptions of the European Union continue to be conditioned by the Anglo-Saxon media, which impedes a more nuanced understanding of the processes and dynamics of European integration as well as the intricacies and roles of EU institutions. China, Europeans argue, has been a much greater supporter of European integration whereas India has tended to stay away from the debate. Even though India was one of the first countries to establish diplomatic relations with the European Economic Community, India has tended to take a comparatively more measured approach towards European integration. To many Indians, Europe is like "the dawdy old lady," known for over four centuries. There is "no excitement, no passion" between India and Europe.[3] India, the Europeans often complain, "like" Europe, but "love" the United States even though it is "tough love."

China, the Europeans feel, have over the years developed a far more sophisticated approach towards Europe. Even though EU officials concede that the core of the relationship with both China and India is economic, but China, they insist, functions more like a demandeur constantly seeking to widen interaction and dialogue. People in Brussels often argue that India was neither proactive nor entrepreneurial enough like China to avail of existing opportunities. This may partly stem from the fact that on most things which are of vital concern to India, the EU as a collectivity is either not able or willing to make a difference with the result that most deliverables are perceived to essentially lie in bilateral relationships.

EU officials are fond of saying that India does not devote adequate human resources commensurate with the need to meaningfully engage the Union. In this context, they are fond of stating that while China has a separate embassy accredited to Belgium, besides a separate 60-member embassy to the European Union, India, has a combined embassy of about one-third its size for Belgium, Luxembourg, and the European Union. While Beijing has about half a dozen officials closely following the work of the European Parliament, India has none. There are about two dozen Chinese officials dealing with political affairs, whereas India has a few. At summits and other dialogues, the Chinese are said to follow a structured approach with usually several rows of participants followed by note-takers whereas EU officials say they confront a random democracy on the other side. Despite about 45-odd issues on which there is dialogue and consultations with India under the Strategic Partnership, Brussels feels that it encounters the problem of capacity and resources in the Ministry of External Affairs.

Whereas the Union respects China as a great power, some in India feel that Brussels tends to regard India as a regional South Asian power and does not adequately appreciate its rise in the Asia-Pacific. Europeans tend to consider India still as "an emerging country" whose status is being slowly enhanced, but the process of its global empowerment is just beginning whereas China is clearly ahead in terms of GDP, defence capabilities or diplomatic clout.[4] To most Indians, a Sinocentric Europe has been more willing to accommodate China rather than India. There is a tendency to draw comparison with China, that India should emulate China in its dealings with EU; often trying to introduce a competitive spirit ("you have only yourselves to blame for the lower level of interaction and engagement").

Beijing views the European Union as a pole in an emerging multipolar world and as a potential counterbalance to the United States. To that end, it has been keen that Europeans develop a more united voice. Indians however feel that it is going to be "a long, long way" before Europe is going to act as a pole largely because of the inherent constraints of the Common Foreign and Security Policy in a heterogenous EU of 27 member states. Indian analysts, as well as the upper and decision-making classes, do not see the EU as a counterweight to the United States, but as "a building process and a construct" that could be able to deliver long-term gains for the Indian subcontinent, while maintaining intact the diverse range of Indian bilateral relations with specific European countries.[5] EU displays a lack of geopolitical coherence and has not yet shown signs of acting as a credible power.[6] While Europeans aspire for a multipolar world, they seem to endorse Chinese views of a unipolar Asia, and not a multipolar Asia which also takes into account the growing profile of India and Japan in the region. In fact, both Japan and India will not satisfy themselves with a mere balancing of China, but they will also vigorously contest Beijing's attempts at establishing its dominance in various parts of Asia.[7] The romantic notion that Asia is a "naturally" Sinco-centric continent, Indian observers argue, should be discarded.[8]

Perhaps in no other strategic partnership has Brussels invested so much political, diplomatic, and financial resources as the one with China. As a permanent member of the UN Security Council, China has all the advantages of "great power exceptionalism"[9] (which India does not). Because of its membership of the UN Security Council, it was natural for EU-China interaction to be more significant in the resolution of key problems because in 2007, China had become the largest trading partner of Iran, North Korea, and Sudan and the second-largest of Burma and Zimbabwe.

China is perceived by most Europeans as a direct and immediate threat to European jobs since it is with China that the Union has the largest bilateral trade deficit. The EU's trade deficit with China was rising by € 15 million an hour and reached € 170 billion in 2007. The Pew Global Attitudes Survey of June 2007 noted that China's expanding economic and military power was triggering considerable anxiety in Western Europe, where the number of those with a favourable image of China declined in several West European countries between 2005 and 2007.[10] In a survey is June 2008, a majority in Western Europe believed that either China has already replaced the United States as the world's leading superpower or that it will at some point replace the US.[11] On the other hand, the Union's trade with India was nearly six times less than with China – € 55 billion in 2007 compared to € 300 billion with China. India is perceived by Europeans as a latent and potential threat taking away service-sector jobs, though pressure would increase as both China and India move up the value chain.

In recent years, many Europeans fear "a threat to their economic interests" by the rise of China and India. Indian officials however stress that the tendency to equate India with China in the sense that they constitute a threat to European employment structures is "unfair" because EU's trade with China is 12 per cent as compared to two per cent with India.[12] Some Europeans concede that there is no empirical basis for this, but there is an unsubstantiated fear of a rapidly growing Indian economy having the potential of posing a danger at some time in the future.

There is also an attitudinal difference on how China and India deal with the European Union. Europeans do not exactly relish the more vocal approach of a rising India and its confident and articulate elite keen on gaining a position at the high table. China tends to articulate subtely, rather indirect, and makes allusive statements than the brazenly direct pronouncements that India tends to make in the manner of Western foreign offices. In diplomatic discourse and conduct, India has tended "to carry many chips on its shoulder, almost always moralistic, needlessly arrogant, argumentative, mistaking such attitude as being an assertion of national pride."[13]

Europe is not yet central to Indian priorities which appear to be US-centric. India accords greater importance to the United States than the EU because as the principal foreign policy interlocutor, it is perceived as having the biggest impact on our national security environment. There is a societal bias towards the United States in terms of the importance given to Washington, to cultural and intellectual ties with the US, and the million-strong Indian diaspora. The US has the capacity to act in ways which are more benefiting to India than long European declaratory statements. As an aspiring power, India is more sympathetic to the American effort to "rework the rules of the global game," whereas Europe is a staunch defender of the present order. Europe appears increasingly as "a conservative force: protectionist, in relation to markets but also much else, hoping to keep what it has."[14] A key difference between the EU and American documents on India's strategic partnership with them is that while gradual incrementalism through dialogue and discussion is the hallmark of the Union, there is a more practical, direct American approach, which focuses on vital issues to India like geopolitical, energy, and technology.[15] India also finds it comparatively easy to deal with the United States on a one-to-one basis which is characterized by an effective leadership whereas decision-making in the EU is inherently time-consuming in an increasingly heterogeneous EU-27, driven forward by committees and compromises. US is making greater efforts to understand India's foreign policy priorities and strategic preferences, whereas the Europeans come with their own foreign policy preferences, expecting us to conform to them or explain why we are not in sync with them.

Indian Perceptions of EU-China Relations

The elite and decision-makers in India maintain that the European Union and EU policy-makers have a fixation on China. A veteran Brussels-based Indian observer, remarked that for long the EU had single-mindedly focused on China, since India was overshadowed by China, both politically and economically.[16] As Asia started to really come together and see how China's "peaceful rise" could be kept peaceful for Asia, the EU seemed to have abandoned its traditional focus on India to concentrate on Southeast Asia and Northeast Asia.[17] There has also been resentment in many quarters that until the turn of the millennium, the European Union maintained its Cold War policies of "equidistance" between India and Pakistan. Most stakeholders in India feel that a Sino-centric Europe has been more willing to accommodate China rather than India, which, as Commissioner Mandelson said, "is getting there, but not quite arrived."[18] India is perceived to be in the Commonwealth Games league whereas China in the Olympic Games league.

Many stakeholders in India feel that there is a degree of discrimination in the European Union's interest in and treatment of democratic India and in the favour of undemocratic China, with which the Union has few common political values. Thus, many in India feel that the EU has been less sympathetic to and supportive of "a democratic secular India, one of the few countries to practice democracy in the developing countries against overwhelming odds."[19] India's democratic polity and shared values does not necessarily earn it any brownie points in Europe. Many Indian stakeholders wondered how EU espousal of human rights and promotion of democracy reconciled with political expediency to hug military rulers, responsible for ousting democratically-elected rulers in Pakistan.

The rise of India and China offers two developmental models to the world, especially to developing countries: in China, development has been spearheaded by a "non-democracy" or one-party state relying on policies associated with "managed" economies whereas economic growth in India has been an open and democratic regime in a free market economy. Despite the imperfections of Indian democracy, it has the worked and that too in more than a decade of coalition governance. Many countries, particularly in Africa, welcome Chinese support as an alternative to the Western pattern of interfering in their development. China's spectacular growth is proof to many developing countries that reform and economic opening need not necessarily lead to democracy.

Indian policy-makers feel that Europe does not seem to be unduly perturbed by the potential security implications of a rising China, about its military modernization and rising defence expenditure. Most Europeans tend to feel that they should convince Washington that China should not be regarded as "a strategic threat, but a crucial partner."[20] This is partly because Asian issues and nations are too distant for them to directly impinge on its own security and partly because the EU is not militarily present in East Asia and unlike the United States, does not play the role of an external balancer in Asia. It is difficult to say if most Europeans tend to see China as an economic threat and India's rise as a benign and stabilizing development around the world. Europe tends to either regard the growing Chinese market as an economic opportunity or are increasingly concerned about the mounting trade deficits, which may possibly fuel protectionist sentiments. China continues to pose difficulties in India's immediate neighbourhood – economically, politically, and strategically. Their competition is intense in Myanmar. Sino-Indian relations will continually see elements of both competition and cooperation. It is also equally certain that India will not accept a secondary role to China in Asia and waver from its determination to emerge as an indispensable element in the Asian balance of power.[21]

There are more numerous and deeper institutional links between the EU and China than between India and the Union. India's interaction and institutional engagement with the European Union is less intense, and dense in terms of visits, dialogues, and consultations, than that of the Union with China. For instance, officials from the European Commission, responsible for initiating and implementing the EU's China policy, made 206 trips to China in 2004, on average four visits per week.[22] Between 2002 and 2004, there were 12 visits to India by EU Commissioners and the High Representative for CFSP, Javier Solana whereas there were nine Commissioner visits to China alone in the first half of 2004. However, in recent years with India and EU talking across the board the number of visits of Commissioners and officials has increased, but it still does not equal to those to China.

Similarities in Chinese and Indian Approaches towards the EU

There are basic differences in both the perceptions and interests of China and India with the European Union in many fields including trade, development, globalization, and WTO negotiations, the International Criminal Court, climate change, etc. where the EU has taken a stand contradictory to them.

China and India argue that the structures of global governance (including the G8) must be more democratic, representative, and legitimate. The two new big kids on the block are wary of the creeping "regulatory imperialism" of the North. What they want is "a different set of rules" to safeguard the interests of their populations which constitute more than one-third of humanity.

Both China and India have similar attitudes towards the role of the United Nations and multilateralism. During the UN debate on the eve of the Iraq war (2002-2003), the Europeans were at the forefront of questioning the American attempt to oust Saddam Hussein based on a perceived threat of weapons of mass destruction. China and India were vehemently opposed to European aspirations to transform the United Nations into a supranational organization which can get and implement a mandate to interfere in domestic affairs. Both Asian giants resent European efforts to talk down to them from the high pedestal of post-modernism. They remain acutely sensitive about their sovereignty and internal autonomy against intrusive human rights issues and remain wary about humanitarian intervention and the circumstances in which force may be used. Both feel that hard power is as necessary as post-modernist Europe's fascination for and advocacy of the merits of "soft power."

Both China and India are unanimous that the Commission often tends to assume a patronizing attitude – "Engage and we shall teach you."

As the two most populous economies, China and India continue to have consultations and policy coordination in multilateral trade negotiations. Since the Cancun Ministerial (2003), the advanced industrialized countries are being challenged in multilateral trade negotiations because of effective coalition-building by emerging powers. Senior EU officials have generally expressed a preference of China's low profile and its general caution about assuming a leadership role inside the WTO in sharp contrast to the higher profile that India tends to occupy in multilateral trade negotiations. The greatest challenge, Trade Commissioner Mandelson, recently remarked, is to have "a Chinese negotiator to start talking and an Indian negotiator to stop talking."[23] Some European think-tankers wonder why China has "bizarrely allowed Brazil and India to speak for the developing world" in the Doha Round.[24] At the Geneva Ministerial, however, the Chinese were just as vocal as India about the rigid Western approach jeopardizing the future of millions of poor and subsistence farmers.

India and China have sought to coordinate their policies regarding climate change, especially as the North seeks to incrementally transfer the ecological burden of the entire planet at the door of developing countries despite its "historic responsibility" for cumulative emission levels. China and India are willing to take voluntary measures to curb carbon emissions. They are however unwilling to accept any mandatory carbon emission limits because only continuous growth offers a real possibility of lifting millions out of poverty. India argues that it is imperative to maintain a distinction between "lifestyle emissions" of the West and "survival emissions" of developing countries. "Capping or reducing emission levels in India may mean that 600 million Indians, who do not have access to electricity today, must be permanently denied this very basic energy service."[25] Both Asian countries argue that it is necessary for low emission technologies to be made available to poorer countries at a price they can afford and that technology needs to be shared generously and easily without stringent constraints of intellectual property rights. Climate change is increasingly becoming the next WTO-type of North-South divide. Neither is willing to allow the West to constrain their autonomy in determining their developmental priorities and ensuring continued economic growth which is contingent on ensuring energy security.

Conclusion

The relentless rise of China has presented the Indian business and political community with an example and opportunity to become an alternative, to become collaborative, and to foster its own rise. There are perhaps three lessons which India can learn from how China engages the European Union. **Firstly,** India should more intensively engage the Council and the European Parliament. In the past, India concentrated almost entirely on the European Commission in its dealing with Brussels, primarily because it was the main interlocutor in dealing with trade irritants and seemed reluctant to more intensely engage other EU institutions. For decades, New Delhi regarded the European Parliament as a mere "talking shop" and confined itself to fire-fighting or damage control (mostly on Kashmir). With growing appreciation of the greater profile and role of the European Parliament in the Union's institutional architecture, the Indian attitude towards it seems to have changed significantly. This has been reflected in a number of recent high-profile visits, the establishment of (like China) a separate India Delegation. Senior Council officials continue to complain that there is hardly much contact between them and Indian diplomats/visitors to Brussels and the Indian proclivity to deal mostly with the Presidency.

Secondly, India should emulate China in developing a more robust framework of educational exchanges and encourage Indian elites to study in Europe. There is a need to strengthen media relationships, academic and intellectual linkages as well as foster greater intellectual and elite interaction. The number of Indian students studying in Europe has been rather limited partly because of the limited number of courses in English and because Europe does not provide a structure of post-doctoral fellowships and employment prospects that is available in the United States. There is a continuing need to re-profile and reorient our mindsets about the growing prominence of the EU as a collectivity. While India will not be able to match China in the setting up of Confucius Institutes across the world, the Indian Council of Cultural Relations has established 20 India Cultural Centres around the world of which only two are in Western Europe (Germany and the United Kingdom; with a third one coming up in Paris shortly). India also maintains 19 Chairs of Indian Studies and 5 Chairs of Indian studies on a semester basis, mostly for teaching Indian languages. Of these, there are six for Hindi in Europe (Poland, Hungary, Bulgaria, Romania, Belgium, and Spain), one for Sanśkrit (France), one for Tamil (Poland). India has set up a Chair of Indian Economics at Sciences Po, Paris. Obviously, more needs to be done in this context.

Thirdly, a catalytic role can be played by the think tank community in Europe which for too long have been obsessed with China. The number of think tanks in Europe that remain continuously engaged and committed to research and dissemination of information and debate on India are far and few. There is an urgent need to develop a sustained specialist and policy level dialogue between Indian and European think tanks.

References

1. Chris Patten, cited in Rashmee Z. Ahmed, "EU asks India to ditch narrow view of Pakistan," *The Times of India*, 10 October, 2002.
2. Cited in Meenakshi Shedde, "Indians seem to favour US because of Hollywood movies," *The Times of India*, 24 November, 2001.
3. C. Raja Mohan, "India, Europe and the United States", in Rajendra K. Jain (ed.) *India and the European Union in the 21st Century* (New Delhi: Radiant Publishers, 2002), p. 62.
4. Jean-Luc Racine, "The India-Europe Relationship in the US Shadow," in Rajendra K. Jain (ed.), *India and the European Union: Building a*

Strategic Partnership (New Delhi: Radiant Publishers, 2007), pp. 53-54.

5. Joel Ruet, Pramit Pal Chowdhury and Hari Vasudevan, "India's Europe: Cultural Footprints and Conflict Resolution Processes," in I.P. Khosla (ed.) *India and the New Europe* (New Delhi: Konark, 2004), pp. 105-106.
6. Karine Lisbonne-de Vergeron, *Contemporary Indian Views of Europe* (London: Chatham House, 2006), p. 5.
7. C. Raja Mohan, "India and the Emerging Non-Proliferation Order: The Second Nuclear Age", in Harsh V. Pant (ed.) *Indian Foreign Policy in a Unipolar World*. (London: Routledge, 2009), p. 51.
8. Varun Sahni, "China-India Partnership: Defining an Agenda", *China Report*, 44(1), 2008, p. 37.
9. G. John Ikenberry, "The Rise of China and the Future of the West", *Foreign Affairs* 87(1), 2008, p. 32.
10. Pew Global Attitudes Project, "World Publics Welcome Global Trade — But Not Immigration: 47-Nation Pew Global Attitudes Survey," 4 October, 2007, p. 35. Online at: http://pewglobal.org/reports/display.php?ReportID=258.
11. Pew Global Attitudes Project, "Some Positive Signs for U.S. Image, Global Economic Gloom – China and India Notable Exceptions, 24-Nation Pew Global Attitudes Survey, 12 June, 2008," p. 5. Online at: http://pewglobal.org/reports/pdf/260.pdf.
12. Shyam Saran, *The EU-India Partnership Summit 2005* (New Delhi: Konrad Adenaeur Foundation, 2005), p. 4.
13. Jaswant Singh, *A Call to Honour: In Service of Emergent India* (New Delhi: Rupa and Co., 2006), pp. 276-277.
14. Sunil Khilnani, "India and the World," in Manmohan Malhoutra (ed.) *India: The Next Decade* (New Delhi: Academic Foundation, 2006), pp. 490-491.
15. Racine, n. 4.
16. Malcolm Subhan, "India and the European Union: A View from Brussels", in Rajendra K. Jain (ed.) *India and the European Union in the 21st Century* (New Delhi: Radiant Publishers, 2002), p. 51; Harsh V. Pant, "India and the EU: A Directionless Courtship", 7 October 2008. Online at http://in.rediff.com/news/2008/oct/07guest1.htm.
17. Shashank, "India and the European Union", in Rajendra K. Jain (ed.) *India and the European Union: Building a Strategic Partnership* (New Delhi: Radiant Publishers, 2007), p. 23.

18. Cited in H.S. Rao, "Kamal Nath makes a point with 'fat cows," 14 December, 2007. Online at: http://www.rediff.com/money/2007/dec/14nath.htm.
19. A.N. Ram, "India and the European Union in the New Millennium," in Rajendra K. Jain (ed.) *India and the European Union in the 21st Century* (New Delhi: Radiant Publishers, 2002), p. 5.
20. Christopher Patten, *Not Quite the Diplomat: Home Truths about World Affairs* (London: Allen Lane, 2005), p. 278.
21. C. Raja Mohan, "Japan and India in a Rising Asia," public lecture at Fukuoka, Japan, 30 July, 2007. Online at: http://www2.jiia.or.jp/pdf/kouenkai/070730-Raja_Mohan_Speech.pdf.
22. Cited in Malcolm Subhan, "Beneath unrest lies symbiotic harmony", *The Financial Express*, 9 July 2005.
23. Cited in Vijay Dutt, "Banter at Kamal Nath's book release," *Hindustan Times*, 15 December, 2007.
24. Charles Grant and Tomas Valasek, *Preparing for the Multipolar World: European Foreign and Security Policy in 2020* (London: Centre for European Reform, 2007), p. 30.
25. Shyam Saran, Speech by Special Envoy of the Prime Minister, on Climate Change at Mumbai, 21 April, 2008. On line at: http://www.meaindia.nic.in/speeches/13883.

8

China's Rise: EU Perception & Approaches

S. Y. Surendra Kumar

The international security environment is witnessing a power shift from the West to Asia, led by the rapid rise of China and India. More than India, it is the rise of China that is a major concern for major powers like US, EU, Russia, and Japan. Although, this concern has not been expressed formally by these countries, their bilateral and multilateral strategic dialogues obviously indicate the increasing threat from China.

Generally, the rise of China in the last few decades is attributed to rapid economic growth i.e., a sustained average growth rate of 6.7% per year since 1950, which accelerated to an average of 8.3% per year since the post-reform period of 1978[1], and more than 10% per year in the last two decades. Subsequently, China today stands as either the second or third largest economy in the world and has also emerged as the largest trading partner to major powers like US, EU, and Japan. It is also estimated that China's economic size will match America's by 2035 and double it by mid-century.[2] Interestingly, China is holding around $800 billion in US treasury bonds and some $2 trillion worth of currency reserves wielding financial terror against the US. If China were to turn a part of its huge dollar holdings to other currencies, say the euro, it could seriously hurt the US economy.[3] This explains the growing strength of China.

China's economic growth has also enhanced its military power. From time to time China has modernized its military in a rapid manner. In 2009, China announced a 14.9% increase in its defense budget to a total of US$70 billion, compared with US$58.8 billion in 2008.[4] Apart from defense spending, it is transforming from a mass army designed for protracted wars of attrition on its territory to one capable of fighting and winning short-duration, low or high-intensity conflicts. It is generally perceived that China's increased military spending and modernization of its armed forces will pose a long-term threat to US and India's interest.

Furthermore, to address its energy security needs it has established a substantial naval presence along vital maritime chokepoints, which is popularly known as China's 'String of Pearls", a plan to acquire several strategically placed ports, naval bases and listening posts in friendly countries like Gwadar (Pakistan), Hambantota (Sri Lanka), Sittwe (Myanmar) and Chittagong (Bangladesh) to protect the billions of dollars worth trade that pass through strategic sea lanes such as the Strait of Hormuz or the Malacca straits to Middle East, Africa, and Latin America.[5] This string of pearls also allows China to access several preferential resources and a market access at highly subsidized terms. This strategy does not have any parallel strategy either by US, Japan or any power. Thus, this strategy has also enhanced the rise of China.

While growing economically, China has also won diplomatic recognition from other countries, broadened its diplomatic activity, participated more in international institutions, and wielded more geopolitical influence in Asia and around the world. China is undoubtedly the second most influential country in the world after the US. Its role in stimulating world economy and even containing nuclear proliferation in the Korean Peninsula (North Korea) and the Persian Gulf (Iran), is certainly crucial.[6] In this new order, China is becoming a more responsible player on the global stage and is involved in a growing number of issues on the international agenda, such as counterterrorism, environmental degradation and global warming, energy security, international crime, international peacekeeping and nation building, nuclear nonproliferation, public health, and the stability of the global financial system.[7]

Thus, China's rise is more often characterized in terms of threats and opportunity, more neutrally as challenges. The Chinese leaders, for their part, insist that China is on the road to 'peaceful development," working for a peaceful, harmonious world, not seeking hegemony and not threatening anyone.[8] Nevertheless, China's increasing economic, diplomatic, and military power is compelling countries to rethink on the existing security arrangements and take steps that may lead to the formation of bilateral and regional groups of nations with common interests and values. Against this background it would be interesting to assess the EU perception and approaches towards a rising China.

EU Perception and Approaches

Although, all nations perceive the rise of China as a significant development, however, consensus does not exist with regard to the assessment of and the reaction to China's presumed rise. In this regard, even major powers like US and EU have wide differences in their perception and approaches over China's rise. For instance, (a) many American scholars and decision-makers see China as a future peer competitor and possible threat to its security interest. However, a majority of the European Union (EU) and its member states do not perceive the rise of China as a clash with western interest (US and EU). (b) Europe has long believed in the wisdom of binding China into the international institutional order. This perspective is based on several beliefs that predominant powers should be counterbalanced and that a multi-polar world is more stable than a hegemonic or anarchical order; that nations should adhere to international law and codified norms of behaviour; that international institutions should be strengthened and empowered to achieve effective global governance; that sovereignty has its limits and, under certain conditions (such as in the EU), can be shared; and that soft power should be more influential than hard power.[9] These core elements indicate the way Europeans think about China and its potential role in the international system. (c) Although, both EU and US share a common interest in the improvement of human rights in China, they tend to differ in the tactics used to achieve it, like US leans towards public diplomacy, as well as introducing a resolution on China at successive UN Human Rights Commission meetings. On the other hand, EU prefers private diplomacy and has consistently encouraged China to ratify and adhere to various human rights treaties. With regard to human rights status in China, the US has always placed a priority on the rights of political prisoners and dissidents, freedom of religion, forced abortions and female infanticide; religious and cultural repression in Tibet. However the Europeans emphasize more on workplace safety, reducing gender discrimination, decreasing state control of the media, improving prison conditions, and eliminating the death penalty.[10] (d) Generally, US sees the rise of China in terms of increasing hard power; the growth in Chinese military power and its effects on US national security interest in East Asia; trade deficit, loss of US manufacturing jobs resulting from outsourcing and so on. Europe, on the other hand considers China's rise more in terms of China's domestic transitions – as a large developing country in the midst of multiple transition leading it away from socialism and towards a market economy, open society, more representative and more accountable government.[11] Thus, EU focuses primarily on China's internal scene. (e) US perceives the rise of China as a direct threat to US interest in the region, however EU believes that the main threat to its security are transnational issues and not necessarily China. Moreover, there is no fundamental conflict of interest (unlike with the US) between China and EU, as a result neither side poses a threat to each other. However, given their differences in historical background, cultural heritage, political system, and economic development level, it is natural that the two sides have different views or even disagree on some issues.

Overall, the US policy towards China is a combination of engagement, hedging, and containment. The EU has pursued a course of comprehensive engagement and co-operation. Thus, it would be interesting to identify the guiding factors for EU perception towards China's rise.

Guiding factors

Shared values

Generally, both EU and China share many common values such as their belief in changing the global structure of power to a multi-polar world and support 'effective multilateralism' to dilute the US dominance in the international arena.[12] Subsequently, they want to strengthen alternative poles of national power and regional organization, such as EU, Association for South East Asian Nations (ASEAN), Shanghai Cooperation Organization (SCO), and so on. They also share a common opinion on reforming global institutions, like the United Nations (UN) and ensuring all countries including the big powers to abide by the international law. Thus, both China and EU look to each other as a potential balancer to balance US predominant power through use of effective multilateralism at international forums.

Concerns over global issues

Apparently, both China and EU have moved beyond their regions and are undertaking greater and challenging roles in world affairs. In the process both realize that to address the challenges in the international arena, they need each other's support to achieve the goals. For example, EU's attempt to achieve key global issues such as reforming the UN, preventing Iran and North Korea from building nuclear bombs, intervening in failed states, it needs China's consent or cooperation. So EU wants to make sure that it works closely with China as both could increase their global power.[13] Furthermore, they also have vital roles in shaping the outcome of many transnational issues like terrorism, illegal immigration, international crime, contagious diseases, energy, environment, poverty elimination, sustainable development, spread of Weapons of Mass Destruction (WMD), poor governance, and so on. Thus, EU and China's concern over shared global issues is very well reflected in successive summits in which leaders agreed to strengthen cooperation between them to address global challenges.[14]

Economic Factor

Apparently, the EU is a developed economy having advanced technological and strong financial resources while China boasts a steady economic growth, a huge market, and abundant labour force. Thus, economic opportunities have a strong impact on EU polices and its approach towards China's rise. Strong economic relations have been one of the key factors for EU's varied approach. That is, from 2000 to 2009, the EU trade in goods with China tripled in value. EU export to China rose steadily from Euro 26 billion (2000) to € 82 billion (2009), while imports rose from € 75 billion (2000) to € 215 billion (2009).[15] For EU, China is the second most important trading partner after the US, accounting for 8.5% of EU exports and 17.8% of EU imports. Furthermore, EU companies have also taken advantage of the Euro's strength in recent years to finance growing levels of direct investment in China, especially since China's needs for infrastructure investment plans adds to the strengths of EU companies.[16] As a result, EU's Foreign Direct Investment (FDI) into China has increased from 0.3 billion in 2000 to 5.3 billion in 2009. However, EU's trade deficit in goods with China has increased from € 29 billion in 2000 to € 170 billion in 2009. At the same time, the EU trade in services with China has been surplus of € 5.4 billion in 2009.[17] Thus, these economic trends are also an important guiding factor to EU's approach and perception towards a rising China.

Not a Strategic competitor in Asia

Generally, the US and China both perceive each other as a strategic competitor in the spheres of economic, political, military, and strategic interests in Asian, Latin American, and African regions. However, China does not perceive EU as a strategic competitor in Asia and beyond, since the latter has limited strategic interest in the region (unlike US) and does not have military troops stationed in Asia. As a result, Beijing perceives that Brussels is not seeking to expand its global military profile in Asia or beyond, thus, both agreed for strategic partnership rather than being strategic competitors.

As a result of the above stated factors, EU differs from US in its perception and approaches towards China. Nevertheless, both the US and EU want China to be a status quo rather than a revisionist power and believe that emerging China in the widest possible range of international institutions might help ensure this outcome by socializing Beijing into international norms of behaviour. Thus, the United States and the EU welcome China's rise but differ in terms of perception and approaches.

EU-China Relations: The Challenges

Although, EU-China bilateral relations have expanded over the decades and both sides will continue to invest significant political and diplomatic capital and resources in the expansion of bilateral relations. There are many challenges confronting the bilateral relations such as:

Both EU and US had slapped an arms embargo on China in reaction to the 1989 Tiananmen Square incident. Since then, US has not made any serious efforts to lift the embargo, on the other hand, the EU has made serious efforts from time to time towards lifting the ban, however has failed to reach an agreement due to lack of consensus among its members. Even the recent EU Foreign Ministers informal meeting held at Brussels in September 2010 failed to reach an agreement.[18] As countries like France, Germany, and Spain have strongly supported lifting the ban to enhance relations with China and also to capitalize from the large Chinese market, the Scandinavian countries along with US, Japan, and Taiwan have opposed on the grounds that there is continuing human rights violations in China, which has not changed since 1989, like increasing number of death sentences; administrative detention, curtailing of minority and religious rights. Lifting of the embargo will change the balance of power in the region favouring China; Russia will also lift its restrictions on arms sales to China in fear of EU competition in the Chinese market;[19] China's record on proliferation is far from satisfactory, which will benefit third states like Pakistan, Iran, North Korea; and the embargo is complementary and EU should not break out of the common front with US on this issue.[20] Nevertheless, those members in support of lifting the embargo argue that China being a strategic partner, it will not be appropriate to put China into the same category as Zimbabwe or Mynmar, that are also subjected to the arms embargo. Further, China has come a long way since 1989 and the lifting of embargo would be seen as the last step in normalizing relations with China rather than as a reward for anything. [21] Interestingly, China sees the lifting of embargo as a signal that EU is accepting and acknowledging China as an equal partner on the international stage, rather than China being desperate for EU weapons. Thus, lifting of the ban will surely strengthen EU-China relations. Furthermore, US President Barack Obama is presently discussing a major policy change in US-China military relations. This was reported by the Chinese media on the possibility of US lifting its twenty year old arms embargo on China. The US may sell China the C-130 military transport aircraft manufactured by Lockheed and used extensively by the US military.[22]

manufactured by Lockheed and used extensively by the US military.[22] If this happens it would be easier for EU to do the same and enhance its military relations with China.

Although, economic issues shaped the EU-China relations and will continue to do so, there are many economic issues challenging the bilateral relations like the issue of Yuan currency, of which European policymakers including the European Central Bank Chief Jean-Claude Juncker have being urging China to appreciate its currency and correct its currency exchange imbalance, and want Beijing to focus more on its growing internal market rather than on exports, since, China's depreciated currency and low labour costs keep Chinese exports cheap for European consumers. As a result, China is now Europe's biggest source of manufacturing imports, while just two decades ago there was almost no trade at all between the two blocs. Subsequently, European industries that have been slow to adapt to the global market over the past decade have been severely hit by the new Asian competition, with the textiles and steel sectors suffering the most.[23]

Apart from this, EU is concerned over Beijing dumping cheap products on its market and has raised punitive tariffs on imports it says are illegally subsidized by the Chinese government. China's cheaper goods have hit the EU companies badly, as EU companies have to compete harder, both for their own markets and for export markets with China. According to a Dutch study, an average European family saves about 300 Euros a year through cheaper Chinese goods.[24] Even on the issue of intellectual property rights (IPRs) China has failed to implement the transparent IPR legislation protecting European intellectual property in China and has also been lukewarm in enforcing WTO compatible intellectual property rights and regulations. Thus, China needs to address the major concerns of EU for long lasting strategic partnership.

Domestic issues like democracy, rule of law, protection of human rights and minority rights, and the use of force is still a major cause of concern for the EU. It is very unlikely that China would address these issues the way the EU wants given China's stiff opposition. For example, on the issue of promoting and strengthening democracy in China, the Chinese leaders emphasize that they believe in socialist democracy and not necessarily in the western form of democracy. They staunchly oppose multi-party democracy or genuine elections that would diminish the power of the China Communist Party. On the issue of protection of human rights, despite the launch of specific dialogue on human rights in July 1995, followed by human rights dialogue since 2001, and the 29th EU-China human rights dialogue in June 2010, little progress has being made by China. Hence, these issues will continue to hinder the growth of EU-China relations.

EU has the challenging task of balancing its relations vis-à-vis US and China, since EU's deepening ties with China could damage its relations with its key global ally, the US, as many Americans see a rising China as a potential threat to its strategic interest that needs to be contained. This is precisely the reason for US to persuade EU not to lift the arms embargo on China and support anti-China resolutions at the UN and other international forums.

Hence, both EU and China should address these above stated issues to further strengthen its relations. Overall, EU perceives the rise of China as an opportunity and less as a threat to its strategic interest in the regional and international arena. In this context, EU would continue its efforts to further engage China in political dialogue; support China's transition to an open society; encourage China's integration into the world economy and pursue a policy of raising its own profile towards China.[25] On the other hand, China would also continue its engagement with EU to achieve its long-standing quest for greater power status and in the process it wishes EU to recognize China's market economy status; strictly observe the 'One China policy'; not to support separate Tibet tendencies; continue the dialogue process on human rights issue;[26] and enhance the economic and military cooperation. Apart from bilateral cooperation, EU and China would continue its multilateral cooperation in addressing the transnational issues, strengthening multilateralism and also addressing common international security threats which requires some actions like terrorism, proliferation of WMD, instabilities, regional conflicts and failing states, organized crimes, environmental issues and pandemics, and securing energy resources.[27] Thus, a strong EU-China partnership would go a long way in shaping both, regional and international issues.

References

1. Tao Xie and Benjamin I. Page, "American's and the Rise of China as a World Power," Journal of Contemporary China, Vol.19, No.65, June, 2010.
2. Albert Keidel, China's Economic Rise—Fact and Fiction (Washington, DC: Carnegie Endowment for International Peace, 2008), p. 1.
3. Bharat Wariavwalla, "Name of the game is Interdependence," Strategic Analysis, Vol.34, No.4, July 2010, p.514.
4. Zhu Liqun, China's Foreign Policy Debates, Chaillot Papers (Paris: EU Institute for Security Studies, 2010), pp.38-40.
5. Iskander Rehman, "Keeping the Dragon at Bay: India's counter-containment of China in Asia," Asian Security, Vol.5, No.2, 2009, p.122; Lawrence S. Prabhakar, "China's String of Pearls in Southern Asia-Indian Ocean: Implication for India and Taiwan" in M.J. Vinod, Yeong-Kuang Ger and S.Y. Surendra Kumar,Security challenges in the Asia-Pacific Region (New Delhi: Viva Books, 2009), p.44; Walter Ladwig III, "Delhi's pacific ambition: Naval Power, look East and India's Emerging influence in.the Asia Pacific," Asian Security, Vol.5 No.2, 2009, 87-113.
6. Chintamani Mahapatra, "Fairy tale of America decline and China's rise," Strategic Analysis, Vol.34, No.4, July 2010, p. 520; Chris Patten, "The Rise of China," The RUSI Journal, Vol.13, Issue.3, June 2010, pp.54-57.
7. David Shambaugh, "The New Strategic Triangle: US and European Reactions to China's Rise" The Washington Quarterly, Vol.28, No.3, 2005, p.7.
8. China State Council, White Paper: China's Peaceful Development Road, 22 December, 2005, http://english.peopledaily.com.cn/200512/22/eng20051222_230059.html.
9. David Shambaugh, "The New Strategic Triangle: US and European Reactions to China's Rise," The Washington Quarterly, Vol.28, No.3, 2005, p.9.
10. Ibid, p.11.
11. Ibid, p.15.
12. Yong Deng, "Remoulding Great Power Politics: China's Strategic Partnership with Russia, The EU and India," The Journal of Strategic Studies, Vol.30, No.4-5, August-October 2007, pp.863-903;David Shambaugh, "China and Europe: The emerging Axis," Current History, September 2004, pp.243-248.

13. Katinka Barysch, Embracing the Dragon: the EU partnership with China (London: Centre for European Reform, 2005), p.2.
14. "13th EU-China Summit, Joint Press Communiqué," 6 October 2010, Brussels, 14577/10.
15. "Strong increase in EU27 exports to China in the first half of 2010," Eurostat News Release, 5 October 2010. www.ec.europa.eu/eurostat.
16. "China, the EU and the Transatlantic Alliance," 22 July 2005, A statement by Robin Niblett, Testimony before the US-China Economic and Security Review Commission, p.3.
17. Eurostat News Release, op.cit. 15.
18. "EU Remains Torn On Lifting China Arms Embargo," 11 September 2010. www.defensenews.com/story.php?i=4775528; Kristin Archick, Richard F. Grimet and Shirley Kan, "European Union's Arms Embargo on China: Implications and Option for the US Policy,"CRS Report for Congress, May 2005, pp.1-47.
19. Sonika Gupta, "Politics of arms embargoes: US-China-EU," 20 October 2010. http://www.ipcs.org/article/china/politics-of-arms-embargoes-us-china-eu-3262.html.
20. Gudrun Wacker , "Lifting the EU arms Embargo on China, US and EU Position," Bates Bill and Gudrun Wacker (eds.), China's Rise: Diverging US-EU Perception and Approaches (Berlin: Stiflung Wissenschaft and Politik, 2005) p.31.
21. Ibid, p.35.
22. Sonika Gupta, n.19.
23. Gabriele Steinhauser, " EU, China to lock horns on Yuan, trade," 10 October 2010, http://www.forbes.com/feeds/ap/2010/10/06/business-eu-eu-china_7989096.html.
24. Axel Berkofsky, "The EU-China Strategic Partnership: Rhetoric Versus Reality," Marcin Zaborowski, Facing China's Rise: Guidelines for an EU Strategy (Paris: Institute Security Studies, 2006) p.105.
25. Eberhard Sandschneider, "Is China Military Modernisation a Concern for the EU?," Marcin Zaborowski, Ibid, p.43.
26. Terry Narramore, "China and Europe: Engagement, Mulitpolarity, and Strategy "The Pacific Review, Vol.21, No.1, March 2008, pp.7-8.
27. For details see, May-Bitt Stumbaum, "Opportunities and Limits of EU-China Security Cooperation," The International Spectator, Vol.42, No.3, September 2007, pp.351-370.

9

Strategic Engagement of India: A Comparative Study of the European Union & the United States

M. J. Vinod

Introduction

India and the European Union (EU), as large democracies share common values and beliefs that make them natural partners given their common commitment to democracy, pluralism, human rights, rule of law, an independent judiciary and media. Both are also factors for stability in the world order, besides being multi-cultural, multi-religious and multi-lingual societies. India is a microcosm of the globe and accounts for nearly one-sixth of humanity. The EU, with its expanding geographical boundaries is one of the most demographically diverse entities in the world and yet able to synthesise the rich diversity of its member states into a viable coherent whole. These are areas where both India and the EU could benefit from an exchange of experiences. The United States' and the European Union's strategic engagement with key players of the world like India needs to be compared and contrasted from the following perspectives:

a) They all share common values and beliefs that make them natural partners as well as factors of stability in the present world order.

b) They all share a common commitment to democracy, pluralism, human rights, rule of law, to an independent judiciary and media.

c) They are all multi-cultural, multi-religious, and multi-lingual societies

India maintains strategic partnerships with important EU countries independently — like Britain, France, and Germany. Annual summits are critical to these partnerships, as is the case with the EU, since the year 2000. Moreover, strategically the notion of a common European foreign and security policy has been evolving. The first EU-India Summit held in Lisbon in June 2000 heralded a new political willingness to foster closer bilateral relations in a variety of areas. Since 2000 regular annual summits have been held, accompanied by the setting up of joint Working groups and a plethora of joint initiatives. The culmination of these rapprochement initiatives was the signing in June 2004, of a New Strategic Partnership Agreement, which defined five priority areas of cooperation:

a. Multilateral cooperation in the international sphere with an emphasis on conflict prevention, anti-terrorism, non-proliferation, the promotion of democracy, and the *defence* of human rights.

b. Strengthened economic cooperation involving sectoral dialogues along-with jointly drafted regulatory policies.

c. Cooperation in development so as to enable India to achieve the 'Millennium Goals' as framed by the United Nations.

d. Intensifying intellectual and cultural exchange.

e. Improving the institutional framework of Indo-European relations[1]

Accordingly, India and the EU are committed to working towards:

- Promoting effective multilateralism;

- To regularly hold consultations on thematic issues prior to the UN General Assembly (UNGA), and work together on negotiation and implementation of the outcome of major international conferences and summits that focus on security, trade, environment, development, and human rights.

Indian Foreign Policy Outlook and Context: Implications for India-US and India-EU Ties:

Indian foreign policy is characterised by perceptions of self-reliance and independence, and has used a mixture of hard and soft power guided by a strong sense of 'strategic autonomy', which puts the degree of engagement with other countries in perspective. This dimension matters in the context of India-US and India-EU strategic engagement too. The moot questions to be raised are the following:

1) What does the United States and India expect from these partnerships?
2) Can we say that the India-EU strategic partnership is vibrant and multi-faceted, and not merely ritualistic?
3) To what extent is the EU as a global player ready to share in the responsibility of global security?

The EU and US engage Asia in different ways. The US has discovered the power potential of India which is critical to the Asian strategic calculus. On the contrary, the EU seeks to engage India because of its economic growth. The EU is less a strategic security actor and mainly focuses on soft power capabilities and avenues.

In terms of India-US ties, the rationale for Washington's strategic interests can be summarised as follows:

- Increasing overlapping of national and geo-strategic interests of India and the US.
- No single area of India-US cooperation highlights the transformation in bilateral ties more than defence and strategic cooperation.
- India-US defence and strategic cooperation has risen to "unprecedented levels." It has taken the shape of "dialogues," "periodic policy reviews," and reciprocal visits of senior military commanders and officials" as well as "joint military exercises." The indications are that any failure to recognise the strategic importance of India to the US and vice versa could jeopardise the balance-of-power in Asia.

Extended Reach of India-US Strategic Coop.; Overall Implications for the Asia-Pacific:

If one were to list the critical strategic factors that have impacted on the evolving strategic partnership between India and the US, the following deserve to be highlighted:

1. Short and long-term security threats that China poses to India.
2. The impact of China-Pakistan nexus and its implications for India's security.
3. Pakistan's status as a nuclear weapons state and its implications for India.
4. State-sponsored terrorism and India's security.
5. Arms peddling/drug trafficking/money laundering – implications for India.
6. Spread of WMD's and associated materials/data/technologies.
7. Protecting the free flow of commercial land/sea/air lanes.

The increasing U.S. focus on the political and economic relationships in Asia and the rise of China and India have increased India's strategic importance in U.S. eyes. "India's democratic heritage," "its impressive economic performance," and "civilian control of the military" are all seen as attractive factors in pursuing a closer strategic relationship. U.S. officials expect India to play a major role in shaping Asia's strategic environment. They see India as a uniquely valuable participant in this type of flexible structure for working together. Moreover, the practical experience of working with India following the Asian Tsunami of 2005, lead the United States to stress the importance of inter-operability in its emerging relations with India.

Some options at the EU's disposal

The first of these is to strengthen a sense of European unity and to fight against the overriding trend of each member state to go it alone in its relations with India.

a) This occurs even in areas where common European policies have been agreed, for example, in the area of joint research activities.

b) In India the "every member state for itself," approach is not merely unworkable, but could also be counterproductive. It could compromise on the EU being perceived as a single entity.

c) Given India's size, its burgeoning economy and its increasing political and military power, the only possible European partner for India is the European Union as a whole. The sooner this reality is realised the better for the whole of Europe.

Secondly, European diplomacy vis-a-vis India and China, needs to be rebalanced.

a) In India, the 'pro-Chinese bias' of the European Union is ill received. For Indians the Sino-centrism of Europeans is paradoxical, given Europeans' perceived concern with promoting democracy and the Rule of Law. On both these fronts China's record leaves much to be desired, and this is well known to the Europeans.

b) A more balanced European policy would be well received in India if it also involved actively supporting India's campaign for a permanent seat in the UN Security Council, an objective opposed by China. U.S. President Obama's visit to India in November 2010 and his open admission of the need to admit India as a permanent member of the Security Council are certain trends that the EU can no longer afford to ignore, though it will still be some time before this becomes a reality.

Realpolitik Factors

The European Union and its member states will need to act more strategically so as to bring Europe's true weight to bear internationally. The security dialogue (November, 2008) held shortly after the Mumbai 26/11 attacks was more substantive than any of the previous ones, but meaningful cooperation on security issues will be with the Member States and not the EU because it is *they* who have the assets and competences, not the Union.[2]

India and the EU also have much to contribute towards fostering a rule-based international order - be it through the United Nations (UN) or through the World Trade Organisation (WTO). We hold a common belief in the fundamental importance of multilateralism, and in the essential role of the UN for maintaining international peace and security, promoting the economic and social advancement of all people, and meeting global threats and challenges.

It is critically important to expand our multifaceted relationship and build upon these foundations. One perhaps needs to note the distinction between 'the modern world' of assertive states, based on balance and the 'post-modern' world of multilateral cooperation, based on openness.[3] Hence, India and the EU need to commit themselves accordingly to:

- Strengthening dialogue and consultation mechanisms;
- Deepening political dialogue and cooperation;
- Bringing together People and Cultures;
- Enhancing Economic Policy Dialogue and Cooperation;
- Developing Trade and Investment.

India and the EU believe that a multilateral approach, in which the UN plays a central role; is the best way to address global challenges such as development which is economically, socially and environmentally sustainable; effective management of globalisation; terrorism; drug trafficking; organised crime; natural disasters; pandemics; and energy security. The following are the areas where India and the EU need to further strengthen their collaboration.

Peacekeeping, Peace-Building and Post-Conflict Assistance

India and the EU have a common interest in UN peacekeeping and in post-conflict political and economic rehabilitation and reconstruction. Both sides propose to work together in the following areas:

- Engage in consultation prior to major UN debates on peacekeeping and peace-building.
- Establish official level dialogue on UN peacekeeping and peace-building. This could help exchange ideas on conceptual and operational aspects of peacekeeping operations. This could also include post-conflict reconstruction and rehabilitation. The following initiatives are being contemplated;

– Training for military and civilian components of peacekeeping missions, including police and other security forces;

– Exchange of trainees and instructors between Peacekeeping Training Centres of India and EU Member States;

– Joint support of UN peacekeeping and peace building efforts, including improved analytical capacities and greater cooperation between EU and Indian components of UN peacekeeping missions.

Disarmament and Non-Proliferation of Weapons of Mass Destruction (WMD) and Security Dialogue

India and the EU have to build on their shared interest in working towards achieving the goals and objectives of universal disarmament and non-proliferation of weapons of mass destruction (WMD's). The proliferation of WMD's and its linkages with terrorism pose a threat to international peace and security.

Multilateral consultations and the pooling of all efforts and resources. Effective export control measures for dual use goods can play an important role in preventing proliferation, and at the same time, such measures should not hamper international co-operation in materials, equipment, and technology for peaceful purposes. Given this heady agenda, India and the EU need to strengthen their security dialogue.

Fight Against Terrorism and Organised Crime

India and the EU have identified terrorism as one of the most serious threats to international peace and security. Both sides have been working together to strengthen cooperation in counter-terrorism efforts in accordance with the UN Charter and applicable principles of international law. In this respect India and the EU have been collaborating to seek full implementation of all relevant UN Security Council Resolutions (UNSCRs) and UN conventions on terrorism. Critical issues in this context include:

- The fight against trafficking and psychotropic substances, and the diversion of chemical precursors are matters of concern;
- Tracking terrorist access to financing and money laundering in particular, to be pursued by India and the EU. This has to take

into account international standards adopted by the Financial Action Task Force (FATF);

- Expand the EU-India cooperation to meet the threat posed by the link between drug trafficking and terrorism, illicit arms trafficking, and cyber-terrorism;
- India and the EU are also in the process of enhancing cooperation between Europol and the Central Bureau of Investigation, to deal with these multifarious threats and challenges.

The US and the EU engage a rising Asia in different ways, which underscores who shapes what aspect of global politics. The US has discovered the power potential of India, crucial to the Asian strategic calculus. However, Indian foreign policy does not contemplate becoming part of a military alliance. In this context India-EU relations assume importance. The EU seeks to create a multi-polar world in which it identifies India and China as the emerging Asian power centres, and seeks to engage India because of its economic growth. However there is a 'deficit' in the India-EU relationship because the EU is not a strategic security actor and its ability to bring security deliverables to the partnership is extremely limited.[4]

The EU is not in the business of balancing or bandwagoning other powers and that should be clearly understood by its partners. Instead, the EU should take the lead in filling the gap between interdependence and power politics, engaging old and new global players in the management of common challenges through multilateral frameworks. To this end, strategic partnerships can play an important role. As strategic partnerships deepen, the divide between interdependence and power politics narrows.[5] The sheer diversity of the EU partners, the sometimes unconvincing performance of the EU and the mismatch between the priorities of the EU and those of the partners are the three major challenges facing the EU in the context of building up strategic partnerships.[6]

The European Union should be best placed of all major political blocs to navigate the interdependencies of the emerging international system.[7] Unfortunately, due to its fragmented institutional arrangements, it has lacked coherent leadership and presence on the international stage, while its constituent economies have suffered badly during the financial downturn. Its member states are over-represented in most parts of the international system, and are seldom prepared to do the hard work of agreeing on a common policy position. As a result, Europe continues to punch far below its weight – a problem seen clearly at Copenhagen, where despite a credible policy position ahead of the summit, the EU found itself largely irrelevant to the outcome.[8]

Conclusion

The EU-India strategic partnership is to a certain extent overshadowed by the India-US and India-China partnerships, both of which deal with issues of immediate interest for India. Perhaps it was the US and Chinese focus on India that may have influenced the EU to seek a partnership with India. Realpolitik factors should influence EU relations with India along with the "normative factors" of pluralist democracy. Internally India is yet to come to grips with the "EU as an umbrella institution" for European countries. Within India, EU member countries are perceived as being more active diplomatically than the EU is.

The European Union's strategic partnerships with key players in the world provide a useful instrument for pursuing European objectives and interests. This is where India-EU relations come in. This will only work if they are two-way streets based on mutual interests and benefits and on the recognition that all actors have rights as well as duties. Indian foreign policy is characterised by perceptions of self-reliance and independence, and a mixture of hard and soft power. Indian foreign policy is guided by a strong sense of "strategic autonomy," which puts the degree of engagement with other countries in perspective. This dimension matters in the context of India-US and India-EU strategic engagement too.

The background is however different. The urge of the EU to build strategic partnerships with various parts of the world like China, India, Japan, Canada, indeed emanated from security imperatives. The first-ever European Security Strategy (ESS), adopted in December 2003, could be described as the harbinger. India also responded positively. Next year at The Hague Summit, India and EU entered into a strategic partnership. A Joint Action Plan was adopted in 2005. India-EU ties are largely embedded in a dense institutional web compared to many other countries. As there is a wider political consensus in India to deepen the EU-India strategic partnership, innovative ideas are required to make the strategic partnership more vibrant and multi-faceted and not annually ritualistic.[9]

India and EU need a strategic dialogue that goes beyond the articulation of normative principles. The time has come for concrete action and this calls for "strategic vision" and "sagacity". The EU will need to respect India's "strategic autonomy" and its freedom to "set its security priorities". The challenge for the India-EU strategic partnership is to 'balance norms and realism'.

India is also trying to become a 'norm setter' seeking to change the 'status quo' in matters of global governance. The EU's reactions in this context are very critical. Hence, when the US upgrades its ties with India it is a "global signal" that cannot be ignored. India is largely being perceived as a 'trading bloc' and "not as a significant political actor." The United States has been much more a "norm setter," while the EU has been a more status quoist in its approach.

Both the US and the EU have recognised the power potential of India. Yet one wonders whether the time has come for the EU to move beyond its "soft power" approach, so as to also address India's security concerns. Though there has been convergence of some strategic interests between the US, India, and the EU, yet there are divergences at the level of global and regional aspirations as well as India's security concerns. The India-EU security dialogue since 2006 has now gone beyond a platform for sharing views. The US on the other hand, has gone a long way in upgrading its ties with India. Perhaps this is a signal to the EU which it cannot ignore. A major challenge for the EU would be to expand India-EU relations from the current "economic" focus to "political and security" issues of common concern. The importance of India's power potential as being critical to the Asian strategic calculus deserves to be recognised by the EU.

References

1. Christopher Jaffrelot, India and the European Union, March 2006,http://www.ceri-sciences-po.org.
2. Rajendra Jain, India and the European Union: Perceptions and Policies, (Paper presented at the European Studies in Asia (ESiA) Network Public Panel, "EU-Asian Relations: Policies and Perceptions of the EU in Malaysia," Asia- Europe Institute, University of Malaysia, Kuala Lumpur, 19 June, 2009).
3. Robert Cooper, The Breaking of Nation (Almanac Books: London, 2004).
4. Ummu Salma Bava, "The EU and India: Challenges to a Strategic Partnership," in "Partnerships for Effective Multilateralism: EU Relations with Brazil, China, India and Russia," Chaillot Paper, Institute for Security Studies, European Union, May 2008, p.113.
5. Giovanni Grevi, "The Rise of Strategic Partnerships: between Interdependence and Power Politics," in 'Partnerships for Effective Multilateralism: EU Relations with Brazil, China, India and Russia' Chaillot Paper, Institute for Security Studies, European Union, May 2008, p.172.
6. Roberto Menotti and Maria Francesca Vencato, "The European Security Strategy and the Partners," in Sven Biscop and J. Andersson (eds),The EU and the European Security Strategy – Forging a Global Europe (Routledge: London, 2007).
7. Alex Evans, Bruce Jones and David Steven, Confronting the Long Crisis of globalisation:Risk, Resilience and International Order (Washington D.C.;Brookings Institution, 2006).
8. Ibid.
9. Jaffrelot, n.1.

Section-IV

EU-South Asia-India

10

EU-South Asia Economic Linkages

Gulshan Sachdeva

1. Introduction

The history of economic relationship between the Indian subcontinent and Europe is very old. At the end of the fifteenth century, European traders came to India and started exporting goods to Europe and other parts of Asia. Slowly India became an important centre of European trading activities in Asia and the Indian Ocean, by the activities of the Portuguese as well as the Dutch, English, and French East India companies. The initial Portuguese monopoly was later challenged by the English and Dutch East India companies at the beginning of the seventeenth century. Later, these two companies dominated the trade between the two continents. Apart from the French East India company, other companies like the Danish, the Ostend, and the Swedish never became very significant players in trade with the subcontinent.[1]

These East India companies acted as the main vehicle of trading and financial exchanges between Europe and Asia. Over a period of time, the influence of European companies together with that of private traders reshaped the maritime trading patterns. As a result of their important position in the market, these companies also imposed themselves upon local production, financial, and agrarian systems. A particularly powerful influence was exerted upon Indian production by its exposure to competition from British manufactured goods.[2] Various studies have established that as a result of these interactions, economies of the region expanded, further monetized and were integrated to the pre-modern global economy. Some studies, however, question the benign view of the "age of partnership" between the Europeans companies and Indian states. It is argued that this was a period of "contained conflict" between the trading companies and Indian states. Blockades, bombardments, ship seizures, massacres and abductions were regular options for European traders in the seventeenth century.[3]

The English East India Company also exerted its military power in Bengal in the mid-eighteen century. This facilitated its transition from a purely commercial company into an imperial power. The market determined economic relationship between India and Europe changed with the establishment of the colonial relationship between Britain and the subcontinent. With the advent of industrial revolution in Britain, many fundamental changes in economic interactions happened. Instead of being the source of textile products, the Indian subcontinent became an important market for the textile products of Manchester and Lancashire.[4]

At the time of independence, the countries of the region were host to a large body of foreign capital, mainly British. As a feature of colonial heritage, foreign investments were concentrated in extractive industries. For example, in India about 85 percent of tea plantation areas were foreign owned. Similarly, trade and ancillary services were dominated by foreign capital. Even in 1951-2 (four years after independence) about 40 percent of India's imports and exports were handled by foreign firms.[5] A survey of 41 subsidiary companies in India, which had Rs. 10 lakhs (1 million) of paid-up ordinary share capital registered in Calcutta and Bombay, were either British or mixed with British majority. Two of them were Anglo-Dutch (Philips and Unilever) and one American (General Electric)[6].

The London *Economist* reported in 1955 that British investors (who retained a major share of foreign investment in India) still had large percentages in the tea industry (60.4%), mining (28.9 %), jute (25.3%) ,and coal (14.5%).[7] But in all these years there were continuing sales of British interests to local entrepreneurs. While in 1938, there were 61 large business groups controlled by British in India, and by 1962, no more than 25 business groups remained British.[8]

Although a number of estimates have been made, it is difficult to calculate the exact amount of foreign (and European) capital in pre-independent India. Several estimates confuse British investments with foreign investments and other's focus on foreign control over areas of the Indian economy. Despite serious problems, some excellent works have been produced on foreign capital during that period. The following table summarizes various estimates of foreign capital in India between 1920 and 1960.

Table 1: Summary of Different Estimates of Foreign Investment in India 1921-1960(in Rupees Crores*)

Authority	Year for which estimated	Amount
V K R V Rao	1926-7	328
Economist	1928-9	180 (including Ceylon)
G D Birla	1929	585
Prof Findley Shirras	1930	190
Sir Robert Kindersley	1930	142
Associated Chambers of Commerce	1931	741
Sir Robert Kindersley	1936	130 (including Ceylon)
Statist	1939	866-931
Prof B R Shenoy	1939	565
Dr A K Banerji	1921	302 (British share 240 crores)
Dr A K Banerji	1938	413 (British share 302 crores)
Reserve Bank of India	1948	320(British share 230 crores)
Reserve Bank of India	1948 (net valuation)	226(British share 206 crores)
Reserve Bank of India	1953(net valuation)	392(British share 326 crores)
Reserve Bank of India	1960(net valuation)	566(British share 442 crores)

*One Crore= 10 million

Source: B R Tomlinson, "Foreign Private Investment in India 1920-1950," *Modern Asian Studies*, Vol.12(4), 1978.

Although in the earlier decades after independence, most of the foreign capital invested in the region came from Britain, newly established authorities drew on a wide range of countries for technical assistance. For example, India focused on the USA for oil refineries, on Germany for steel making, on France for ship building, on Switzerland for rail coach and drug manufacturing.

During the first decade of independence, the economies of the South Asian region had been very open economies. However, by the late sixties they had become some of the most protectionist economies in the world. State interventions in economic activity had become pervasive. Tariff and non-tariff barriers were extremely high. Attitudes towards foreign investments were hostile and stringent exchange controls were in place.[9] The sheer presence of multinationals was regarded a threat to host countries, raising concerns that these companies could influence domestic economic and political affairs. FDI and MNCs were also viewed as modern forms of colonialism[10]. Consequently, the region was not seen by international investors as attractive investment destination. By mid-1970s, however, Sri Lanka started the process of economic liberalization, which was later hesitantly followed by others in the mid-1980s. It was only with the 1991 economic liberalization of India, the biggest economy in the region, that the economic policy discourse changed in South Asia.

2. Economic Development and Liberalisation in South Asia

With about 1500 million people having PPP per capita income of about $2700, the South Asian region today is one of the densely populated regions of the world. With about six per cent average economic growth during the last fifteen years, the region is also among one of the fastest growing regions of the world. Starting with Sri Lanka in the 1970s, all South Asian countries embarked on an economic liberalisation that accelerated significantly in the 1990s. These liberal policies were driven by a general disillusionment with state control and planning implemented in individual countries, and the feeling that the region was missing the growth and development opportunities that East and Southeast Asian countries were enjoying. The collapse of the central planning in the former Soviet Union also played its part. During the 1990's, real GDP growth in the South Asian region was above 5 per cent per year. Gross domestic investment was about 22 per cent and per capita income grew at 3.3 per cent per year. Inflation also remained low throughout the region.

Before the economic crisis hit the world economy, the regional GDP growth was growing fast. This growth was the result of good performance by the Indian and Pakistani economies. More than half of the regional economy is contributed by the service sector, which has grown rapidly in the last decade. Agriculture is also an important sector, which is still largely dependent on the monsoon. In the last few years, agriculture has remained weak in all big economies. In the last few years, the average agriculture growth was between 3 to 4 per cent in India, Bangladesh, and Pakistan. To improve the situation policy makers are planning substantial public investments in agriculture along -with private investments in mechanisation. Due to global economic crisis, the regional economy has slowed down. Still, the region has been able to perform reasonably well. And growth prospects remain good. South Asian economies, however, will need greater investments in infrastructure and human resources to sustain high growth rates. Future prospects for Afghanistan and Nepal would depend on achieving solutions to political conflicts.

Table 2: South Asia: Basic Economic Indicators

	India	Pakistan	B'desh	Sri Lank-a	Afgha-nistan	Nepal	Bhutan	Maldives	South Asia
Polution, mid 2008 (mn)	1140	166	160	20	29	29	0.7	0.3	1545
Population Density, 2008									324
Surface Area (000 sq km), 2008	3287	796	144	66	652	147			5131
GNI ($billions) 2008	1187	157	83.4	36	10.6	11.5			1487
GNI, PPP ($billions) 2008	3340	430	232	90	32	32			4163

PCI $ (2008)	1040	950	520	1780	370	400	1040	3640	963
PCI, PPP $ (2008)	2930	2590	1450	4460	1100	1110			2695
Average Annual Growth Rate (2000-200-7)	7.3	5.4	5.8	5.1		3.8	8.0	6.7	
GDP Growth 2008	6.7	3.7	6.2	6.0	2.3	6.1	5.0	5.8	
GDP Growth 2009	7.4	1.2	5.7	3.5		4.9		-2.6	
Sectoral Share in GDP, 2009									
Agriculture	17.1	21.6	18.7	12.6	32	32.6	18.3	--	
Industry	28.2	24.3	28.7	29.7	26	15.8	43.6		
Services	54.6	54.2	52.6	57.7	42	51.6	38.2		
Average Annual Sectoral Growth Rates, 2003-2009									
Agriculture	3.6	4.0	3.7	3.7	4.6	3.4	0.9	-3.2	
Industry	8.9	6.4	7.8	6.4	16.0	2.4	11.6	7.1	
Services	9.7	5.8	6.2	6.5	15.2	5.3	9.9	6.7	
Consumer Prices									
2008	8.0	12.0	9.9	22.3	33.2	7.7	8.3	12.3	
2009	6.1	20.8	6.7	3.4	-9.6	13.2	4.4	4.0	
Gross Domestic saving (%of GDP, 2008)	30.4	11.4	20.1	18.0	-7.9	9.8	42.3		
Gross Domestic Investment (% of GDP, 2008)	43.9	22.1	24.2	27.1	27.6	30.3	40.5		

Fiscal Balalnce (% of GDP, 2008)	-5.9	-7.3	-5.3	-7.0	-4.0	-2.1	0.7	-12.6	
Current Account Balance (%of GDP, 2009)	-3.0	-5.9	2.8	-0.5		4.2	-8.8	-28.5	
External Debt (%of GNI 2008)	19.0	28.7	27.7	28.1		28.9	49.7	81.7	
Internat-ional Reserv-es (US $ bn. 2008)	274	13	10	2.5					

GNI-Gross National Income; PCI- Per Capita Income; PPP-Purchasing Power Parity

Sources: Asian Development Indicators 2010 (ADB); *World Development Indicators 2010(World Bank)*

Macroeconomic policies in the region have historically generated some fiscal imbalances. Fiscal deficit is still high in major economies viz., India, Pakistan, Sri Lanka, and Bangladesh. The unsustainable nature of fiscal deficits has been widely recognized by policy makers in the region. Monetary policy in the region generally involves depreciations aimed at shoring up foreign reserves and promoting exports through increased competition. These policies were facilitated by relatively weak inflationary pressures. Although regional inflation remained low in the past, the last few years has seen rising inflation. Due to high import growth, the current account deficit may also increase slightly in the coming years. Still, there are enough reserves to face any challenge. Although global economic crisis has reduced foreign exchange reserves, India was still holding about US$ 275 billion reserves in 2008. Impressive economic growth in the last decade has also helped to reduce poverty. In Bangladesh, India, and Nepal, poverty fell by 9, 10, and 11 percentage points respectively. In Sri Lanka it fell by 6 percentage points and only in Pakistan it increased by 8 percentage points due to stagnation in the 1990's.[11] According to estimates, however, if the growth accelerates to 10 percent a year, the region could see single-digit poverty rates by 2015.[12] Studies comparing the region with East Asia show that South Asia's export orientation, inflows of foreign direct investment, workers' skill levels, infrastructure, and the ease of doing business, savings, productivity are less favourable. However, remittances in South Asia played an important role. In 2004-05, remittances by South Asian nationals working abroad totalled $22 billion.[13] To sustain and improve growth rates, the region will have to focus on improving investments, productivity, regional inequalities, and regional cooperation. In the external sector, the decade of 1990s witnessed comprehensive reform programmes in almost all South Asian countries. Except for Sri Lanka, which had opened up much earlier in the mid-1970's, all other countries have reduced tariffs and quantitative restrictions and liberalised foreign investments.

3. Europe South Asia Trade Linkages

As European countries are major economic partners of South Asia, their share in trade and investment is very substantial. For example, FDI from Europe to India is higher than investments from the USA and Japan put together. This kind of investment relationship has developed from a very extensive trade and political relationship between the European countries and the countries of South Asia. This is illustrated from the brief account of South Asian countries' linkages with EC/EU and individual European countries.

EU-India Trade

As a result of new economic policies in the early 1990s, India has become one of the fastest growing economies of the world. Despite some serious challenges related to energy, security, poverty, infrastructure, regional disparities, and internal security, there are strong indications that rapid growth will continue. Although major world economies are in a recessionary mode, Indian economy is still growing at a respectable pace. Due to increasing global linkages, the growth rate has come down from average 8.8 per cent achieved between 2003-04 and 2007-08.[14] Despite adverse global conditions, India is able to achieve about 7 per cent growth even for the year

2008-09. With exports worth $163 billion, Indian's merchantable trade reached $ 414 billion in 2007-08. It has been growing at an average annual rate of more than 30 per cent in the last four years (2003-04 and 2007-08). In addition, the service sector, which accounts for about 55 per cent of Indian economy, continues to perform well and contributes to growing service exports, which touched $142 billion in 2007-08. Within the services, Information Technology-Business Process Outsourcing (IT-BPO) industry was growing at an average of 31 per cent between 2003-04 and 2007-08. In 2007-08, this sector alone was responsible for $ 40 billion exports of IT and related services.[15]

Realizing the importance of economic relations with European countries, India was amongst the first few countries to establish diplomatic relations with the EEC in 1962. Later India and EEC signed some agreements in 1973 and 1981. The Commercial Cooperation Agreement (CCA) signed in December 1973 (which came into force in April 1974) was the first one to be signed by the EEC with any "non-associated developing country embodying the concepts of commercial and economic cooperation linked with trade."[16] Remarkably, this agreement focused on trade promotion with India in such a way that would not affect India's bilateral relations with individual EEC member-states. As a comprehensive agreement, it covered a wide range of economic issues including trade, economic cooperation, industry, services, energy, telecommunication, tourism, private sector investment, science and technology, intellectual property, agriculture, development cooperation, environment and human resource development.[17] It provided for a Joint Commission and three Sub-commissions on - (i) trade and commercial cooperation, (ii) economic cooperation, and (iii) development cooperation. Later, six working groups in areas of agriculture and marine products, information technology, environment, textiles, and consular issues were also set up. In 2001, India and EU signed a science and technology agreement. They also signed a custom cooperation agreement in 2004 to simplify customs procedures to facilitate trade as per international standards.

In the first summit meeting held in Lisbon in June 2000, India and EU agreed to enhance their trade and cooperation. As a result, the 11th EU Joint Commission encouraged the industry to launch the "Joint Initiative to Enhance Trade and Investment." These meetings led to the 'India-EU Strategic Partnership' in 2005. At the sixth summit in 2005, a 'Joint Action Plan' was also launched.[18] These meetings have been supplemented by 'India-EU Business Summits' organised by the apex Chambers of Commerce and Industries on the Indian side and Union of Industrial Employers' Confederation of Europe (UNICE) and local chambers of commerce from the member states representing the Presidency on the EU side.

In 1960-61, West European countries accounted for about 37 per cent of India's total trade. A large amount of this trade was still with two countries, viz., UK and West Germany. UK accounted for about 27 per cent of total exports and 20 per cent of total imports.[19] In later years, trade with some other countries also became important, particularly with Belgium. Trade with the EEC was an important component of the Indian foreign economic relations in the 1960s and the 1970s. Its relative importance declined as India forged special trade and economic relations with countries of the former Soviet, bloc. In 1971, the EC granted 'Generalised System of Preferences (GSP) facility to India, the first among the Asian countries, aimed at encouraging exports of manufacturing goods of poor developing countries. Some studies have, however, concluded that owing to structural rigidities and list of sensitive goods, the impact of the scheme was marginal.[20]

In recent years, Indian exports to the combined EU-27[21] have increased from about US$ 8.8 billion in 1996-97 to about US$ 40 billion in 2008-09.[22] Similarly, Indian imports from EU-27 have grown from about US$ 10.6 billion in 1996-97 to about US$ 43 billion in 2008-09. These imports were from India's major trading partners in the EU-27, i.e., Germany, UK, France, Belgium, Italy, Netherlands, Spain, and Sweden. In 2007-08, these eight countries accounted for about 89 per cent of India's trade with EU. The remaining 19 countries accounted for only 11 per cent of the total trade with EU-27. Imports from Belgium, France, Germany, Italy, and UK constituted about 76 per cent of total imports from EU. In fact, UK has retained its importance as a major export market within the EU. In 2007-2008, it accounted for 19 per cent of total exports to the

EU. In recent years, imports from Sweden have also increased at a very high rate. As a result of the economic recession in Europe, bilateral trade has come down to about US$ 75 billion in 2009-10 from its peak of about US$82 billion in 2008-09, (See, Figure 1).

Figure 1:

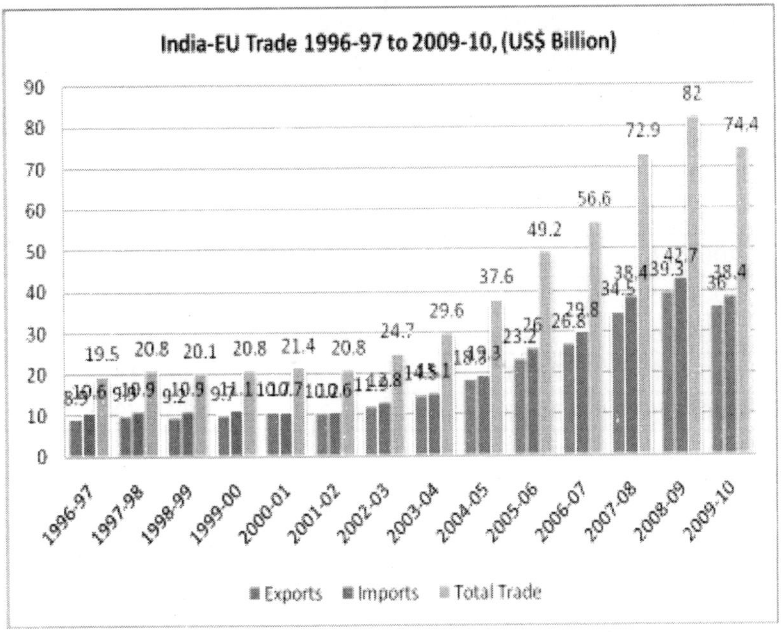

Source: Calculations based on data provided in *Export Import Data Bank*, Directorate General of Foreign Trade (DGFT), Ministry of Commerce & Industry, Government of India.

Although in absolute terms, India's trade with EU has increased, in relative terms as a percentage of India's total exports and imports, it has declined consistently in the last decade. As indicated in Table 3, in 1996-97, India-EU-27 trade constituted about 26.5 per cent of the total Indian trade. However, in 2007-2008, it declined to its lowest level, i.e., 17.6 per cent, despite some marginal increase in 2005-06.

Table 3: Percentage Share of EU-27 in India's Trade, 1996–97 to 2007–08

Year	% of Total Indian Exports	% of Total Indian Imports	% of Total Indian Trade
1996-97	26.49	27.15	26.48
1997-98	26.83	26.22	27.21
1998-99	27.70	25.68	26.57
1999-00	26.24	22.38	24.04
2000-01	23.99	21.12	22.47
2001-02	23.17	20.71	21.84
2002-03	22.54	20.89	21.65
2003-04	22.73	19.28	20.84
2004-05	21.84	17.30	19.25
2005-06	22.53	17.42	19.51
2006-07	21.21	16.06	18.14
2007-08	21.17	15.27	17.59

Source: Author's calculations based on DGFT Databank, Ministry of Commerce and Industry, Government of India.

In fact, India-EU trade has grown at a comparatively slower pace than India's total external trade during the last one decade. Against an average of about 28.9 per cent growth of Indian trade in four years (between 2003-04-and 2007-08), India-EU trade grew at about 25.4 per cent. Similarly, compared to about 34 per cent growth of Indian imports during these four years, imports from EU grew at an average of about 26.5 per cent, annually. These factors indicate that the European economies have not been able to take full advantage of the expanding Indian economy. In comparison, during this period India's trade with various other countries grew significantly. For example, India-US trade grew at an average rate of 26.3 per cent and its trade with China registered a growth of nearly 53 per cent per year. This rising level of trade indicates that India has been quite proactive in signing trading arrangements with a number of Asian countries.

The composition of main trading items between India and EU shows that India exports a wide variety of products to EU. Major export items are readymade garments, gems and jewellery, pharmaceuticals, organic chemicals, leather goods, vehicles, and machinery. The rate of growth has been the highest in food items, iron and steel, etc. Major items of import include gems and jewellery, machinery, electronic goods, chemicals, iron and steel, aluminium, etc. Similar items in both lists also indicate that considerable intra-industry trade is also taking place. For many years, India had balance of trade problems with many EU countries. The last few years have witnessed a deficit in the balance of trade with countries like Belgium, Germany, France, Finland, and Sweden. On the other hand, there has been a surplus with Italy, Netherlands, Spain, Portugal and even UK, with which India had a trade deficit for a long time. In the earlier decades, the trade debate in India was dominated by balance of trade issues. However, with India poised for growth at a rate of 8-9 per cent per year and with large foreign exchange reserves,[23] this sense of insecurity has given way to pragmatism. India is likely to expand its trade in spite of relatively large trade deficits in the next few years. Therefore, trade deficit, which influenced trade talks between India and Europe in the past, may not be an important issue in the coming years.

Trade in Services

There is no denying the fact that services are assuming centre-stage in the economies of both India and EU in recent years. In 2006, services accounted for about 69 per cent of EU economy.[24] The same year, the comparative figure for India was about 55 per cent. In 2006, the total global trade in services amounted to about Euro 4400 bn. Of this 25 per cent was in travel, 24 per cent in transport, and the rest 50 per cent in other services. In fact, EU is the biggest global player in international trade in services. In 2006, EU recorded a surplus of Euro 68.5 billion in this sector and its total trade in services was Euro 814.7 billion (Euro 441.1 bn in exports, and Euro 373.1 bn in imports). India is also becoming a significant player in global trade in services and in 2006, it ranked sixth, behind EU-27, US, Japan, China, and Canada. In international transactions worth about Euro 100 bn., India recorded a surplus of about Euro 20 bn (exports worth Euro 60.0 bn and imports worth Euro 39.3 bn). As can be seen from Tables 2-3, between 2004 and 2006, India's trade in services almost doubled. Its trade in services with EU-27 grew from Euro 7.8 bn. in 2004 to about Euro 15.6 in 2007 and there was an overall surplus in travel, computer, information and communication services. However, in all other categories, India recorded a deficit of about Euro 2.4 in 2007.

Moving Towards India-EU FTA

Some of the above discussed factors are encouraging EU-India trade deals, while others are proving adverse. The collapse of the Doha development round of WTO negotiations has pushed many countries including India to look for alternatives to multilateral negotiations to improve their trade positions. Since 2005 India has put its proposed regional trade agreements on fast track. In the past, India had adopted a cautious approach to regionalism, and was engaged in only a few bilateral/regional initiatives, mainly through Preferential Trade Agreements (PTAs) or through open regionalism.[25] In recent years, it has started concluding Comprehensive Economic Cooperation Agreements (CECAs) with many countries. These CECAs cover FTA in goods,[26]services, investment, and other identified areas of economic cooperation. India has already signed an agreement on South Asian Free Trade Area (SAFTA) as well as individual trade agreements with Afghanistan, Bhutan, Sri Lanka,[27] and Nepal.[28] India-Singapore CECA, India-Chile PTA as well India-MERCOSUR PTA have also been signed. In addition, trade and investment deals are being negotiated with Gulf Cooperation Council (GCC), South Korea, Malaysia, Mauritius, etc. India-Japan negotiations are also at a very advanced stage. Similarly, India-Israel, India- Brazil, South Africa (IBSA), and India-Russia joint study groups have been set up.[29] Against this backdrop, the time has been ripe for an India-EU FTA.

On the recommendations of the High Level Trade Group (HLTG), which was set up under the 'Joint Action Plan' in 2005, it was agreed at the seventh summit in October 2006 in Helsinki that both sides would negotiate for a broad based trade and investment agreement. They also agreed to begin negotiations on - (a) trade in goods (achieving elimination of duties on 90 per cent of tariff lines and trade volume within seven years of the entry into force of the agreement); (b) trade in services (all modes); (c) investment; (d) public procurement; (d) technical regulations (cooperation on technical barriers to trade and sanitary and phyto-sanitary measures) ; (e) intellectual property; (f) competition policy; and (g) dispute settlement provision.

It is clear that the agenda for negotiations have been quite broad. Despite the prevalence of a favourable environment for a trade deal, bureaucrats on both sides are remarkably slow in negotiations. The HLTG took one year (with only five one-day meetings in Brussels and Delhi) to come out with a report which could easily have been produced in a few weeks. Actual negotiations started only in June 2007, eight months after the Helsinki summit. In the first meeting, the broader objectives of negotiations were agreed and working groups were established. Since then more than ten rounds of negotiations have taken place.

According to official sources, India and the EU have submitted their initial proposals where they have offered to cut tariffs on 90 per cent of goods in terms of volume. From the Indian side, it has been proposed that 90 per cent tariff lines as well as 90 per cent of import trade value will be liberalised within seven years from the starting date. Current discussions are on increasing this figure, with India asking the EU to abolish tariffs on 95 per cent of the goods, while EU wants India to offer a tariff slash on 98 per cent of goods. On the issue of non-tariff measures, some broad objectives have been finalised and on rules of origin, objectives have been cleared and some texts have been exchanged. On the crucial issues of services and investment, some negotiations have started while on other issues like IPR, competition, and public procurement, both sides are in the process of finalisation of the broad objectives.

In 2008, at the ninth summit in France, India and the EU agreed to conclude the agreement by 2009 and double their trade in five years.[30] However, this has proved difficult without serious political pressure. Already the Federation of Indian Chambers of Commerce and Industry (FICCI) have expressed concerns that all items of export interest to India, like leather, textiles, and garments, may not get covered in FTA being negotiated with the EU. It suggests expansion of the scope of the agreement to cover 95 per cent of the merchandise goods.[31] The Communist Party of India (Marxist) asserts that unless details of the agreement are discussed in the Indian Parliament, no commitments should be made. The Politbureau of the party warns that "such FTAs can turn out to be much more damaging for the livelihoods of our farmers, workers and other sections of the working people than the WTO agreements."[32] A campaign group led by trade unions and non-profit organizations have already asked the government to halt the talks.[33] Some domestic opposition, difficult global economic situation and developments on other bilateral pacts (like India-Japan and India-US) may further derail the India-EU CECA.

Meanwhile, some academic studies have looked at the implications of a possible EU-India trade and investment agreement. A joint study by the Consumer Unity & Trust Society (CUTS) International and Sussex University assert that instead of shallow integration (the removal of border barriers to trade, typically tariffs and quotas) it would be far more effective if India and the EU go for deeper integration, which involves policies and institutions that facilitate trade by reducing or eliminating regulatory and behind-the-border impediments to trade. These policies could include issues such as customs procedures, regulation of domestic services production (which discriminate against foreigners), product standards (which differ from international norms or where testing and certification of foreign goods is complex and exclusionary), regulation of inward investments, competition policy, intellectual policy protection, and rules surrounding access to government procurement.[34] The study also suggests that an EU-India FTA is likely to increase FDI flows from the EU by 27 per cent, and FDI stocks by 18 per cent. Another report by Decreux and Mitoritonne[35] argues that the impact of an agreement will be positive for India and the EU. However, in the case of India, the service sector will be more likely to reap full benefits of FTA with the EU. FICCI has estimated that bilateral trade could touch $572 billion by 2015, if the deal goes through.

EU's Trade with the Rest of South Asia

Pakistan, Bangladesh, and Sri Lanka have also developed wide-ranging relations with EC and its member states. Pakistan established relations with the EC in 1962, followed later by commercial agreements in 1976 and 1986. From 1992, a bilateral political dialogue has also been instituted. In 2004, a bilateral third generation agreement was concluded with the provision of a Joint Commission. In trade, the EU is Pakistan's largest trading partner, accounting for (3.6 billion) in exports (3.9 billion) in imports in 2008 (See Table 4). Within the EU, UK is Pakistan's major trading partner, followed by Germany, France, Italy, Netherlands, and Belgium. Pakistan's main exports to EU are textiles, clothing as well as leather products while its imports from the EU mainly comprise mechanical and electrical machinery as well as chemical and pharmaceutical products. In development cooperation, the EC has committed more than 500 million in poverty alleviation and social sector development since 1976.[36] In May 2007, the EU and Pakistan agreed to set up a Sub-Group on Trade under the auspices of the EU-Pakistan Joint Commission. Now the EU and Pakistan have initiated a strategic dialogue and at the second EU-Pakistan summit in June 2010 the EU agreed to increase funding for trade related technical assistance to Pakistan.

Table 4 : EU- Pakistan Trade 2002-2009 (Million Euros)

Year	Exports	Imports
2002	2914	2149
2003	3003	2175
2004	3251	2839
2005	3861	3078
2006	1641	2184
2007	3461	3808
2008	3622	3908
2009	3318	3612

The EC-Bangladesh commercial agreement was signed in 1976. In 2001, under the third generation agreement, the scope has widened to cover areas of trade and development, human rights, good governance, and environment. For Bangladesh, the EU is the biggest export market which benefits from preferential market access, i.e. duty and quota-free access. As a Least Developed Country (LDC), Bangladesh enjoys quota- and duty-free access to the EU under the

1986 Textile Agreement and General System of Preferences (GSP) and under "Everything But Arms" initiative of the EU. In 2008, Bangladesh exports to the EU were 5.5 billion and imports from the EU amounted to 1.1 billion. In fact, the EU is the biggest export destination of Bangladeshi products, accounting for 56% of the country's total exports in 2007. The main items that Bangladesh exports to the EU are readymade garments (90%), frozen food (6%), leather, jute, and tea. Bangladesh's main imports from the EU consist of machinery and mechanical appliances (55%) and chemical products (14%). In development cooperation, the EC's development support to Bangladesh with the main objective of poverty alleviation has totalled 1.7 billion since 1976.[37]

EU-Sri Lanka economic relations intensified with the cooperation agreement in 1975. In 1995, a third generation agreement also came into force. EU has also played an important role as a co-chair, which regularly monitored the peace process. EU is Sri Lanka's top export partner. In 2009, Sri Lanka exported 2.2 billion worth of products to the EU, which represents 39 percent of Sri Lanka's total exports. After India, the EU is also Sri Lanka's number two import partner. Sri Lanka imported 1.3 billion worth of products and services from the EU – 14% of its total imports. Overall, in 2009, the EU was Sri Lanka's largest trading partner accounting for 2.88 billion trade - almost 20 percent of Sri Lanka's total trade. Textiles and clothing account for more than half of the country's export value (58.7% for exports to the EU) with machinery, rubber-based goods, jewellery, and agricultural products making up for the rest.[38]

The major trading partner of Bhutan and Nepal is India and Europe is important in the field of development assistance. In 2009, EU-Nepal bilateral trade was about Euro 140 million. From 1982 to 2006 community assistance to Bhutan was about 60 million Euros in the areas renewable natural resources, health and trade development, and export diversification. Between 1977 to 2006, assistance to Nepal was about 240 million in areas such as irrigation, watershed management, livestock, reproductive health, primary education, refugees, and institutional capacity building. Maldives has also received about 20 million for different post-tsunami humanitarian and reconstruction assistance projects.

Europe is also making significant contribution to military, development and reconstruction activities in Afghanistan. Individual member states and the European Commission together have committed around 8 billion for reconstruction activities. EU nations are participating in the NATO-led International Security Assistance Force (ISAF) with around 30,000 troops.

This wide-ranging relationship is also supported by European diplomatic, business, and cultural presence in South Asia. Except the Baltic Republics, all European countries have their diplomatic missions in India. Big European countries also have their consulates in major cities like Mumbai, Kolkata, Chennai, Bangalore, Hyderabad, etc. Apart from French, Italian, German and European Business Group, there is also a Council of EU Chamber of Commerce in India. Major countries are represented in Pakistan, Sri Lanka, Bangladesh, and Nepal. The EU has seven delegations in the region. In the information and cultural side, British Council, Alliance Française, German cultural institutions, Goethe Institute, etc. have their presence throughout the region. Delhi even hosts the Hungarian Information and Cultural Centre.

4. Investment Flows

As a result of the liberalised policies as well as a strong growth performance, the South Asian region has become an important source of FDI inflows in the late 1990s and in the first decade of the 21st century. In recent years, led by India, it has also become an a source of FDI outflows. Even in the period of global recession, Indian economy attracted about US$100 billion between 2007 and 2009, while in turn half of this investment was also invested by Indian companies abroad. Other economies of the region, mainly Pakistan is also attracting investments (Table 5).

Table 5: FDI Inflows, Outflows & FDI Inward Stock & Outward Stock in South Asia (Million US $)

	India	Pakistan	Bangla -desh	Sri Lanka	AFG	Nepal	Bhutan	Maldive
FDI Inflows								
2007	25,001	5,590	666	603	243	6	73	15
2008	40,418	5,438	1,086	752	300	1	30	12
2009	34,613	2,387	716	404	185	39	36	10
FDI Outflows								
2007	17,233		98	21	55			
2008	18,499		49	9	62			
2009	14,897		14	15	20			
FDI Inward Stock								
1990	1,657	1,892	477	679	12	12	477	25
2000	16,339	6,919	2,162	1596	17	72	2162	18
2009	163,959	17,789	5139	4687	1550	166	5139	231
FDI Outward Stock								
1990	124	245	45	8			45	
2000	1,733	489	69	86			69	
2009	77,207	2,201	91	334			91	

Source: World Investment Report 2010, pp.170, 175.

Since the region has started attracting investment, the extensive relationship with Europe has resulted in major FDI inflows from Europe. Its share in India's total FDI approvals from January 1991 to December 2005 was around 25 per cent. Investment approvals from EU rose from US$ 78 million in 1991 to US$ 2,314 million in 2001. This trend continued and cumulative actual FDI inflow from EU-25 during 1991-2005 reached US$ 7.6 billion, which was more than combined investments from US and Japan. Of course, this figure excluded the acquisition of existing shares (up to 1999), Reserve Bank of India's Non Resident Indian schemes, stock swaps, and advances pending for issue of shares. During this period, Netherlands was EU's top investor in India, followed by UK, France, and Germany. Moreover, FDI data provided by Indian government sources may be misleading. It is difficult to accurately find out country-wise data as large number of investments by European and American firms to India are being allegedly routed through Mauritius. In fact, between April 2000 and January 2009, about 43 per cent of total FDI in India came from Mauritius.[39]

Figure 2

Actual FDI from EU-25 to India, 1991–2005 US $ Millions

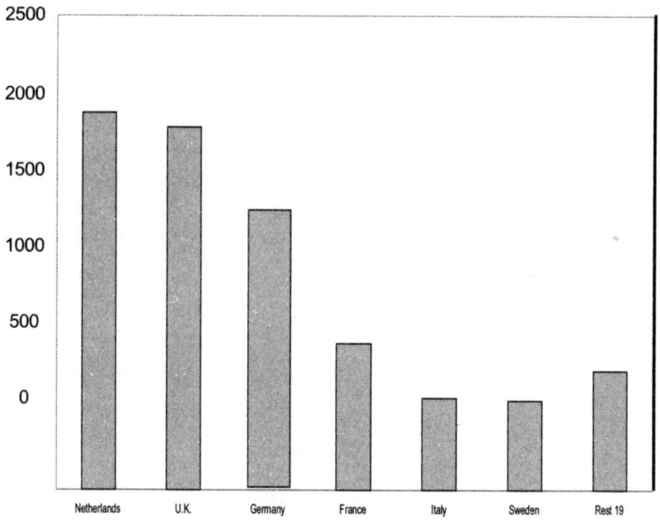

Source: *Foreign Direct Investment Policy 2006*, .Ministry of Commerce & Industry, Government of India, April, pp. 80-83.

During this period, the main sectors which attracted FDI from the EU were electrical equipments, fuels, transportation industries, chemicals, and services. Eurostat data shows that between 2001 and 2006, EU companies invested about Euro 9 billion in India, likewise Indian companies invested about Euro 1.9 billion in EU member states. After reaching peak in 2007, EU FDI flow to India has decreased.

Table 6

FDI Flows between India & the EU

(2001- 2009, in Million Euros)

Year	EU FDI in India	Indian FDI in EU
2001	348	108
2002	1074	133
2003	747	614
2004	1562	0
2005	2546	548
2006	2390	879
2007	4019	
2008	3272	
2009	3207	

Source: Eurostat database

In its earlier publications, Eurostat had indicated very high FDI inflow to India in 2007. However, in its latest database, it has moderated its figures. Overall, by the end of 2008, EU-27 countries had about 20 billion Euro FDI stock in India. Germany has emerged as the biggest investor from Europe to India.The UK, Netherlands, France, Sweden, Italy, and Finland are other big investors from Europe. Outside the EU, Switzerland has also invested Euro 1589 million in India.

Figure 3

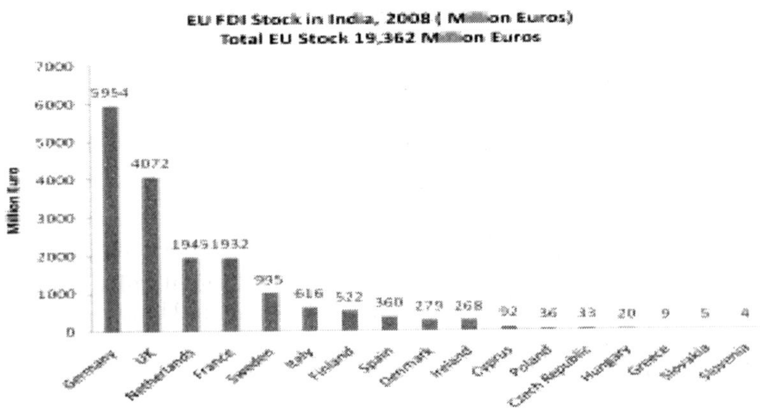

However, this flow of investment was not a one way traffic. According to some estimates, between 2000 and 2007, around 900 Indian companies invested about $12 billion in different EU member states. This was about 76 per cent of Indian greenfield investments[1] in developed countries abroad. UK has been a major attraction for Indian companies where more than 500 of them have invested about $9 billion during 1990-2007. Netherlands and Cyprus have also received substantial Indian FDI. In UK, a majority of the earlier investments were in the service sector. In recent years, there have been major investments in the manufacturing sector as well.

Table 7

Indian FDI in EU, 1990-2007(Million US$)

	1990-99	2000-2007	No. of Investing Firms
European Union	**1021**	**12061**	**857**
Austria	37	5	12
Belgium & Luxembourg	17	187	41
Cyprus	20	1359	36
Czech Rep.	1	35	5
Denmark		27	5
Finland	2	-	4
France	3	109	28
Germany	24	138	131
Greece	3	-	2
Hungary	3	2	9
Ireland	38	13	13
Italy	42	54	16
Latvia	1		2
Malta		64	1
Netherlands		1701	79
Poland	1	2	9
Spain	1	13	10
Sweden	3	10	8
UK	798	8353	531

Source: Jaya Prakash Pradhan, India's Emerging Multinationals in the Developed Region, New Delhi: Institute for Studies in Industrial Development, 2008.

Apart from greenfield investments, Indian companies have also been actively involved in overseas acquisitions. According to some estimates, 306 Indian firms were involved in 596 acquisitions worth $ 47 billion during 2000-2008 in the developed world. Of these acquisitions, European deals represented more than 50 per cent in value terms. Some important acquisitions in the years 2006 and 2007 were led by Tata Steel, Suzlon Energy, Dr Reddy's Laboratory and United Spirits (Table 9).

Table 8

Overseas Acquisitions by Indian Firms in Europe, 2000-2008

(Million US$)

Region/Country	Value
European Union	**23536**
Austria	133
Belgium	910
Czech Rep.	43
Denmark	16
Finland	101
France	316
Germany	3115
Greece	16
Hungary	44
Ireland	169
Italy	363
Netherlands	486
Poland	8
Portugal	69
Spain	173
Sweden	87
UK	17488
Other Europe	**1829**
Monaco	25
Norway	1646
Switzerland	158

Source: Pradhan,2008, op.cit.,

Table 9

Some Important Acquisitions by Indian Companies in Europe, 2006-07

Indian Company	Target	Sector	Acquisition in US$ Mn.	Year
Tata Steel	Corus, UK	Metal	13650	2007
Suzlon Energy	75% stake in Repower, Germany	Electrical machinery & Equipment	1816	2007
United Spirits	100% stake in Whyte & Mackay, UK	Food & Beverages	1178	2007
Aban Llyod Chiles Offshore Ltd.	Sinvest ASA, Norway	Oil & Natural Gas	800	2007
Dr. Reddy's Lab.	Betapharm Arzeinittel GmbH, Germany	Pharmaceuticals	597	2006
Suzlon Energy	Hansen Transmissions Belgium	Non electrical machinery	558	2006

Source: Pradhan, 2008, of cit.

Technology Transfer

EU is also one of the major sources of technology transfer to India. Between August 1991 and December 2004, Indian authorities approved more than 3600 technical collaborations from EU countries that accounted for about 38 per cent of total technical collaborations during this period. The highest number of technical collaborations was in the area of electrical equipment (including computer software), industrial machinery, and chemicals. Germany had the maximum number of 1,088 technical collaborations. UK and Italy were in second and third place with 843 and 473 approved collaborations. In financial collaborations, UK was the leader with more than 1,600 collaborations. The total number of technical and financial collaborations signed between Indian and the EU companies during 1991-2004 was 9,745, which was about 37 per cent of total collaborations signed by Indian companies during this period. In comparison, about 6,080 financial and technical collaborations were approved with US companies. According to the Indo-German Chamber of Commerce, Indo-German collaboration companies have been market leaders in product groups in India.

Figure 4

No. of FDI and FTC Approvals from EU-25, 1991–2004

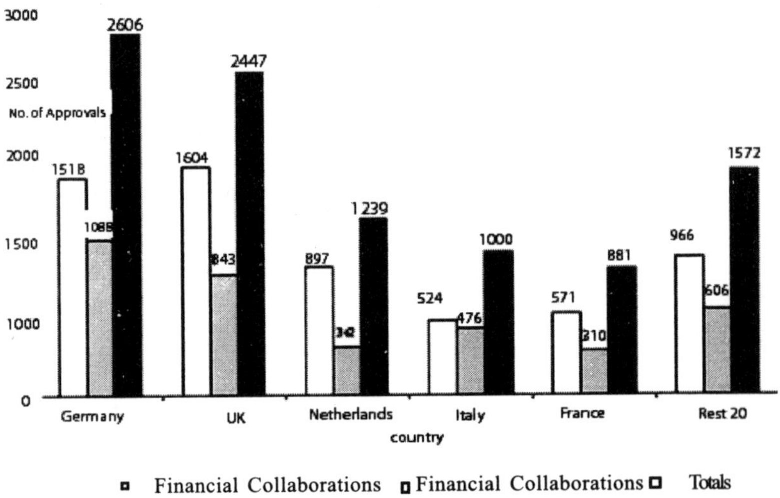

Source: Author's calculations based on publications of the Ministry of Commerce and Industry, Government of India.

Country-wise analysis of FDI inflows to Pakistan shows a slightly different trend. The US is the biggest investor in Pakistan. UAE is also a significant investor in Pakistan. Major European countries like UK, France, Germany, Netherlands, and Italy accounted for about 21 per cent of total FDI investments between 1989-90 and March 2006. In 2006-07, investment from EU countries amounted to about one-third of total FDI into Pakistan. Since then it has declined. Apart from these five major countries, small investments also came from Sweden, Austria, Belgium, Ireland, and Denmark, (Table 10).

Table 10: Net Flow of Foreign Direct Investment to Pakistan 1989-90 to 2008-09

	1989-90 to 2005-06		*2006-07*	*2007-08*	*2008-09*
Country	**Total FDI US$ millions**	*% of Total Million*	*US$ Million*	*US$ Million*	*US$*
USA	3,633.5	*31.5*	*914.4*	*1309.3*	*875.3*
European Union			*1720.4 (33.4% total)*	*663.4 (12.35 of total)*	*412.7 (11.1% of of total)*
Major EU Countries	2,445.80	*21.1*			
U.K	1,862.2	*16.1*	*860.0*	*460.2*	*263.4*
Germany	282.5	*2.4*	*78.9*	*69.6*	*76.9*
France	82	*0.7*		*8.4*	*6.4*
Netherlands	201.4	*1.7*	*771.8*	*121.6*	*41.8*
Italy	17.7	*0.2*			
Belgium			*2.5*	*25.9*	*48.9*
Austria			*1.1*	*14.5*	*19.1*
UAE	1541	*13.4*	*661.5*	*588.6*	*178.2*
Japan	464.8	*4.0*	*64.4*	*131.2*	*74.3*
Korea	199.9	*1.7*			
Saudi Arabia	474.6	*4.1*	*104.9*	*46.2*	*-92.3*
Hong Kong	138.5	*1.2*	*32.6*	*339.8*	*156.1*
Canada	21.2	*0.2*			
Switzerland			*175.9*	*169.3*	*227.3*
China			*712.1*	*13.7*	*-101.4*
Others	2611.5	*22.6*			
Total	**11,530.8**	*100*	*5139.6*	*5410.2*	*3719.9*

Source: Board of Investment, Government of Pakistan.

The available official information on FDI proposals in Bangladesh shows that European counties are becoming important contributors to the FDI flows to the country. According to the Bangladesh Board of Investment in 2003 and 2004, western European countries' share accounted for more than 45 per cent of total investments.[41] However, one or two major projects from a single country in a year can influence these proportions. For example in

2003, French and Norwegian investments in cement and telecom sectors respectively changed proportions. Similarly, in a particular year, only Norwegian investment constituted the bulk of the European investment.

5. European TNCs in South Asia

Moving from broad FDI data to financial and technical collaborations/joint ventures/ foreign companies, etc., official information in South Asia becomes more complicated. Many foreign companies are operating in this region in a variety of ways because of different kind of laws and regulations, incentives or disincentives. Definitions of foreign companies/collaborations are also changing since the early 1990's. Since there is lot of variation among countries in the region, it is not really possible to neatly summarise European companies' data in a regional manner. Although the *World Investment Report 2005* provided some information about the parent corporations and foreign affiliates operating in the region, many of these figures are not identical with the publications of different government ministries and departments as well as publications of the European diplomatic missions operating in the region, (Table 11).

Table 11: Number of Parent Corporations and Foreign Affiliates in South Asia

Country	Year	Parent corporation based in economy*	Foreign affiliates located in economy
Afghanistan	2004	1	2
Bangladesh	2004	2	28
Bhutan	1997	-	2
India	2004	1700#	1181
Maldives	2004	1	3
Nepal	2004	1	9
Pakistan	2001	59	582
Sri Lanka	2004	-	1430
South Asia		1764	3237

*Definitions varies from country to country

Data refers to number of approved FDI projects as of 2003

Source: World Investment Report 2005, UNCTAD, p.265

In India, "foreign companies" (other than banking companies) are those which are not incorporated in India and are subjected to special regulations relating to their business activities, etc. through the provisions of sections 28, 29, and 30 of FERA, 1973. Acquisition/ disposal of immovable properties is also subject to regulation under Section 31 of FERA, 1973. Until 1992, Indian companies, in which non-resident interest exceeded forty per cent, were also subject to these regulations. However since January 1993, FERA companies are treated on par with other Indian companies except those engaged in "agricultural or plantation" activities in India.[42] The number of these companies has grown from 565 in 1960 to about 3000 in 2009. In 1981, the number of foreign companies operating in India was only 300. In the last ten years, there is a very significant increase in the number of foreign companies in India. In addition, there are large numbers of foreign technical and financial collaborations, etc., many of which are governed under contract law and many are treated as Indian companies, (Table 12).

Table 12: Number of Foreign Companies in India 1960-2009

Year	Foreign Companies*
1960	565
1665	582
1970	561
1975	510
1980	315
1981	300
1985	324
1990	469
1995	619
2000	1045
2001	1141
2002	1285
2003	1497
2005	2007
2006	2040
2007	2546
2009	3105

* As defined under Section 591 of the Companies Act, 1956

Source: Ministry of Company Affairs, Government of India.

Table 13 provides detailed analysis of the foreign companies operating in different Indian states. It shows that out of the total 1,754 foreign companies, 623 (35.5%) are from 8 major European countries. Of these 623 companies only 307 are from the UK. There are 91 companies from Germany, 67 from France, 52 from Netherlands, 33 from Italy, 31 from Switzerland, and 19 from Sweden. There are 383 (21.8%) foreign firms from USA and 130 (7.4%) from Japan. Interestingly foreign firms from smaller Asian countries are increasing their presence in India at a very fast rate. There are 168 (9.6%) firms from Singapore and 81 companies (4.6%) from Hong Kong.

Majority of the European companies (about 70 per cent) are operating in Delhi, Mumbai and surrounding areas (457 out of 623 are only in Delhi, Maharashtra and Haryana). Only 12 percent European companies (76 companies) operate in the Southern region. Due to its historical background, UK companies have a strong presence in West Bengal. Many of the UK tea industry companies operate from Kolkata. In recent years, many foreign companies are moving towards Southern Indian States, particularly to Karnataka (India's Silicon Valley, Bangalore). This trend is clearly visible from the number of American and European companies present in Karnataka (34 and 48 respectively). Interestingly, except for British companies in West Bengal, the rest of Eastern and North-Eastern India (Bihar, Orissa, Assam, Arunachal Pradesh, Sikkim, Tripura, Manipur, Meghalaya, Nagaland, Mizoram) do not have a single European firm operating in the foreign company category. Similarly, they have no presence in Punjab, Rajasthan, Madhya Pradesh, and Jammu & Kashmir. The biggest state of India, Uttar Pradesh has only 3 European companies.

Table 13: Distribution of Foreign Companies Operating in Different Indian States, as on 30September 2004.

	UK	Germany	France	Nether-lands	Italy	Switerzer-land	Belgium	Sweden	European - 8	USA	Japan	Australia	Hong Kong	Singapore	Others	Total
Northern Region																
Delhi	115	38	43	25	14	12	7	14	268	168	64	24	39	66	145	774
Haryana	7	-	-	1	1	2	-		11	4	3	-	4	-	4	28
Himachal Pradesh	1	-	-	-	-	-	-	-	1	-	-	-	-	-	1	2
Jammu & Kashmir	-	-	-	-	-	-	-	-	0	-	-	-	-	-	-	0
Punjab	-	-	-	-	-	-	-	-	0	-	-	-	-	-	-	0
Rajasthan														1	4	4
Uttar Pradesh	2	-	-	-	1	-	-	-	3	1	1	-	-	-	3	8
Chandigarh	-	-	-	-	-	-	-	-	-	-	-	-	-	-	2	2

Western Region																
Gujarat	2	1	-	1	-				4	2	-		-	3	7	16
Madhya Pr	-	-	-	-	-	-	-	-	0	-	-	-	-	-	0	0
Maharashtra	71	33	19	17	10	13	12	3	178	117	34	10	20	59	85	503
Goa											1				1	2
Southern Region																
Andhra Pr	11	1	-	-	1	1	2	-	16	9	2	-	1	4	2	34
Karnataka	18	7	3	1	2	2	-	1	34	48	4	1	8	23	17	135
Kerala	1	-	-	-	1	-	-	-	2	-	-	-	-	-	3	5
Tamil Nadu	8	5	2	3	3	1	1	1	24	22	10	4	7	13	21	101
Pondichery	--	-	-	-	-	-	-	-	-	-	-	-	-	-	-	0
Eastern Region																
Assam & Other 7 NE States	1	-	-	-	-	-	-	-	1	-	-	-	-	-	1	1
Bihar	-	-	-	-	-	-	-	-	-	-	-	-	-	-	-	0
Orissa	-	-	-	-	-	-	-	-	-	-	-	1	-	-	1	2
West Bengal	56	6	-	4	-	-	1	-	67	8	11	2	1	-	17	106
Other	14								14	4			1		12	31
Total	307	91	67	52	33	31	23	19	623	383	130	42	81	168	327	1754

Source: Parliament (Lok Sabha), Unstarred Question No.2935, dated 17.12.2004.

Since Europe is a major investor in India, thousands of European companies operate in India either as foreign companies, joint venture partners or technical collaborators. Almost all big European names are present in India Since the list will be too exhaustive; it would be better to have a snap shot of European companies in India. Major British companies which operate in India are as follows:

Table 14: Some Major British Companies Operating in India

Company name	Sector	Remarks
Aviva India Ltd.	Insurance	JV with Dabur India
British Petroleum	lubricants	JVs with Tata, Castrol, about US$ 900 million investment
Barclays	Financial services outsourcing	JV with Intelnet
British Telecom	ICT	JVs with VSNL,Bharti, Mahindra & Mahindra
Cable & Wireless	ICT	
Cadbury	Confectionary, food products	
Cairn Energy	Oil & gas exploration	
GSK Pharmaceuticals	Pharma	
HSBC	Banking	
ICI Ltd.	Paints, textiles	
Johnson Matthey	Chemicals, catalyst & ceramics	
Logica CMG	ICT	
Marconi Telecom	Telecommunications	
Marks & Spencer	Retail	
P & O Ports	Ports management	JV with Chettinad group
Reuters	Media	
Scope Internal	BPO	

Shell India	Energy	
Tesco	Resource base for apparel/IT	
Unilever	Home & personal care, food & beverages	
Virgin Atlantic	Airlines	

According to Indo-German Chamber of Commerce (IGCC), which currently has about 6700 Indian and German members, there are about 1500 German companies operating in India in 2004. These companies were mainly medium sized firms from German Mittelsland. They operate in more than 50 product groups concentrated mainly in machinery and high technology goods, precision instruments, chemicals and pharmaceuticals, and electrical and electronic goods. According to IGCC, there are a further 1,595 collaboration agreements also in operation. Of them 611 are technical-cum-financial collaborations, that is, joint ventures (including 100% subsidiaries). The remaining ones are only technical collaborations. The total number of Indian and German firms involved in these agreements is 780 and 777 respectively. Since many firms sign more than one agreement the number of firms and agreements vary.[43] The largest are in the field of machinery and components followed by heavy vehicles, chemicals, technical consultancy services, computers, electrical appliances, etc. During the year 2004, the Indo-German collaboration companies were market leaders in as many as fifteen product groups. Many of the German companies are also listed in the stock exchange. According to IGCC, IGCC-15 index (index of 15 major Indo-German companies listed in the stock exchange) has performed better than the Bombay Stock Exchange index as well as the National Stock Exchange index. Companies included in IGCC-15 index are Aventis Pharma ,BASF India, Lanxess ABS, Bayer Cropscience , Merck Ltd., FAG Bearings India , Goetze (India), Henkel SPIC India, Insilco, Krone Communications, MICO, Siemens Ltd., Thomas Cook, KSB Pumps, ZF Steering Gear.[44]Currently some of the major German companies present in India include Abicor Binzel, Adidas Marketing, Baerlocher Additives, Bajaj Allianz, BASF, Baumuller, Bayer, Beiersdorf, Bosch Group, Braun Medical,

Burgmann, Carl Bechem, Carl Zeiss, Daimler Chrysler, DHL Express, DMG, Durr, Fichtner, Henkel, Kluber Lubrication, Knorr Bremse, Lahmeyer International, Lapp, Pharmaplan, Schuler, Steag Encotec, Stollberg, Suspa Pneumatics, Wurth, Zeppelin Mobile Systems, and Zwick Roell.

According to the French Agency for International Development, there were about 250 subsidiaries of French companies as well as about 50 representative's offices in operation in India. The list includes many major French companies like Airbus, Air France, Alstom, France Telecom, Alcatel, L'oreal, Lafarge, Saint Gobain, and Thales.[45] The French companies' presence in India is diversified. They are in telecom, IT, fashion, machinery, transportation, and chemicals. French companies have also invested in India's infrastructure, primarily in roads and railways. French companies widened the 60 km pathway between Delhi and Jaipur and also participated in the Delhi Metro.

According to the Dutch official sources, more than 100 Dutch countries operate in India in areas like building and operating LPG gas stations, LPG conversion systems, ,engineering industries, hybrid seeds, chemicals, software, pharmaceuticals, measurement solutions, banking, insurance, consumer electronics, dredging, transportation systems, fleet management, oil and gas industry, market research, logistics, freight forwarding, and consultancy. Similarly, Swiss official sources indicate that there are 128 Swiss-Indian collaborations working in India in the areas of engineering and equipment (22), services (19), textiles (19), chemicals and pharmaceuticals (18), information technology (10), instruments (9), printing and packaging (5), electrical equipments (4), trading (4), construction (3), auto components (3), metals (3), processed food (2), and others (7). Although the number of collaborations in sectors such as power, processed food, and construction is low, big Swiss companies such as ABB, Nestle, and Holcim are very much present. In fact, they are amongst the leaders in their respective product markets in India. In pharmaceutical, all major Swiss companies are present in India. About 25 companies from Luxembourg including Arcelor, Amercil, CTI, Ceratizit, Cebi, Dometic, Eurofoil, GMH, etc. are active in steel, power, telecom, gold imports, white goods, almunium foil, etc. Norway is represented in India through its fifty or so companies working either in joint ventures or independently. These companies mainly operate in areas like ship management, ICT, refrigeration, hydro power, chemicals, engineering, aluminium, etc.

In the case of another South Asian country, Pakistan, according to a former President of Pakistan, about 600 foreign companies (both public and private) were working in Pakistan in 2006.[46] The Overseas Investors Chambers of Commerce and Industry of Pakistan, which represents all major private foreign investors of Pakistan has 180 members. Of the 167 members in 2005, 45 were from the UK, 41 were from continental Europe, 43 were from America and Canada, 11 from Japan, 9 from the Middle East, and 17 from other countries. Sector-wise 11 operated in industrial undertakings, 15 in banking, 15 in chemicals/pesticides/fertilizers, 17 in engineering and industrial products, 12 in finance and leasing companies, 15 in food and consumer products, 2 in information technology, 4 in insurance, 23 in oil gas and energy, 25 in pharmaceutical, 30 in shipping, airlines, trading, and other services, 9 in tobacco and other manufacturing companies.[47] It was a mix of large and medium international enterprises working in Pakistan.

About 27 German collaborators operate in Karachi (21), Lahore (5), and Quetta (1). These companies include Lufthansa, Siemens, Allianz, Asta Medica, BASF, Bayer, Deutschebank, Eurocentra, Gemex trading, Hansa Management, Johs Rieckermann, Karl Gross, Keller Grundbau, KSD Pumps, Kuhne and Nagel, Pakgro Trans, Prinz, Schering Asia, Merck Marker, etc. Similarly, more than thirty French firms are active in Pakistan. These companies include Air France, Airbus, CFM, CMA-CGM, DCN International, Eurotradia, Intra-Keck, Michelin, Pride Forasl, Rhodia, Thales, Total Atlas Lubricants, Total Parco, Alcatel, Archifile, Avantis, Dassaualt Aviation, Prepac, Publicis, Reinforced Earth, etc.

According to a recent list prepared by the Federation of Nepalese Chambers of Commerce and Industry, of the total 395 technical and financial joint ventures already operating in the country, 79 are with European partners of which the highest number of collaborations is with Germany. Country and sector-wise classification are shown in Table 15. A list prepared by UNCTAD in 2003 listed 60 major foreign investors in Nepal. Of them, 13 are from Europe (see table 16).

Others major investors are from India (18) and USA (6). Table 17 also illustrates some of the European collaboration projects in Nepal.

Table 15 : List of Technical and Financial Joint Ventures in Nepal , April 2005

Country	No. of joint ventures	Areas
Germany	19	Hotels, readymade garments, carpets, olive plantation, transformers, herbal products,
UK	13	Tea, hotels, garments, consultancy, organic farming
France	9	Restaurants, software, garment herbal medicine, recycled paper, hotels
Switzerland	9	Hotels, carpet, power generation
Italy	6	Restaurants, cargo
Austria	6	Restaurants, readymade garments
Norway	6	Hydropower, construction, transformers
Netherlands	5	Hotels, tissue culture, training
Denmark	2	Beer, Drilling industries
Finland	2	Software, readymade garments
Spain	1	Restaurants
Belgium	1	Hotels
European total	79	
India	116	
USA	47	
Japan	41	
South Korea	20	
Others	92	
Total	395	

Source: Federation of Nepalese Chambers of Commerce & Industry

Table 16: Major European Investors in Nepal, 2003

Company Name	Ownership	Business
Gorka Brewery	Denmark	Beer
Gorkha Lawrie	UK	Tea
Himal Hydro	Norway	Civil construction
Himal Power	Norway	Hydro Power
Maccaferri Gabions	Italy	Wire mesh box
Nabil Bank	Ireland	Banking
National Drilling	Denmark	Drilling
NCC Tunnelling	Norway	Construction
Nepal Bayem	Germany	Transformer
Standard Chartered Bank	UK	Banking
Surya Nepal	India/UK	Cigarettes, garments, seeds
Tiger Mountain Group	UK	Safari camp
Voicol Industries	France	Bitumen Emulsion

Source: *An Investment Guide to Nepal* (New York and Geneva: UNCTAD, ICC, 2003).

Table 17: Some Important European Collaboration Projects in Nepal, 2009

Company Foreign Collaborator
Amtronics Pvt. Ltd (GE Co., UK)
Food Specialities Nepal Pvt. Ltd. (Nestle Company, Switzerland)
Ganesh Cold Storage Pvt. Ltd. (Swiss Association for Technical Co-operation, Switzerland)
Gorkha Ayurvedic Co. Pvt. Ltd. (Center for International Development & Research, France)
Gorkha Brewery Pvt. Ltd. (Industrialization Fund for Development Countries IFU, Danbrew Consult, Denmark)

Gorkha Lawrie Pvt. Ltd.(Lawrie Group Plc. Ltd., UK)
Himalayan Encounters Pvt. Ltd. (Encounter Overland, UK)
John Sanday Consultants Pvt. Ltd. (Ms. Linda Kentro, UK)
Jyoti Spinning Mill Pvt. Ltd. (Werner Blaser, Switzerland)
National Drilling Co. (International Water Contractors, Denmark)
Nepal Agro-Industrial Products Pvt. Ltd. (Mr. M. Suchak, UK)
Nepal Colour Lab Pvt. Ltd. (Mr. D. Koops, Germany)
Nepal Hydro-electric Pvt. Ltd.(Kvaerner Brug A/S Sorumsand Verksted A/S, Norway)
Nepal Indo-Suez Bank Ltd. (Banque Indo-Suez, France)
Nepal Italia Leather Industries Ltd. (Belvedre Chemicals & Plants, Italy)
Sports and Nature Pvt. Ltd. (Mr. Nils Hallen Berg, Germany)
Summit Hotel Pvt. Ltd. (Dr. J. A. Noordijk, Netherlands)
Tiger Mountain Pvt. Ltd. (Explorasia Ltd. & others, UK)
Vaicol Industries and Products Pvt. Ltd. (Colas, SA, France)
West Nepal Adventure Pvt. Ltd. (Mr. Jim Hardward, UK.)

Source: Foreign Investment Promotion Division, Nepal.

A similar list for Bangladesh was also complied by UNCTAD in 2000. Of the total list of 50 major investors, about half were European companies. 7 companies were from the US, 2 from Japan, and the rest were mainly Asian investors, (See Table 18).

Table 18: Major European Investors in Bangladesh, 2000

Comapany Name	Ownership	Business
Aventis Bangladesh	France/Germany/ UK/USA	Pharmaceuticals
Aventis cropscience	France/Germany	Pharmaceuticals
Beghabari Power	UK	Power
BASF	Germany	Chemicals
Berger Paints	UK	Paints
British American Tobacco	UK	Cigarettes
BOC Bangladesh	UK	Industrial medical gases
Bureau Varitas	France	Inspection services
Clariant	Switzerland	Chemicals
Credit Agricole Indosuez	France	Banking
East West Seod	Netherlands	Agro seeds
Glaxo	UK	Pharmaceuticals
Grameen Phone	Norway	Telecommunications
James Finley	UK	Tea
IBCS Primax	UK	Software
Koramphuli Fertilizers	UK/Netherlands	Fertilizer production
Lafarge	France	Cement
Lever Brothers	UK/Netherlands	Cosmetics
Nestle	Switzerland	Food products
Novartis	Switzerland	Pharmaceuticals
Organon Bangladesh	UK/Netherlands	Pharmaceuticals
Picard	Germany	Leather products
Reckitt & Colman	UK	Consumer products
Robintex	Germany	Textiles
Scancem	Sweden	Cement
Shell	UK/Netherlands	Oil & gas exploration
Siemens	Germany	Electronics
Standard Chartered Bank	UK	Banking
HSBC	UK	Banking
Van Ommeren Tank	Netherlands	Storage

Source: *An Investment Guide to Bangladesh* (New York and Geneva: UNCTAD &ICC, 2000)

According to the Sri Lanka Board of Investment, the UK is one of Sri Lanka's major investors from the EU. British companies have invested in areas such as textiles, garments and accessories, electronic products, security printing, tourism, infrastructure development, rubber based products, activated carbon, prawn farming, agriculture, food processing, computer software development and data entry services, business, financial, and educational services. Major British companies operating in Sri Lanka include Unilever, British Tobacco, Glaxo, Smith Kline Beecham, Brook Bond/Liptons, Lloyd's of London, Courtaulds-Textile Pic, Oxley Threads, Price's Patent Candle Company Ltd., Coats Viyella, Marks & Spencer, P & 0 Steam Navigation Company, and Thomas de La Rue. After UK, Germany is the second largest European investor with over 170 approved projects. The areas in which German companies operate in Sri Lanka include apparels, hosiery, knitwear, surf sails, textiles, electronic products, light/heavy engineering, rubber based products such as tyres and automobile parts, coir products, wooden/soft toys, chemicals and dyes, gems and jewellery, tourism, and recreational products. Some of the major German collaborations include Aqua Dynamics, BASF-Finlay, Bodyline, Eskimo Fashion Knitwear, Globe Knitting, Kramski Lanka, etc. Many French companies also operate in Sri Lanka. These include Alcatel, Biogrow Lanka, VMA-CGM, Degremont, Intissel, Lafarge, Noyon, and Periceyl. Some significant investment is also made by companies from Scandinavia.

6. Conclusion

Due to the historical link between Europe and South Asia their economic association was very strong at the time of independence. A major portion of South Asian trade was either with Britain or its colonies and allies. This pattern continued for some years after independence. However, the critique of colonialism later on formed the basis of the policy for "self reliance' in the region. As these countries established their independent relations with other countries, economic relations got diversified. In later years, the former socialist bloc countries also became important economic partners, particularly of India. Despite all these changes, economic linkages between South Asia and Europe remained strong and important. India and Pakistan were among the first few countries to establish diplomatic relations with the European Economic Community (EEC) in 1962. EC also granted the Generalised System of Preferences facility to South Asian countries. There is extensive diplomatic, business, and cultural presence of Europe in the region, which has resulted in strong economic ties.

In the last two decades, the process of European economic integration and the economic liberalisation in South Asia created tremendous new opportunities for renewed economic interaction. Since the late 1980's, FDI has become an important element of reform strategies throughout the South Asian region. In this environment, Europe is emerging as an important trade and investment partner of all South Asian countries. The EU is the largest trading partner of all major economies of the region. It is also a leading investment partner of India and Bangladesh. Since 2000, India and EU have established the institution of annual summit meetings. These summits have resulted in the *India-EU Strategic Partnership*. At the sixth summit meeting in 2005, a *Joint Action Plan* has also been agreed. These political summits have been supplemented with *India-EU Business Summits*. The EU has "third generation" agreements with Pakistan, Bangladesh and Sri Lanka along with a number of institutional arrangements. The EU has also initiated the process of EU-Pakistan strategic dialogue. Similarly, the EU and its member states are also playing an important role in the reconstruction of Afghanistan.

Although traditionally the UK has been the biggest investor in the region from Europe, other countries like Germany, Netherlands, France, and Sweden are also becoming very active. In technical collaborations, Germany is much above all other European member states. The presence of European businesses is much higher in South Asia than normally perceived. For example in India, FDI flows, technical and financial collaborations, and the number of foreign companies from Europe are more than USA and Japan put together.

Almost all prominent European companies are active in South Asia. Although European firms are active in a wide variety of activities, most of them are centred in a few urban centres like Delhi, Dhaka, Karachi, Kolkata, Mumbai, and Lahore. But they are no exception to the rule as most of the local private and foreign investment is also concentrated in a few well connected urban areas. Apart from traditional areas like the tea industry, European companies are also concentrating on services, telecommunications machinery, automobiles, and energy sector throughout the region. Along-with the latest trend, they are also moving into Southern Indian states, particularly in the IT industry.

There is a clear need to further sensitize South Asian policy makers about the importance of European economic presence in the region. Similarly, more awareness about the growing opportunities in the South Asian region is also needed at the European level. Further integration of both regions would improve the competitiveness of both the partners in a globalized economy.

References

1. For details see, Om Prakash, European Commercial Enterprises in Pre-Colonial India, (Cambridge: Cambridge University Press, 1998).
2. K N Chaudhuri, The Trading World of Asia and the English East India Company(New Delhi: S Chand & Company, 1978).
3. See Sanjay Subrahmanyam, The Political Economy of Commerce: Southern India, 1500-1650 (New York: Cambridge University Press, 1990).
4. Om Prakash, n.1.
5. Pradeep K Chibber and Sumit K Mazumdar, "Foreign Ownership and Profitability: Property Rights, Control and the Performance of the Firms in Indian Industry" Journal of Law & Economics, Vol.42, No.1,1999, pp. 211-12.
6. See, Appendix II, B R Tomlinson, "Foreign Private Investment in India, 1920-1950" Modern Asian Studies, Vol.12, No.4, 1978.
7. " India- Progress & Plan," The Economist, January 22, 1955, cited in Daniel Lloyd Spencer, "Foreign Participation in South Asian Enterprises", Far Eastern Survey, Vol.24, No.3, March 1955, p.41.
8. Chibber and Mazumdar, n.5.
9. Institute of Policy Studies, Sri Lanka, Foreign Direct Investment and Economic Integration of the SAARC Region, mimeo, paper presented at second SENAI conference, Kathmandu, 28-29 August 2000.

10. "Foreign Direct Investment in Developing Asia", in Asian Development Outlook 2004 (Manila: ADB, 2004).
11. Shantayanan Devarajan and Ijaz Nabi, Economic Growth in South Asia:Promising, Un-equalizing ,...Sustainable? (Washington DC: The World Bank. 2006).
12. Ibid., p.1.
13. Ibid. p.3.
14. Indian financial year runs from 1 April to 31 March.
15. Figures used here are taken fron various publications of Ministry of Finance and Ministry of Commerce & Industry, Government of India.
16. Commission of the European Countries, Communication from the Commission to the Council, 'The Community's Relations with India,' Com (79) 176 Final, 5 April 1979, Brussels, p.2, http://aei.pitt.edu/4335/01/001276_1.pdf. Accessed on 3 April 2009.
17. For details see, Cooperation Agreement between the European Communities and the Republic of India on Partnership and Development, http://europa.eu.int/comm/external_relations/india/intro/agree08_94.pdf.
18. For details of all these summit meetings and related documents see, political dialogue section of the European Commission delegation to India, http://www.delind.ec.europa.eu/en/political_dialogue/official_documents.htm.
19. See sections 7.4(A) and 7.4(B) in Economic Survey 2000-2001, Ministry of Finance, Government of India. http://indiabudget.nic.in/es2000-01/tables.htm.
20. Swapan K. Bhattacharya, India and the European Union: Trade and Non-Tariff Barriers (New Delhi: Aakar Publications, 2005).
21. EU-15: Austria, Belgium, Denmark, Finland, France, Germany, Greece, Ireland, Italy, Luxembourg, the Netherlands, Portugal, Spain, Sweden and the United Kingdom.EU-25: EU-15 plus Cyprus, Czech Republic, Estonia, Hungary, Latvia, Lithuania, Malta, Poland, Slovakia, Slovenia (these 10 countries joined EU on 1 January 2004).EU-27: EU-25 plus Bulgaria and Romania which joined EU on 1 January 2007.
22. Unless otherwise indicated, all figures used in this article are from various publications of the Ministry of Commerce and Industry, Government of India.
23. Indian foreign exchange reserves rose to $315 bn. in May 2008. Due to global financial crisis, it has declined somewhat in the last few months. Reserve Bank of India informed that as of 9 January 2009,

Indian foreign exchange reserves amounted to US $254.7 billion. For details see, http://rbidocs.rbi.org.in/rdocs/Bulletin/PDFs/T_44.pdf. Last accessed on 23 April 2009.

24. The actual shares were 69.6 per cent and 68.6 per cent of EU economy in terms of value added and employment respectively.

25. There is no single definition of open regionalism. The concept was mainly developed by APEC countries where members of a trade bloc undertake trade liberalization together and extend it worldwide on a "most favoured nation" basis.

26. Which means zero customs duty regime within a fixed time frame on items covering substantial trade, and a relatively small negative list of sensitive items with no or limited duty concessions.

27. See, http://commerce.nic.in/trade/international_ta_indsl.asp.

28. http://commerce.nic.in/trade/nepal.pdf.

29. Details of all these agreements and negotiation status can be found at http://commerce.nic.in/trade/international_ta.asp?id=2&trade=i

30. 'India- EU Set to Ink Trade Pact by 2009, Set 100 Bn Euro Target'The Economic Times, 28 September 2008, http://economictimes.indiatimes.com/News/Economy/Foreign_Trade/India-EU_to_ink_trade_pact_by_2009_set_100_bl_Euro_target/articleshow/3541388.cms,accessed on 03 May 2009.

31. 'FTA with EU Must Cover 95% Goods for Real Benefit to India', Business Line, 26 September 2008, http://www.thehindubusinessline.com/blnus/14261831.htm,accessed on 03 May 2009.

32. See, Press Statement by the Polit Bureau of the Communist Party of India(Marxist) on the proposed India-EU Free Trade Agreement, http://cpim.org/statement/2008/09272008-india-eu%20fta.htm.

33. 'Amid Protests, EU India Talks Begins Today', available on http://www.livemint.com/2009/03/16222358/Amid-protests-EUIndia-trade.html, accessed on 03 May 2009.

34. Michael Gasiorek, Qualitative Analysis of a Potential Free Trade Agreement between the European Union and India ,Sussex: Centre for the Analysis of Regional Integration and Jaipur: CUTS International, 2007.

35. Yvan Decreux and Christina Mitoritonne Economic Impact of a Potential Free Trade Agreement Between the European Union and India, Paris: CEPII-CERAM, 2007.

36. Pakistan-European Community Country Strategy paper for 2007-2013, p. 13.

37. Bangladesh-European Community Country Strategy paper for 2007-2013, p. 12. http://ec.europa.eu/comm/external_relations/bangladesh/intro/index.htm.
38. http://ec.europa.eu/trade/creating-opportunities/bilateral-relations/countries/sri-lanka/.
39. For official statistics about FDI in India see FDI Statistics section of the Ministry of Commerce and Industry, Government of India website: http://www.dipp.nic.in/fdi_statistics/india_fdi_index.htm. Last accessed on 23 April 2009.
40. Greenfield investment is a form of FDI where a parent company starts a new venture in a foreign country. The alternative to this is a brownfield investment where a company acquires an already existing firm in a foreign country.
41. See FDI in Bangladesh in 2004 (Dhaka, Board of Investment, 2005).
42. See chapter on " Foreign/FERA companies and Foreign Nationals" in Exchange Control Manual http://www.rbi.org.in/scripts/BS_ECMCatDisplay.aspx?catid=10.
43. For details of all German companies operating in India Indo-German collaborations see Directory of German Companies in India : Collaborations, Joint Ventures, Subsidiaries (2 volumes) 12th edition, (Mumbai: Indo German Chamber of Commerce, 2003).
44. For details see http://www.indo-german.com/english_htms/indo_german_index.htm.
45. For details see,Les Implantations Françaises en Inde et en Asie du Sud (Paris : UBI France, 2005).
46. http://www.presidentofpakistan.gov.pk/PRPressReleaseDetail.aspx?nPRPressReleaseId=1781&nYear=2006&nMonth=2.
47. http://www.oicci.org/index.asp.

11

India and EU in Multilateral Trade Negotiations

Sukalpa Chakrabarti

Introduction

On December 12, 2008, the WTO's Doha negotiations collapsed, proving the arresting effects of what had already surfaced, that the substantive divisions on central issues were too deep and the political will too frail to bridge the gaps. This break followed several unsuccessful attempts to agree on modalities for reducing agricultural subsidies and protection. Consequently, it has put a big question mark on the credibility of world leaders and also of the fora through which they express themselves. The U.S. and European Union trade chiefs have already acknowledged that it may not be possible to complete the Doha round of negotiations by 2010, as demanded by leaders at the last G20 summit and other meetings.

Despite the scepticism of the leading negotiators to conclude the Doha round by 2011, it remains to be seen if the bilateral and regional trade initiatives could generate any positive momentum to revert to Doha, arguably in a more viable format. Major trading nations are already making frequent forays into regional and bilateral trade deals. The Indo-EU FTA is an obvious illustration. Being the largest trading partner and second largest source of foreign direct investment, the European Union (EU) is one of the most important economic partners as far as India is concerned. At the same time, being one of the fastest growing economies of the world over the decade or so, as also being the producer of the largest pool of technically skilled manpower, India certainly offers an attractive option to the EU for building a durable and prosperous economic partnership. The growing levels of trade and investment flow between India and the EU bear testimony to the fact. The growing relation between India and EU are important; nevertheless, the focus of this paper is the analysis of the nature of relation between the two in the specific context of international strengthening of WTO and a successful conclusion of the DDR.

The EU and India have cooperated closely under the aegis of the World Trade Organization (WTO) and this remains the core framework for their trade relations. EU-India relations go back to the early 1960s. India was among the first countries to establish diplomatic relations with the (then) EEC. The 1994 cooperation agreement signed between EU and India took the bilateral relations beyond mere trade and economic cooperation. Together with the Joint Political Statement signed in 1993 it opened the way for annual ministerial meetings and a broad political dialogue. In 2004 India became one of the EU's "strategic partners." Since 2005, the EU-India Joint Action Plan, revised in 2008, aims at realizing the full potential of this partnership in key areas of interest to India and the EU (political, strategic, humanitarian, and economic).

India-EU relations have grown exponentially from what used to be a purely trade and economic driven relationship to one covering all areas of interaction. In the bilateral discussions of January 2005, held between Mr. Peter Mandelson (Trade Commission, European Commission) and Shri Kamal Nath (former Union Minister of Commerce & Industry, India) both had agreed to find areas of common interest in the ongoing negotiations in the World Trade Organization (WTO) and to work for the progress of the Doha Round to have a positive outcome.

Also within the WTO frame, there are numerous opportunities of collectivized pursuit by nations of their shared interests. The EU and India, both global players in world trade, have a shared belief in the benefits of the rule-based multilateral trading system and are deeply committed to the successful outcome of the DDA negotiations. India as a leader of the group of (advanced) developing countries known as the G20, and also as part of G4 (along with the EU, US, and Brazil) is steering the current negotiations. A successful conclusion of the Doha round would contribute significantly to a more open and stable environment for trade and investment for both the EU and India.

If there was any incompatibility in the early years of the multilateral negotiations, it did not affect the basics and it did not take long to smoothen out any differences between India and EU. It is remarkable that the EU has emerged not only as a powerful economic bloc but also wants to establish its special identity in the sphere of drafting foreign policy. Understandably this quest for foreign policy identity would very much depend on a meaningful convergence of outlook of the two countries regarding major problems affecting the world.

Against this backdrop, this paper proposes that India and EU can work more closely at the WTO on issues where our stances are already synchronous namely policies to promote rural development, preferential market access for developing countries, codification of special and differential extended by the WTO to developing countries, protection of geographic indicators, etc.

Given the expanding areas of convergence, it is not impossible to foresee an Indo-EU joint position on the Doha Development Agenda. True there are certain areas where the policies of the two countries have not fully converged and where the two have several major points of difference. For instance, when one looks at the Indo-EU trade and investment regime through the Indian lens, Indian exporters to EU register various complaints and grievances relating to the procedural aspects and treatment of Indian exports in the EU, especially those relating to steel, textiles and clothing, and agriculture. This paper, however, is not directly concerned with such issues and would rather explore possibilities for a convergence on multilateral trade negotiations. In particular, the paper would focus on a possible Indo- EU leadership role in ensuring an early resumption of the DDR leading to substantial market access for developing countries in agriculture, non-agricultural products as well as key areas of services.

SECTION I: Exploring Reasons for the Breakdown of the Doha Round and examining the stands taken by India and the EU

Let us now take a brief look at the various factors that contributed to the breakdown of the DDR talks:

The most contentious disagreements have been on issues of agriculture like cuts in overall trade distorting support (OTDS), percentage of products to be declared as sensitive products, tariff rate quota expansion for such products, tariff capping, special products, and the Special Safeguards Mechanism (SSM). As for market access, developing countries want trade in agriculture to be freed from domestic supports and other non-tariff distortions and the tariff escalations for labour-intensive products such as textile, clothing, and leather products in developed countries to be removed. The main concern has been that the developed countries that provide over $15 billion of subsidies a year to agriculture would like to keep their bindings higher so that there are no real cuts in subsidies. The major developed country players, especially the US, pinpoint the SSM as the sticking point of the entire negotiations. This is a new safeguard that a majority of the developing countries, led by the G33 group, had advocated to allow them to raise agricultural tariffs above the bound levels in the event that the volume of imports rises above a certain level or the prices of imports fall below a certain level. The SSM is seen by the developing countries as essential to protect their food security and the farmers' livelihoods from import surges that in the past had already damaged the local agriculture sector guised as local products. Under the normal safeguard (the WTO's existing Agreement on Safeguards), a country has to prove serious injury or threat of serious injury before it is allowed to take action (raise the tariff above the bound level). For agriculture, this is inappropriate; once damage is done, it is difficult to get farming started again, unlike industry. Hence the need for a special safeguard. There is already a special agricultural safeguard (SSG) which was set up in the Uruguay Round, but it is mainly used by developed countries as the condition is that it can be used only for products that underwent a "tariffication process" in that

Round. The developing countries wanted the use of the special safeguard to be extended to them, through the SSM.

There is also speculation that the SSM was not the real conflicting issue. The most widely held view was that the US did not want to face the cotton issue, which would have been the next item on the G7 agenda once the SSM was settled. Since the US had agreed to cut its overall trade-distorting domestic agricultural support by 70%, it would have to agree to reduce cotton subsidies by more than that as the mandate is that these subsidies be cut more deeply and faster than the normal or average rate. The 2008 US Farm Bill having planned that cotton subsidies be maintained or increased in the next five years, it would have been difficult, politically or diplomatically to offer a plus 70% cotton subsidy cut. The failure of the Geneva talks would then have been placed squarely on the United States.

Another area of concern was the negotiation on industrial goods containing an important aspect of what the developed world calls "real tariff cuts" by "emerging nations." This primarily means that the BRIC nations accept tariff cuts below the existing applied rates of duty. Although this may seem logical to some exponents, it goes against the basic tenet of the WTO agreement that only calls for cuts in bound tariffs and not to applied duties. India, for instance, is only expected to cut its existing bound tariff levels of 40 per cent or 25 per cent to lower levels of, say, 14-15 per cent at the most. It would also be expected to bind about 95 per cent of its tariffs at that level as well. The industrialized nations have been seeking "voluntary" negotiations for eliminating or substantially reducing tariffs in sectors that would constitute over 60 per cent of the world trade. These include products like chemicals, industrial machinery, electrical and electronics, auto parts, raw materials, sports goods, toys, and forest products among others. Naturally, developing countries like India have been resisting the inclusion of this agenda.

Next was the tricky part of the negotiations for reducing tariffs on environmental goods. The developed countries are of the view that the there is a need to eliminate tariffs on environmental goods, while the mandate is clearly not seeking such an elimination. It only seeks a reduction and, only if appropriate, elimination. There is also a lack of clarity on the approach for identifying environmental goods.

In services, the main spot of concern for developing countries are the new protectionist measures developing across the world which are likely to hurt market access in movement of professionals.

Thus, differences between rich and developing nations have been the major stumbling block. India and other developing nations have been defending their agricultural market to protect millions of subsistence farmers from easy imports that may result from the multilateral agreement. The US and the other developed countries, however, seek more market access in developing nations, including India.

The key aim of India's negotiating strategy in the WTO negotiations is to protect the interests of farmers, particularly with regard to their food and livelihood security and to protect sensitive industrial sectors from the impact of tariff reductions or bindings. To further such interests, India is seeking effective cuts in the trade-distorting subsidies provided to the agriculture sector by developed countries, while at the same time seeking flexibilities for developing countries such as provisions for lower tariff cuts, longer implementation periods, self-designation of Special Products (SPs) that would safeguard the interests of the farmers in the event of surges in import volumes or a fall in price. In SSM, India's position, like that of most developing countries, is that there should be no difference in the triggers leading to increase of tariffs up to and above the UR levels.

In the face of differences on this issue, Pascal Lamy tried to broker a compromise through an alternative proposal involving defining substantial injury and inserting a strict monitoring mechanism. India agreed to negotiate on this proposal but the US turned it down. With the efforts of the EC, the G-7 senior officials worked out an alternative proposal which India was ready to accept, but the US was not.

The EU is committed to an agreement in the agricultural sector that reforms farm subsidy programs throughout the rich world in line with the EU's wide-ranging 2003 reform of the Common Agricultural Policy.[1] As part of the Doha Round, the EU had offered to cut farm tariffs by 60%, reduce trade distorting farm subsidies by 80%, and eliminate farm export subsidies altogether. Recognizing the crucial role that agriculture plays in many developing countries, the EU has granted extensive market access to agricultural imports from developing countries and, with the initiative "Everything but Arms," full duty free quota free access to products from the world's poorest countries. Agriculture has been identified as the most promising area for joint action between India and EU.

Under the non-agricultural market access negotiations (NAMA), India has been negotiating for flexibilities that are both appropriate and adequate, to protect the sensitive industrial tariff lines from the purview of tariff reductions or bindings. In the December 2009 Working Session of the Seventh Ministerial Conference of the WTO on "The WTO's Contribution to Recovery, Growth and Development," Shri Anand Sharma, then Union Minister of Commerce & Industry, while addressing the media persons in Geneva, emphasized that there was no change in India's negotiating position in Agriculture and NAMA. "*....India and its coalition partners were steadfast and united in their commitment to uphold the development dimension, the centrality of the multilateral process and the need to safeguard livelihood concerns, particularly of the poor, subsistence farmers in their countries.*"

The EU does not seek general deregulation or privatization of sectors where principles of public interest are at stake, and the EU is also committed to defending the right of WTO members to promote cultural diversity.[1] Both India and the EU agree that the goal of multilateral trade is not just to create new trade between developed countries, but also between developing countries. Hence, in market access for industrial goods, they want to create significant new trade flows by cutting down on tariffs.

On intellectual property rights (IPRs), India seeks changes in the Trade Related Aspects of Intellectual Property Rights (TRIPS) agreement to accommodate concerns relating to bio-piracy, and is supporting the EC demand for a higher level of protection to all products. Like India, the EU also wants to use the Doha Round to improve the protection of Geographical Indications.

Services liberalization is another important issue for India due to its interest in the movement of natural persons in the category of experts and skilled persons. In areas of its interest like Mode 1 and Mode 4, India received positive signals from EU, among others. Also on The Singapore Issues, EU is of the opinion that India has taken steps "obviously in the right direction."

The EU wants to come to an agreement over a package of development measures including: a special agreement to address trade distortions caused by subsidies to cotton farmers in developed countries; the extension of unlimited markets access to all Least Developed Countries by as many countries as possible; a new global package of "aid for trade" assistance to help the poorest build the capacity to trade; special measures to help the poorest countries implement any Doha Agreement effectively and without long-term harm to their economies.

Thus the common areas of interest may be summed up as follows:

- both the EU and India need market access in industrial goods;
- both agree that there has to be special and differentiated treatment for developing countries;
- both are convinced that agriculture is more than producing food; and,
- both are aware that services is the most dynamic sector in their respective economies and would benefit from further trade opening.

SECTION II: India & EU's efforts at bringing the DDR to a successful conclusion

The international system is experiencing a critical shift of power from the West to the East, with new global actors emerging. The most important change that the WTO has witnessed is the inclusion of three or four large emerging economies like Brazil, China, India, and South Africa among the small core group of negotiators. Parallely, the emergence of the New Quad[2] also marks a major transition in global trade negotiating architecture. It is widely acknowledged today that the time has come for multi-polarism, pivoting on dialogue between all relevant and emerging actors.

For a successful conclusion of the DDR, formation of "issue based negotiating groups" should be actively encouraged and modalities have to be agreed upon to ensure that outcomes and also the negotiating processes are inclusive, equitable, and transparent.

Since 2003, the concept of effective multilateralism has been the basis for EU's external relations, with an aim to expressing the global need for delivering international institutions and momentous international action.[3] Given that both India and EU are contracting parties in several multilateral treaties, it is possible to explore areas of common interest in which both actors can build on their complementarities and deliberate on the need for effective multilateralism for the pursuit of the collective good.

India and the European Union (EU) had formally agreed to find areas of common interest [as indicated during the bilateral discussions between Mr. Peter Mandelson (Trade Commission, European Commission) and Shri Kamal Nath (Union Minister of Commerce & Industry, India)]. At the Tenth India-European Union Summit, the leaders discussed regional and global issues, and the means to prioritize, rationalize, and strengthen EU-India relations.

Both India and the EU agreed on the importance of an effective multilateral system and underlined the importance of successfully concluding in 2010 multilateral negotiations at the WTO for a balanced agreement that fulfils the development objectives of the Round.[1] Such an agreement should significantly foster trade flows in agriculture, industrial goods and services among and between developed and developing countries, as well as promote transparent and simplified rules and procedures and address all other remaining issues.

The Delhi Ministerial meeting in September 2009 exerted a renewed momentum towards a successful conclusion of the DDR. In September 2009, India invited trade ministers of a handful of developing countries for an informal mini-ministerial meeting in New Delhi, which reaffirmed its credentials as a serious player in the multilateral arena. In the December 2009 Working Session of the Seventh Ministerial Conference of the WTO on "The WTO's Contribution to Recovery, Growth and Development," Shri Anand Sharma stated that the first priority should be to conclude the Doha

Round as quickly as possible. Banking on the progress that has been achieved in reducing tariffs, cutting distorting subsidies, opening markets, and removing non-trade barriers would go a long way to increasing world trade and welfare, he said, and stressed the importance of inclusive global development to shore up demand. When asked for his views on the success of the Ministerial Conference, Shri Sharma informed that this was the first full Ministerial meeting in the aftermath of the global economic meltdown and the Conference had provided Members with an opportunity to collectively discuss the world economic scenario, the challenges faced by the multilateral trading system, and to review the working of the WTO.

Presently, India and the EU are bringing together the G-23 group, which includes United States, Japan, Canada, Australia, Switzerland, China, Brazil, Argentina, South Africa, Indonesia, South Korea, Mexico, Egypt, Burkina Faso, Zambia, Pakistan, Mauritius, Barbados, Turkey, Venezuela, Chile, Norway, Malaysia, and Colombia. As the G-23 is a bigger forum, it could be more transparent than smaller groups and help bridge the major gaps in positions between the US and emerging markets like China, India, Brazil, South Africa and Argentina. To ensure the overall progress of the round, unresolved issues in the areas of agriculture, industrial goods (NAMA), antidumping regime, streamlining of fisheries subsidies, fair implementation of IPR and services would be looked at individually in these groups. The resolution of these core modalities and the ambition of the offers under services would be the key to putting the stalled Doha Round back into acceleration mode. While a final deal in the World Trade Organization's nine year-old Doha round may still be far off, but such informal small-group contacts between the big players can definitely go a long way in successfully closing the negotiations.

To quote Brazil's foreign minister, Celso Amorim, *"It all depends on one rather simple thing... It depends on all the players wishing to finalize. If they wish to finalize and they know how to do it, you can do it. There is no big complexity."* Thus, the onus lies on the policy makers to work out concrete measures based on the converging views and translate the same into action. Both India and the EU are committed to finding solutions that promote the successful and balanced conclusion of the Round.

Conclusion

After years of vacuous demands that the negotiators settle their differences and wrap up the round, it is high time to step back and build a political support for the long-term survival of the multilateral system and the WTO. It is time the perception that the WTO and the regime it oversees, exclusively serves the rich countries' interests, is given up. The huge increase in WTO membership and the rising share of emerging economies in world trade shows this is not true. It is clear that the credibility, legitimacy, and ability of the WTO to enforce its decisions in dispute settlement cases and for creation of more open and stable environment for trade and investment, will surely take a beat if DDR is abandoned.

At the World Economic Forum Meet at Davos (28 January, 2011) world leaders were unanimous in their call for the rapid conclusion of a global free trade deal. The former WTO Director-General and Goldman Sachs Chairman Peter Sutherland urged direct involvement from top decision-makers in pushing forward the stalled talks.

"The only chance that we have to conclude the round now, is for the heads of government to become directly engaged in the process to conclude the negotiations," Sutherland said, frustrated at previous G20 and G8 meetings, which he regarded as having produced no more than "statements of general intent." The European leaders were outspoken about their zeal for an end-game. British Prime Minister David Cameron told the Davos gathering of business and political elite: *"This is a stimulus that doesn't cost money, so it's a stimulus that we need."* While speaking about the urgency of concluding the round, Cameron stuck to the developed nations' position, as he called for emerging markets to accept deeper cuts on industrial goods. He also urged the agriculture producers to give *"a little more"*.

Sharing the same spirit, German Chancellor Angela Merkel added: *"We are literally metres away from the finishing line but if we do not reach this finishing line, decades will go by without this opportunity ever offering itself again."* She called for attention to mind the gap between the rich and poor countries and said, *"We have to look at the sheer speed of development in the emerging economies and this dynamism has to be factored in,"* when concluding the Doha Round. Indonesian President Susilo Bambang Yudhoyono meanwhile declared that, *"for leaders ... failure is not an option. It is giving clear instructions to negotiators."* Brazilian Foreign Minister Antonio de Aguiar Patriota also called for a push towards an agreement. *"We're here to see if there is progress, the intention is to try to take the round from the basis of the progress already made, but I have no certainties,"* he said. U.S. Trade Representative Ron Kirk said in an interview, "the *timing is ripe for us to make the hard decisions that are going to have to be made to bring the Doha Round to a conclusion."*

Meeting on the sidelines of the World Economic Forum's annual summit in Davos, trade ministers from two dozen influential WTO member countries agreed to push for a breakthrough agreement in the Doha Round negotiations by July, so that the long-struggling trade talks can be wrapped up by the end of the year. Ministers, from trading powers such as China, Brazil, India, the US, and the EU as well as smaller nations such as Costa Rica, Jamaica, and Peru, echoed the view that 2011 constitutes a *"window of opportunity"* (to quote India's Commerce and Industry Minister Anand Sharma) for concluding a Doha Round accord.

Despite the determined language, none of the political leaders made any concrete offers at Davos to push the deal forward. Being the two important trading regions of the world, it thus becomes incumbent on EU and India to share the responsibility of bringing the Doha round to a successful conclusion. The EU being traditionally seen as representing the 'North' and India the 'South', together they can succeed in bringing the divergent viewpoints of the developed and developing nations on key issues of multilateral trade regime to the table and help sift out the differences while highlighting the areas of convergence. The EU for instance can play a crucial role in convincing the American administration to modify its current position on sectoral tariff reduction by developing countries thereby creating an opportunity for USA and India to break the impasse that has stymied the Doha Round's successful conclusion. India, too, must do its part in convincing the developing economies of the benefits of a successfully concluded Doha round and come up with a balanced give and take position, working on horizontal negotiations.

At the Eleventh European Union - India Summit (held in Brussels, 10 December, 2010), leaders representing both sides welcomed the commitments made at the G20 Seoul Summit to promptly bring the Doha Development Round to an ambitious, comprehensive and balanced conclusion in 2011, consistent with the mandate of the Doha Development Round and build on the progress already achieved. They also reaffirmed their commitment to resist all forms of protectionist measures. Both the EU and India have managed to develop converging views on the main issues that have been stalling the DDR so far, viz., need for market access for industrial goods, need for special and differentiated treatment for developing countries, need for an agreement in the agricultural sector that reforms farm subsidy programs throughout the rich world, need for higher level of IPR protection for all products, and a common realization that services is the most dynamic sector in their respective economies that would benefit from further trade opening. EU-Indian trade and cross-border investments have also picked up, demonstrating that it is possible to move ahead on economic issues. It is time that both the EU and India intensify their mutual relations and use it as an effective leverage for decision-making in existing global governance structures.

In keeping with the expectations, the EU invited a smaller group of seven central players in the negotiations - Australia, Brazil, China, India, Japan, and the US, in addition to the EU - to meet on 28 January for a more detailed discussion on how to proceed at the World Economic Forum Meet at Davos (28 January 2011). Since it is already agreed in principle that the world's poorest countries would not have to make concessions, the difference is between the rich and fast emerging economies like Brazil, China, and India vis-a-vis the rich developed nations. The central tension prolonging the trade negotiations is based on the rich, developed countries desire for more free market access to the economies of developing countries, and the developing countries appealing for more significant contributions from the wealthy countries.

The Davos intervention recognizes that in the wake of the global financial crisis, free trade, far from being a threat to nation states, is an economic lever as vital to recovery as any stimulus package or currency advantage. The developed nations are now struggling to reconstruct their economic growth models. The US is printing money to generate a lower dollar and to revive job growth; Europe is gripped by a sovereign debt crisis and battling to save the euro; Britain has been forced into its most savage austerity since World War II; and Japan too has suffered a sovereign credit downgrade. As the debt-burdened developed nations struggle to appreciate the emerging market-led growth, the time is ripe to come to a multilateral understanding that would reflect the Davos theme of "shared norms for the new reality." The change of mood away from protectionism to free trade has been noticeable in both the camps. The deal aiming to eliminate farm export subsidies and reduce barriers in farm, manufacturing and services trade, is projected to increase trade by as much as $ US 360 billion a year, thus resuscitating the post-crisis global economy.

Thus, all that is now required is a collective political will and cultivating an environment of trust among the WTO member nations. The trust building should focus on achieving some collective success on issues, which may require less compromise for all concerned. To achieve this goal, a pro-active approach from all WTO members is needed now to make progress on all issues of the Doha Development Agenda as well as on the crosscutting issues, in a balanced manner.

References

1. European Commission:http://ec.europa.eu/trade/creating-opportunities/economic-sectors/agriculture/.
2. US, EU, India and Brazil with the latter two replacing Japan and Canada. The negotiating group often includes China and South Africas well.
3. India–EU Joint Statement, 10th Summit (New Delhi, 6 November 2009;Erkki Liikanen, ICWA-EUISS Third India-EU Business Summit, Plenary Session 3 Copenhagen, 9 October, 2002.

12

EU - India Development Cooperation: Nature, Ideology, Politics

Jayaraj Amin

The development agenda of the European Union (EU), though limited in scope, came to be crystallised soon after the inception of the EEC, the predecessor of EU. In spite of several bilateral development frameworks that the member states of EU have with other countries in the world, the development policy of the EU has become important because today EU has exclusive competence over the EU development policy and it also serves the purpose of structuring EU relations with non-European, in particular the developing countries of the world. The competence of the EU to act in the area of development cooperation (without prejudice to the actions of member states) is recognised even in the Lisbon Treaty of 2007.[1]

The EU development cooperation policy has witnessed significant changes in the reach, pattern, and financial commitment over the years. Reflective of the past colonial heritage initially the development framework focused on the countries of sub-Saharan Africa, Caribbean, and the Pacific (ACP) who were associated in the EEC (under Articles 131 and 136, Part IV of the Rome Treaty) framework for technical and financial aid entitling them to duty cuts and financial aid through specially created European Development Fund (EDF).[2] This association was formalized in Yaounde-I (1963) and Yaounde-II (1969) conventions between 18 African, Carribean, and Pacific (ACP) countries and 6 European countries. Subsequently the development framework of EU has widened both its scope and reach. The Maastricht Treaty on European Union (1992) in particular gave for the first time a clear legal status to the development policy and introduced three principles to improve the effectiveness of the policy, namely, Complementarity (of member states' policies, programmes, and EC action), Coordination (between two or more development partners and policies), and Coherence (operation without contradiction in policies and programmes).[3]

Aligned closely with EU's trade policy, today the development policy of the EU encompasses aid, trade, and humanitarian assistance. As Article 177 of the Maastricht Treaty states the objective is to develop and consolidate democracy and the rule of law and to foster in the developing countries, "sustainable economic and social development," "smooth and gradual integration into world economy," and "the campaign against poverty."[4] The thrust on eradication of poverty in the development policy was further highlighted by EU along - with the UN General Assembly adoption of MDG's in 2000 which came to be firmly supported by EU by incorporating it in its developmental policy since the MDG was framed with similar objectives. The objective of poverty eradication in the development cooperation is again highlighted in the Lisbon Treaty of 2007 (Article 188 D, Para 1 and 2).[5]

EU Development Cooperation Structure:

Initially the EU development cooperation framework was designed to provide support to the needy countries of ACP and the structure was more in donor-recipient pattern effected through cooperation agreements. However, over the years the development cooperation perspective has undergone change. Today, the Development Cooperation Instrument (DCI) adopted in 2006 and launched in January 2007 serves as the legal framework for the EU's cooperation with countries, especially of Asia and Latin America. The DCI replaces a wide range of geographic and thematic instruments that were created over time and provides the orientation for the EU's cooperation with countries. The DCI enumerates the programmes that become eligible for cooperation such as, poverty eradication and achievement of MDGs, basic needs, that is, primary education and health; social cohesion and employment; governance, democracy, human rights and institutional reforms; trade and regional integration; sustainable development through environmental protection; sustainable integrated water resource management and fostering greater use of sustainable energy technologies, developing infrastructure and an increased use of information and communication technologies; sustainable rural development and ensuring food security; and, assistance in post-crisis situations and fragile states.[6] Supplementing the geographical orientation is the thematic programmes of the DCI that prominently include "Investing in People" programme that supports good health for all , education, knowledge and skills (vocational), gender equality and other aspects of human and social development such as employment and social cohesion , children and youth, and culture.[7]

As a corollary of the DCI, from 2007 onwards the EU for better delivery and focused developmental assistance, evolved the system of 'Country Strategy Paper' (CSP) for five years (2007-2013) for each country in which the country situation is analysed, the EU objectives of cooperation are spelt out and an action plan is worked out.[8] Complementing the CSP, is the Multi-Annual National Indicative Programme (MIP) that sets out the priority areas and financial allocation. Based on MIP, Annual Action Programmes specifies the objectives and assesses the programme implementation and makes financial allocation. Depending upon the situation in the target country and the objective of EU, the EU adopts different policy frameworks, effected through agreements, to realise the objectives.

These policy frameworks and agreements are not exclusive and may overlap. The EU too has stressed on the improved strategic coherence between EU's aid, trade, and development and treats democratic political setup with liberal values as prerequisite for economic progress. Evidently, the 2005 policy statement entitled 'European Consensus on Development' enumerates that sustainable development includes good governance, human rights, and political, economic, social and environmental aspects (clause 7) and stresses its support to national strategies to this effect.[9] The DCI too focuses on these priority areas. The stress here is to enable "structural reforms" in the target country in line with the general political and economic preferences of the EU.

Therefore, in a large number of 'new generation agreements' that EU has signed with others, especially since 1990's, include EU concerns ranging from human rights to democratic principles to labour standards to good governance. In fact the EU even has introduced a novel 'GSP-Plus' incentive to support "sustainable development and good governance" if any 'vulnerable' country has signed 16 human rights conventions and at least seven (out of eleven) conventions on environment and governance.[10] As Cotonou agreement indicates that in pursuing the objectives of development cooperation, EU seek to establish a comprehensive partnership, "based on **three complementary pillars** of development cooperation, economic and trade cooperation and the political dimension."[11]

Shifts in ideological perspectives:

The development cooperation has witnessed change not merely in its geographical reach but also on the nature of development cooperation. The donor-recipient pattern is being replaced by cooperative framework and developmental projects. The nature and basis of cooperation has become more focussed along-with the articulation of liberal principles and market economy in the integration process. To sum up, today the EU developmental approach is not merely guided by economic considerations and political interventions/ objectives. The "Economic cooperation," a new Commission jargon for new type of development aid, is not without political objectives and appears to be directed more towards creating a favourable macroeconomic and political situation in the recipient countries, backed by trade and investment measures. The use of aid agreement as an economic leverage to compel the recipient country to comply with the preferred political yardstick of EU such as human rights is not unusual.

Second, EU at present prefers to align with national development strategies of the concerned countries than directly aiding the project. The focus here is to bring about change in the delivery capacity of the sectoral management and overall change in the priorities and operation. This shift from project specific to sector specific approach, in which structural reforms are seen as imperative, is complemented by "Donor Coordination" (both at the European level and with global institutions operating with similar broad objectives such as IMF and World Bank) and also by framing of "indicative" five-year programming towards the target country in which attempts are made to establish long term priorities and consistency in the Community assistance. These aspects are reiterated in the Lisbon Treaty of 2007.[12]

Third, there is an increasing interest on the part of EU to enter into bilateral agreements notwithstanding its regional and global policies and strategies. Bilateral agreements provide scope for EU to negotiate and better enforce its preferences than at the global level. Moreover, in EU perspective trade and development goals are linked and the market mechanism is seen as conducive to development and, therefore, to multilateralism.

Fourth, there is a marked emphasis on 'dialogues' as a means to structure development cooperation in the backdrop of market mechanism and its preferred political values. Since the dialogues visualise the final beneficiaries of the programme, the EU prefers increased number of NGOs and civil society actors in the process thereby, giving rise to increased number of players and stakeholders in the EU-recipient country relations. This is also in tune with the EU perspective which views wider participation and involvement of people in developmental activity as not only helpful in implementation but is also an inseparable part of good governance which has now become the main component of EU's development strategy.

Fifth, "reciprocity" more or less has become the order of the day and unilateral concessions are almost becoming events of the past. The stress now is on capacity building, regulatory mechanisms, and 'Aid for Trade' (AfT) policy (to increase trade policy capacity of developing countries) in which the EU preferred values are thrust.[13] So the move gradually pulls away from the GSP scheme based on 'Special and Differential Treatment' (SDT) permitted by GATT/WTO rules under "objective criteria" (such as level of development). This is evident in the ACP-EC-Partnership Agreement or Cotonou Agreement of 2000. Even when concessions are given, for instance under the EU multi-lateralised initiative of 'Everything but Arms' (EBA) which provides duty-free and quota-free access to EU market for exports from LDC's, the net benefit may not be there for the recipient country as its benefits is nullified by the EU's counter measures such as exceptions, NTBs, 'sensitive products' (for instance, sugar, rice, and bananas were initially were not allowed under EBA), etc. In other words, the development cooperation policy has become an important tool for EU to order its relation with the rest and to seek change as per the ideological preferences of EU.

EU-India Development Cooperation - Background

India was one of the first countries to establish diplomatic relation with the six members' EEC in 1962. But, the initial focus of EEC was on Africa and was mostly concerned with food assistance. Nonetheless, with the approval of Food Aid Convention by the EEC in 1967 the countries of Asia and Latin America became the beneficiaries of food aid inflows. India, for instance, during the first food aid convention (1968-69 to 1970-71) received 80 thousand tonnes of cereals of the total 991.04 tonnes.[14] This was less compared to the 165 thousand tonnes given to Pakistan. But the requirement of India was confined to the first year (1968-69) of the food convention and, during the period 1970-74, India was the highest recipient of EEC with 6.5 percent of the total aid committed closely followed by Bangladesh with 6.4 percent.[15] In 1976 EU extended its help by contributing about € 6 million to India towards rehabilitation when the states of Uttar Pradesh and Gujarat witnessed heavy floods.

Nonetheless, it was the GSP provisions evolved in 1971 by EC that became the framework for EC's trade relationship with most developing countries including India. The first agreement with India was signed in December 1973 that stressed on development and expansion of commercial linkages; and, the agreement later paved way for a broader agreement on Commercial and Economic Cooperation in June 1981 moving beyond mere trade issues. So, in the initial stages, the EC did extend humanitarian assistance and economic benefits without expectations of behavioural change. The Cold War choices too had not become a major consideration in its dealing with India despite India's known closer association with the Soviet Union.

However, the 1980's proved to be a turning point in the internal structure and external relations of the EU. The perceived 'Euroscelorosis,' as against the apparent American and Japanese domination of EU economic scenario, coupled with the challenges in new technologies emanating from the Newly Industrialised Countries (NICs), particularly of South East Asia, prompted EU to introspect. The developments led to the adoption of a Single European Act (SEA) with provisions for an internal market that in effect reactivated the EU economic structure. Complementing this process was the end of the Cold War and the increasing trend towards economic issues (globalisation) in 1990's that brought about a significant change in the attitude of EC towards other regions. EU now was determined to have its influence in the world and to protect its economic interests. Not surprisingly, in the emerging perspectives the driving forces of development were reconsidered and state driven development process was presumed to be ineffective in promoting development in an effective way.

So the new thinking that began to crystallise since the days of 'Thatcher-Reganomics' stressed on market as the driver of growth and the neo-liberal policies that allowed more space to the market forces with minimum role to the state, came to supported by most western countries as well as by global financial institutions like IMF and World Bank, although with some variations. In this new thinking the advocacy was in favour of free market, globalisation, liberalisation, and privatisation and these were prescribed as the standard medicine for wherever and whatever economic ills these countries were afflicted with. So the realignment of its policies with Brettonwood institutions and the positions of its own major powers like Britain and France, who were keen on not only increasing global presence but of also advancing issues of governance and conflict resolution were to result in significant reorientation of its external policies and perspectives towards third countries. This is notwithstanding the fact that the welfare and 'social models' most European countries had built internally over time was not sought to be disturbed. Nonetheless, it has to be underlined that market economy was not new to the western countries but what becomes significant is the new drive incorporating these along-with other liberal values in its external front.

So, in the revamped developmental cooperation perspective, regulatory mechanism and rule based effective multilateralism were seen as necessary. This was the time when EU began to adopt a focused and long term perspective incorporating 'European values' instead of ad-hoc positions. In the new development cooperation perspectives focus was on structural reforms in favour of market economy, reciprocal arrangements, and multilateralism for growth. India was not an exception in the new framework. But India had begun its reform process in favour of market economy in 1990s and the perspectives broadly began to converge concerning market economy. EU's altered position came to be reflected in a large number of documents and agreements developed in 1990s. Its position towards Asia was reflected in the Council regulations (EEC) on 25th February 1992 that extended financial and technical assistance and economic cooperation but with due stress on human rights, democratisation, and good governance along-with trade liberalisation.[16] This was the well articulated EU's "Towards a new Asia strategy" in 1994 which advocated a pro-active policy in Asia and foresaw advantages in associating with Asia as well as in helping them "to integrate to the open, market based world trading system."[17]

The EU signed the 'third generation' cooperation agreement with India in 1994 that stressed on broader economic cooperation, beside trade aspects. Together with the Joint Political Statement signed in 1993 it opened the way for annual ministerial meetings and a broad political dialogue. Further cooperation between the two came to be shaped in the backdrop of a number of developments taking place in the Asian region such as the South East financial crisis of 1997, WTO reforms, faster economic development of India, nuclear flashpoint between India and Pakistan, military takeover in Pakistan, etc. that prompted the EU to come out with its revised Asia Strategy in 2001. In these crisis situations India's economic standing was not much affected, which naturally began to attract the position of EU towards India.

Therefore, a regular political dialogue was boosted through the first summit held in 2000 which, since the 2004 Summit, has taken the shape of a Strategic Partnership, making India one of the EU's select global partners. EU-India Cooperation is now characterised by vibrant and regular dialogues with Trioka Ministerial meetings, senior officials meeting, and yearly summits. Complementing this is also the regular meetings on counter-terrorism, human rights, and consular affairs. The Strategic Partnership, in fact, established a linkage between development cooperation, economic growth, and sustainability.

EU-India Development Cooperation at present:

The relationship between EU and India is intense and multilayered; and, it goes beyond mere commercial considerations. The cooperation addresses diverse areas relating to development such as environment, gender, health, human rights, good governance, mutual awareness programmes, and other areas of common interest including educational, scientific and cultural exchanges, and partnership programmes. India is also one of the privileged "Strategic Partner" of EU. Since EU does not appear to have a clear cut priority in establishing the Strategic Partnerships, this can be viewed as a measure for convergence of perspective in the long run that goes beyond the 'technical' aspects with the country that it perceives as important. Hence, the strategic partnership in a way is recognition by the EU of the increasing importance of India in the global scenario and its economic progress, in particular. The large market and the rising number of the middle class have made India an attractive destination for EU companies that are increasingly facing competition from the rest of the world. The plural society, democratic setup, and broad convergence in the liberal market framework enabled by successive governments since 1990's has again brought EU closer to India and it is here that India has an advantages over China.

The interest in India also appears to have been conditioned by the understanding that partnership programmes with important countries are the means to identify or promote sectors and issues of common interest. These are useful tools in shaping global order and multilateralism gradually realising the values dear to EU. The logic of openness and its contribution to the European growth and jobs is well articulated in the *2006 Global Europe Strategy* that aims to reorient bilateral trade agreements through new generations of Free Trade Agreements (FTA) with focus on intellectual property and access to raw materials.[18] Hence, India naturally becomes the country in focus both for its democratic regime and economic progress. India was becoming an active player in the global development scenario and was, interestingly, both a donor (under the "Indian Development and Economic Assistance Scheme – IDEAS) and a recipient of developmental assistance. With EU, for instance, India had € 0.6 billion investment in EU and recipient of € 3 billion EU FDI in India in 2010.[19] Naturally, the CSP for India (2007-13) considering India's present economic progress hoped that India's need for development assistance would gradually decline; and, hence wished to see the present pattern of development assistance move support the pro-poor sector reform policies and other areas of mutual interest, including economic co-operation.[20] In other words, developmental assistance would be replaced by developmental cooperation and this hope is reflected in the increasing trend of joint programmes on diverse fields and complementing Indian efforts.

The deepening of structural reforms (including better governance and infrastructure in order to improve the investment climate, boost productivity, and accelerate growth) and social cohesion (inclusive development) in the CSP for India are seen as necessary to promote growth and substantially reduce poverty. Hence, CSP envisaged providing budgetary support to the social sector (health and education) encompassing best practice models in good governance, decentralised decision-making and development, gender issues, institutional reforms, and public sector management in order to meet the MDGs beside support to the economic, academic, civil society, and cultural activities foreseen in the Action plan.[21] Support was assured in pursuit of economic cooperation and sectoral/regulatory convergence that were viewed as vital to realise the MDGs. For instance, earlier in health care EU was active in supporting sectoral reform when the Government of India initiated in October 1998 the Health and Family Welfare Sector Investment Programme (SIP). In education EU had earlier supported the District Primary Education Programme (DPEP) targeting districts with low female literary rates and Sector Investment Programme (SIP). It had also financed many Rural Development and Natural Resource Management projects. But as CSP for India points out, the multiplicity and geographical dispersion had limited and localised impact with little influence over long term institution building and policy.[22] And now it clearly indicated its move away from project specific to sectoral priorities and reforms in the development cooperation and synchronisation of policies with other players as, for instance, it has done in the education programme (SSA) coordinating with the World Bank and the British Department for International Development (DFID) although all three were involved in negotiations with India.

To give effect, the EU sought to support two priority areas, namely, Social sectors (health and education); and, Support to the economic, academic, civil society, and cultural activities foreseen in the Joint Action Plan (JAP) of 2005, revised in 2008.[23] In the social sector, that is, primarily in health and education, EU aimed to supplement Indian programmes, namely Sarva Shiksha Abhiyan (SSA) and the National Rural Health Mission (NRHM).[24] SSA aims at achieving universal of elementary education. NRHM focuses on basic health-care delivery system in which their special target is the reduction in Infant and Maternal Mortality Ratio. In both of these programmes, beside the programme objectives, the emphasis is on capacity building, inclusiveness, and involvement of civil-society players. In support of the programme the EU in the Multi-annual Indicative Programme (MIP)-I (2007-10) has earmarked an assistance of € 70 million for education, € 110 million for health sector, and € 80 million for India-EU Joint Action Plan (JAP) and indicated that in the MIP-II(2011-13) €100-130 million, € 50 million and € 30-60 million would be earmarked for education, health and JAP initiatives, respectively .[25]

In other areas too programmes are envisaged. There are Economic Sectoral Dialogues and Co-operation (in multiple areas of economy such as trade, energy, S&T, customs cooperation, etc.), Civil Society and Cultural Exchanges, Academic Exchanges (including co-operation in the higher education sector and EU and Indian Studies Centres). Furthermore, policy dialogues and sectoral actions are envisaged for a wide range of areas where the EU and India have jointly identified a scope for enhanced co-operation leading to better governance and policy-making, such as trade and industry, energy, environment, and transport. So the whole exercise revolves around twin pillars of development and pro-poor sector reform that are considered as the central elements of this strategy. Besides, the Commission also indicated "thematic interventions" in the areas of democracy and human rights, migration, and asylum, Human and social development (capacity building for policy making etc.), Environment and Sustainable Management of Natural Resources including Energy and Non-State Actors Development.[26] These are besides the humanitarian assistance that EU has rendered in times of crisis such as floods; drought, and earthquake routed through EU's Humanitarian Aid Office (ECHO). The Commission has allocated close to €100 million in humanitarian aid. Just last year, that is in 2011, when some Indian states were affected by floods, EU provided an assistance of 600,000 and additional € 1million to help the victims of cyclone in parts of Tamil Nadu and Puducherry.[27]

Overview of the Current EU Projects in India

	Sector/Category	EU contribution (in Euros)
1.	Conflict Prevention (Disaster prevention and preparedness in coastal districts)	874,311.00
2.	Environment and the sustainable managementof natural resources	2,345,031.88
3.	Governance, democracy, human rights and support for economic and institutional reforms	4,413,355.53
4.	Human Development (Empowering women, HIV prevention, etc.)	20,358,683.74
5.	Infrastructure, communication, and transport	4,299,300. 00
6.	Multi-Sectors (Community empowerment, developing knowledgebase, health sector, revitalizing sustainable rural livelihoods, etc.)	373,779,931.00
7.	Rural development, territorial planning, agriculture and food security	2,231,680.89
8.	Trade and regional integration	1,582,301.00
9.	Water and energy	7,156,359.00
	Total	**417,040,954.04**

Compilation based on EU List of Projects, http//eeas.eu/delegations/india/projects/ list_of_projects/

In addition, the EU has also signed state partnership programmes with two states in India: Chhattisgarh and Rajasthan and will spend about € 160 million over a period of six years (2006-2012). In Chhattisgarh, the programme is aimed at increasing the efficiency in the delivery of critical social services, especially health and education and the reduction of poverty of tribal communities through environment-friendly economic strategies. EU through its State Partnership Programme in Chattisgarh has allotted € 32 million to education and again € 32 million to the heath care system.[28] In Rajasthan, the project is directed towards state-wide water sector reform and improvement and enhanced water supply and groundwater recharge in selected areas of Rajasthan.[29]

EU, therefore, is undoubtedly an important partner in the development cooperation of India. The programmes envisaged are wide and deep and goes beyond the confines of traditional development cooperation framework. Remarkably, the special report of the Court of Auditors in EU has appreciated the nature of EU cooperation with India for more than 20 years and observed the efficiency of the Commission in targeting the poor by moving "above" classical rural development and infrastructure projects to establishing of sector support programmes in health and education. The report strongly supports the structural reforms and "sustainability" results.[30] Significantly, today the areas of development cooperation have come to include exchange of views on global development issues and exploration of cooperation in development projects in third countries. The dialogues and interactions that have already been established between EU and India, other things remaining the same, are set to reach new heights in the days to come.

Reflections on EU-India Development Cooperation: EU is a major donor of development assistance to India which stood at € 470 million in the period 2007-13. There are concerns that these may be reduced. The EU has launched an aid reform in October 2011that proposes aid cut from 2014 onwards to 19 emerging economies including China, India, and Brazil in order to focus on the "neediest."[31] This might adversely affect the EU development cooperation with India.

A much more concerning factor is the nature of assistance that is increasingly being linked to trade positions of the EU. Especially the requirement stated in the agreements barring few humanitarian assistance for natural disasters, sound more like conditions, and these have become the target of criticism. The official position during the negotiation on these is not publicised much; but, it has often been made clear to the EU on more than one occasion that though Indians do not contest the importance of democracy, good governance, labour clause, environment protection, etc., treat these as domestic matters of the country and India has already put in place the necessary laws and instruments. So India is able to offer some resistance by tough talk and is able to guide its development pace and scope including that of linkages with global economy at its own will and terms. So the EU slogans and norm settings have only a rhetorical value in relation to India and submitting to EU dictates, especially in context of the growing economic strength and confidence of India, have in reality hardly ever happened. EU does not intend to go aggressive on this for reasons of offending the Indian side and the Indian side will not relent on accepting EU dictates through treaty terms. So pragmatism and realist prudence appears to have taken precedence over the normative approach.

Some civil society groups, in particular, those opposed to the indiscriminate globalisation and free trade pacts, however, are critical of the value loaded words and objectives in the agreement. The presumption of universal applicability of the preferred values of EU and the efforts to enforce the same, in particular, is not viewed favourably. [32] Instead there is a call to respect the distinctiveness and sensitivities of the countries concerned. The argument here is that the needs and capacity constraints of the countries need to be considered before integration with the global market is attempted and the institutional and productive capacities need to be strengthened. The aid conditions result in unequal competition with the stronger and these in the global market do not work to the advantage of the large sections and also deprive governments the necessary policy space to implement their own development strategies.[33] Therefore, though 'poverty eradication' is the objective the stress on structural reforms and 'smooth integration into global economy' need not necessarily lead to poverty eradication; instead, could increase the gap between the rich and the poor.

The issue is paradoxical as on one hand EU supports pro-poor policies; on the other, it supports free trade overlooking the fact that the consequent globalisation dominated by MNCs would not benefit all sections of people. Especially when the development is skewed in favour of the rich and powerful the EU's universal propagation of minimum state and multilateral framework is capable of offsetting the poverty reduction drive. The labour clause expectations make situations difficult for countries and worst for the poor without state support. Therefore, the present development cooperation policy coupled with free trade logic, norms, and political preferences is hardly effective in addressing the conditions that breed poverty and tend to lose exclusive focus on the objective of poverty eradication.

But a much more concerning factor is the selective interpretation of principles of multilateralism by the EU. Despite the WTO provisions, EU continues to protect sectors that are extremely important for India such as agriculture, leather, and textiles on dubious grounds and mechanisms like NTBs, anti-dumping clauses, etc. So the selective interpretation of multilateralism and trade liberalisation in areas beneficial to EU such as financial services and manufactured products; and connivance in other areas such as agriculture, textiles, clothing, and footwear and, to a certain extent, in granting liberal access to workers ('Mode 4' services) hardly makes the EU advocacy of liberalisation tenable. Other exports from India have also seen blatant NTBs and discriminatory trade practices as well as anti-dumping measures resorted by the EU. [34] Therefore, EU development cooperation linkages with trade and then trading in a discriminatory manner have raised eyebrows in India.

Moreover, in India most of the products, especially in primary commodities sector, are produced by unorganised and small producers. The EU tabs on exports of these products by conditionalities such as labour clauses, environment concerns, etc. makes production itself difficult, especially in the absence of high investment/resources and technology, lack of procedural awareness, higher costs of compliance and specified production methods not innate to their contexts. Therefore, without adequate strengthening of their capacities exposing them to global competition is not considered advisable.

This is not to undermine the value of EU assistance to India. The resentment is about the incorporation of its preferred values in the development cooperation agreements and its linkages with trade. India has refused to yield to the EU and the EU has not adopted coercive techniques. The other discomforting area is the granting of assistance based on political preferences. For instance, EU's extension of GSP Plus drug regime scheme to Pakistan in 2002 which benefited from increased textile export to EU market invited the ire of India which legally challenged the decision of EU in the WTO dispute settlement body. When the verdict favoured India, EU had to give up its drug regime support and incorporate it under the broader governance framework. Similarly the support on political grounds to Pakistan influenced by its changed Afghan position and "war on terrorism" failed to impress India as it considered itself as a victim of (cross border) terrorism. Indians have wondered whether acts of expediency can ever support the claim of EU as a normative power and its propagation of lofty ideals. This also implied that their development cooperation posture is influenced by extraneous considerations not connected with the high principles of humanitarian considerations or poverty elimination.

Nonetheless, despite the contestation on the EU development perspective on poverty reduction and the *realpolitik* of EU in developmental assistance, the advantage that India derived from the EU development cooperation can not be underestimated. Given the fact that both EU and India are interested in predictable global order and democratic setup it is not difficult for them to convince each other of their peculiar compulsions and requirements. This is particularly important because from India's point of view the complex EU is one of the several entities in international relations with which India has to deal with no foreseen benefits in realisation of its regional and global visions by placating the rhetorical, self-righteous, and normative EU. India has at times become weary of the complex structure of EU decision-making process, extremely cautious approach towards project selection and planning; and, the incrementalist method in stepping up programmes by EU. India would rather prefer bilateral relations with European countries than with EU.

This is in contrast with the experiences of India with the US where the US has provided India a privileged position by signing the civil nuclear deal in May 2005 that facilitated the nuclear ambition of India as well as acknowledged its growing power. Clearly the realist perspectives of India and US match more than India-EU. The rhetoric of EU is responded by the pragmatic approach by India and the two find it difficult to agree on some issues despite the importance one attaches to the other. The normative framework of EU and its attachment with the development cooperation hardly appeals to India that is extra-sensitive to the regional situation and the larger politico-economic and strategic environment in which it operates. America's 'War on Terrorism', for instance, is by and large received favourably in India and wants terror networks in Pakistan to be dismantled. The US, however, is balancing between India and Pakistan and appreciates the role of both in fighting terrorism. Notwithstanding, the EU has demonstrated its lack of such strategic insight in South Asia, partly because of its preference to be a soft power and partly because of its inability to comprehend the political nuances and sensitivities in the subcontinent. Trade alone is not sufficient to boost bilateral ties or to evolve global visions. The EU needs to consider the need to further engage India on issues of deep strategic importance including global security, development and pattern of the emerging global order. The strategic partnership between the two is a significant step in this direction that needs to go beyond rhetoric and translate into reality. Lest the EU, despite being a major donor of development cooperation in the world, will not get the status it deserves.

Reference:

1. Article 2, C 1, Lisbon Treaty, Official Journal of the European Union 17.12.2007,http://eur-lex.europa.eu/LexUriServ/LexUriServ.do?uri=OJ:C:2007:306:0042:0133:EN:PDF.
2. See, R. Enzo Grilli, The European Community and Developing countries (Cambridge, Cambridge University Press, 1993).
3. The donor coordination of aid policies at the global level was stressed at the Paris Declaration on Aid Effectiveness (2005), Clause 39, for

instance, states that, "Donors commit to: Harmonise their activities ..... It should focus on upstream analysis, joint assessments, joint strategies, co-ordination of political engagement;and practical initiatives such as the establishment of joint donor offices." See, The Paris Declaration on Aid Effectiveness and the Accra Agenda for Action,,http://www.oecd.org/dataoecd/11/41/34428351.pdf.

4. Treaty on European Union, European communities (Luxembourg, 1992); Title XVIII, Article 130u. The Article 130u is renumbered as article 177 (Title XX) in the Treaty of Amsterdam.
5. Official Journal, n.3; Article 208 of the "Consolidated version of the Treaty on the functioning of the European Union" that rearranges the Article 177 of Maastricht Treaty again stress on the poverty eradication objective.
6. See, Development and Cooperation–Europeaid,http://ec.europa.eu/europeaid/how/finance/ dci_en.htm.
7. Development and Cooperation–Europeaid, http://ec.europa.eu/europeaid/how/finance/dci/ investing_en.htm.
8. http://ec.europa.eu/development/icenter/repository/F48_consultationNSAs_en_en.pdf; http://ec. europa.eu/development/icenter/repository/COMM_PDF_COM_2006_0088_F_EN_IMPACT _EUROPEEN.pdf; http://ec.europa.eu/development/icenter/repository/Framework_CSP_2006_ en.pdf.
9. http://ec.europa.eu/development/policies/consensus_en.cfm; Official Journal of the European Union C 46/1 24.2.2006 EN,http://ec.europa.eu/development/icenter/repository/ european_consensus_2005_en.pdf.
10. From mid-1990's additional trade preference were given or withdrawn by EU to countries observing social and drug (fighting) policies. But when India challenged in the WTO the addition of Pakistan to the list of the GSP drugs regime the EU abandoned separate social and drugs provisions and incorporated these to a broader 'sustainable development and good governance' principles. Gerrit Faber and Jan Orbie, "The New Trade and Development Agenda of the European Union," Perspectives on European Politics and Society, Vol.9, No.2, June 2008, pp. 192-207.
11. http://ec.europa.eu/development/geographical/cotonouintro_en.cfm?CFID=2311138&CFTOKEN =de5549ec566e53bc-44BE1EAC-BCAD-6AE3-85FE869240E498A7&jsessionid =243062fb88384a375d62.

12. Para 1 (a) and (b), Lisbon Treaty, n.1.
13. http://ec.europa.eu/development/policies/9interventionareas/trade/aid-for-trade_en.cfm.
14. Commission of the European Communities, Press and Information Directorate-General, Information Development Aid, Food Aid by the European Community, 40-73, http://aei.pitt.edu/12325/1/71252_1.pdf.
15. Fegerico Birocchi, "The European Union's Development Policies towards Asian and Latin American Countries," DSA European Development Policy Study Group, Discussion Paper No. 10, February 1999, www. Edpsg.org/Documents/DP10.doc.
16. Council regulation(EEC) No.443/92 of 25 February 1992 on Financial and Technical Assistance to, and Economic Cooperation with, the developing countries in Asia and Latin America. http://europa.eu.legislation_summaries/external_relations_with_thirdcountries/latin_america/r1400/ _en.htm.
17. "Communication from the Commission to the Council", Towards a New Asia Strategy, COM (94) 314 final, Brussels 13-07-1994,http://europa.eu.int/comm/external_relations/asem/asem _process/com95.htm.
18. "Global Europe Competing in the world, A contribution to the EU's Growth and Jobs Strategy", European Commission, External Trade,http://trade.ec.europa.eu/doclib/docs/2006/october/tradoc_130376.pdf.
19. http://trade.ec.europa.eu/doclib/docs/2006/september/tradoc_113390.pdf.
20. India, Country Strategy Paper, (2007-2013),http://eeas.europa.eu/delegations/india/documents/eu_india/country_strategy_paper_07_13_en.pdf.
21. Ibid.
22. Ibid.
23. Ibid.
24. In the earlier CSP (2002-2006) EU had committed an assistance of € 150 million for Sector programme of support for primary education, € 200 million for SSA and € 240 million for Health sector. See, http://eeas.europa.eu/india/csp /02_06_en.pdf.
25. Ministry of Finance, Government of India, Annual Report 2010-2011, http://finmin.nic.in/reports/AnnualReport2010-11.pdf.
26. CSP, no.20.

27. http://europa.eu/rapid/pressReleasesAction.do?reference=IP/11/1188&format=HTML& aged=1& language=EN&guiLanguage=en: http://ec.europa.eu/echo/news/2012/20120131_en.htm.
28. http://eeas.europa.eu/delegations/india/eu_india/development_cooperation/education/index_en .htm; http://eeas.europa.eu/delegations/india/eu_india/development_cooperation/healthcare/ index_ en.htm.
29. http://www.delind.ec.europa.eu/dc-sgi-nrm.asp?links=sgi-link4.
30. Special Report, No. 10/2003 concerning the effectiveness of the Commission's management of development assistance to India in targeting the poor and ensuring sustainable benefits, together with the Commission's replies,Official Journal of the European Union, 2003/C 211/02 http://eur-lex.europa.eu/LexUriServ/LexUriServ.do?uri=OJ:C:2003:211:0021:0037:EN:PDF.
31. Aid reform, http://www.eubusiness.com/news-eu/aid-emerge.dxb/?searchterm=India; http://www.eubusiness.com/news-eu/aid-economy.cwd/.
32. Dick Gupwell & Natalie Gupta , "EU FTA negotiations with India, ASEAN and Korea: the question of fair labour standards," Asia Europe Journal, no.7, 2009, p.91; Jan Zielonka, "Europe as a global actor: Empire by example?," International Affairs, Vol.84, No. 3, 2008, pp. 471–484; Lorenzo Fioramonti & Arlo Poletti, "Facing the Giant: Southern perspectives on the European Union," Third World Quarterly, vol. 29, no. 1, 2008, pp 167 – 180.
33. Marc Maes, "Civil society perspectives on EU–ASIA free trade agreements," Asia Europe Journal No. 7, 2009, p. 97-107.

13

Indo-EU FTA:
Challenges and Opportunities on Horticultural Products with special reference to Karnataka

Vigneshwara Varmudy

The Trade Policy of India has undergone and is still undergoing significant changes over the years. A major move has been the increasing engagement with Free Trade Agreements as compared to unilateral or multilateral trade liberalization through the WTO. Now, Free Trade Agreements between two or few partners have become a tool of much more active form of trade liberalization. This type of shift has had a significant impact on the horticultural sector of India in particular, and the agriculture sector in general.

India and the EU have been engaged in extensive political dialogue on a comprehensive trade, investment, and economic co-operation agreement since 2000. Ever since, there have been several rounds of negotiations. The significance of an Indo-EU agreement is immense since the world's largest trading entity is engaging with the biggest democracy in the world.

As a result of increased investment in horticulture research, extension and production, India has now emerged as a major producer of horti-products in the world following China. In 2008-09, India produced 68.4 MT of fruits, 129.07 MT of vegetables, 1 MT of flowers, 1.13 MT of plantation crops, and 4.15 MT of spices. On the whole, these horti-products contribute around 13 percent of the world's production. As far as fruits and vegetables are concerned India stands second in the world. India leads in the production of mango, banana, sapota, and acid lime. Likewise, it leads the world in the production of Green vegetables, peas, and okra. Apart from these, India is a leading producer in arecanut, coconut, cashewnut, and spices.

Karnataka is the eighth largest state in India and is located in southern peninsular. In Karnataka, a diversity of horticultural crops are grown covering fruits, vegetables, flowers, spices, plantations, medicinal crops, etc. This state stands first in India in arecanut and coffee production, second in flowers and cocoa, third in coconut, fourth in spices, fifth in fruits, sixth in vegetables and cashew. All these crops have good export potential and are required to be developed towards attaining higher export growth in order to make them competitive in the global market. It is on these lines now that there is an opportunity to expand the exports to the European Union through FTA.

From the above it is clear that there is a vast scope for Karnataka to export large volumes of horti-products to EU as there is a huge demand for it. However, there are several challenges in the form of Tariff, SS, and PSY, etc. Hence all these challenges are to be addressed, which will be useful to promote the export to EU.

This paper makes an attempt to examine the existing trade of horticultural products from Karnataka to the EU. In this regard, the available secondary data is adopted to highlight the said aspects. As the FTA between EU and India holds tremendous potential in terms of trade flows, an attempt is made here to note down the challenges and opportunities on the horti-products of Karnataka.

India's Agricultural Trade with EU

India's increasing openness to trade since the early 1990's have increased overall trade flows. If we look at trade sector-wise, agricultural and food products account for a relatively small share of the overall Indian trade. In the year 2007-08, agricultural exports was 12.15 percent of the value of total exports while during the same period the share of agriculture in total imports was just 3.09 percent.

As far as India's agricultural trade with EU is concerned, India features low on EU's partner list, absorbing less than 0.5 percent of the EU's total agricultural exports. Viewed from EU's perspective, India is ranked 12th among the most important EU suppliers and 41st in receiving EU exports.

The total exports from India to EU is equivalent to 2 percent of the EU's global agricultural imports. Amongst the EU-27 countries U.K., Netherlands, and Germany account for 67.65 percent of the total Indian agricultural exports in terms of value. U.K. is the biggest importer of Indian agriculture commodities amongst the EU-27 countries. As far as the commodity- wise breakdown of total exports to EU from India is concerned, Basmati rice is the top exported commodity to EU – 27, and its share in the total agricultural exports from India to EU-27 in the year 2007-08 was 19.29 percent. The second highest exported commodity is processed fruits and vegetables, fresh grapes, dried and preserved vegetables, and guar gum approximately contributing same percent share, i.e., 7.5 percent to the total exports from India contributing to E.U. (Table–1).

Table – 1

India's Exports of Specified Agro products to EU –27 in 2007-08 (Value in 'lakh')

Products	Product-wise Total	% of total
Basmati Rice	5366.00	19.29
Other processed fruits and vegetables	30314.62	10.90
Fresh grapes	21297.99	7.65
Guar gum	21074.69	7.57
Dried and preserved vegetables	20971.25	7.54
Floriculture	16668.26	5.99
Mango pulp	13838.85	4.97
Dried Nuts	11173.20	4.02
Cereal preparations	10723.90	3.85
Jaggery and confectionery	8550.57	3.07
Non-basmati rice	8037.96	2.89
Total	**168017.29**	77.74

Source: DGCIS Annual Export

From Table – 1 it is clear that of the total exports from India to EU the percentage of share of horticultural products is above 41 percent, which clearly indicates that there is a vast scope for the export of the same.

Apart from the above justification it can also be noted that the top ten agri-commodities that EU – 27 countries import from the globe are edible fruits and nuts, peel of citrus fruit or melon (15.70%); residue and wastes from food industries (8.37%); oil seeds and oleaginous fruits (7.70%); Coffee, tea, mate and spices (7.39%); vegetable fats and oil (7.28%); preparations of vegetables, fruits or nuts (5.26%); edible vegetable, plants and tubers (4.92%); overall, EU is a major importer of tropical products.

From the above it is clear that EU-27 countries are importing more of horticultural products from the global economy. This demand need to be tapped by India.

Horticulture in Karnataka

Karnataka is the eighth largest state in India and is located in southern peninsular India, with a geographical area of 190.50 lakh hectares, accounting for 5.84 percent of the total geographical area of the country. Karnataka is a maritime state with a coastline of 287 kms., covering the districts of Uttara Kannada, Dakshina Kannada, and Udupi with nine ports excluding the New Mangalore port.

Agriculture in Karnataka contributes 26.7 percent of the state's GDP and employees 71 percent of the total workers. Horticulture contributes 40 percent of the agricultural income and 80 percent of the agricultural exports.

The diverse agro-ecological conditions prevailing in the state facilitates growth of a variety of horticultural crops ranging from the temperate zone pears, plum, peach, strawberry to the sub-tropical or humid zone fruits like the mangosteen, litchi, rambutan and the tropical mango, banana, grapes, citrus, guava, sapota, jack, pomegranate, pineapple; cabbage, carrot, beet among temperate vegetables; brinjal, okra, tomato, onion among tropical crops; tea, coffee, cocoa, rubber, arecanut, cashewnut, and coconut among plantation crops; pepper, nutmeg, cardamom, ginger, turmeric, chillies and a host of spices; jasmine, rose, chrysanthemum, aster, marigold, and a array of flowers, ornamental foliage crops and a number of medicinal and aromatic plants. These lend the state a unique status in the field of horticulture in India (Table – 2 & Table - 3).

Table – 2

Karnataka's Rank in Area and Production of Important Horticultural crops in India (2008-2009)

	Crop	Area	Production
1)	Fruits	6	5
2)	Vegetables	6	6
3)	Flowers	2	2
4)	Coffee	1	1
5)	Arecanut	1	1
6)	Cashewnut	5	6
7)	Cocoa	3	2
8)	Coconut	2	3
9)	Spices	5	4

Source: Compiled from NHB Database 2008-09

Table – 3

Crop-wise Rank in Area and Production of Fruits and Vegetables and States share in India's total production (2008-2009)

Crop	Rank in Area	Rank in Production	Share in Total Production of India
Banana	4	5	7.3
Citrus	6	6	3.6
Grapes	2	2	14.3
Guava	9	7	6.1
Mango	7	3	10.1
Papaya	7	3	11.3

Pineapple	9	3	13.9
Pomegranate	2	2	17.1
Sapota	2	2	22.8
Brinjal	10	7	3.6
Cabbage	10	9	2.6
Onion	3	2	22.4
Tomato	4	1	14.1
Potato	6	7	1.8
Sweet potato	8	4	3.1
Tapioca	7	7	0.1

Source: Compiled from NHB Database 2008-09.

Karnataka's Exports of horticultural products to EU

Karnataka has a long tradition of overseas trade. Historically, Karnataka has been a major exporter of horti-products like coffee, cashewnuts, spices, mango, coconut products, etc. to EU. At present, Karnataka exports coffee, cashewnuts, processed products, black pepper, grapes, flowers, vegetable seeds, ornamental plants, onion, gherkins, lime, mangoes, pomegranates, chillies and other fruits, vegetables and spices to EU.

These horti-products are exported to EU countries like U.K., Spain, Netherlands, Germany, France, Italy, Belgium, Solvania, Greece, Finland, Austria, Portugal, Hungary and others. Table – 4 presents data on the value of the selected horti-products exported from Karnataka over the years.

Table – 4

Exports of horti-products from Karnataka 2005-06 to 2008-09 (Value in 'crores')

Commodity	2005-06	2006 07	2007-08	2008-09
Coffee products	1103.94	1476.65	1307.60	1579.05
Processed agri-products	381.11	398.36	415.51	712.34
Cashew Kernels	521.81	552.78	527.05	638.48
Spices	169.98	219.72	245.15	479.25
Gherkins	213.96	313.34	244.50	244.50
Flowers	50.00	50.00	50.00	50.00

Source: UITC Bangalore

EU country-wise demand for horti-products of Karnataka

1. **Cashew:** Cashew kernels is exported to Austria, Belgium, Bulgaria, Czech, Cyprus, France, Finland, Germany, Greece, Hungary, Italy, Latvia, Lithuania, Netherlands, Poland, Portugal, Romania, Solvania, Spain, Sweden, and U.K. Among these the major importers are Netherlands, U.K., France, and Belgium.
2. **Flowers:** Flowers like rose, cut flowers, etc. are exported to several EU countries.
3. **Coffee:** Coffee is exported from Karnataka to Italy, Germany, Belgium, Spain, Finland, Solvania, Greece, France, Portugal, Hungary, Netherlands, Poland, U.K., Latvia, Romania, Austria, and others. Among these, Italy is the major importer followed by Germany, Belgium, Spain, Finland, Slovenia, Greece, and France.
4. **Mango:** It is being exported to several EU countries.
5. **Pomegranate**: It is also exported to several EU countries.
6. **Grapes:** Karnataka's grapes are widely demanded in EU states like U.K., Netherlands, and Belgium.

7. **Spices:** Spices like pepper, ginger, chilli, etc. are exported mainly to Italy, U.K., Netherlands, and France. However, other states in EU also prefer these spices.
8. **Arecanut:** Arecanut whole, splited and value added arecanut is exported to Germany, U.K., Italy, and other EU states.

Karnataka has been recording a reasonable performance as far as its share in horticultural exports to EU is concerned. The exports of these products have increased over the years. Even then a large number of horti-products are finding other export destinations, though originating from Karnataka, but are not included in the above. This export performance can be improved significantly in the future if the following challenges or threats are addressed properly.

Challenges or Threats

1. Trade barriers (both Tariff & Non-Tariff) imposed against horticultural exports imposed may hinder the growth. There appears to be a difference in the tariff rates between India and EU. The EU has a much lower tariff than India for almost all products. The EU's high protection with regard to some fruits and vegetables, citrus and grapes, flowers, etc., however, impact India's export of these items.
2. Quality standards fixed by the EU states, e.g., non-harmonised MRL, stringent health and hygienic rules on spices, etc.
3. International prices are unpredictable and volatile.
4. Due to IPR's regime, certain inputs become costlier and access to them becomes difficult; therefore, such possibility may have an impact on export competitiveness.
5. Comparative cost advantages and production efficiency achieved by the traditional exporters may pose a challenge to exporters from the state.
6. EU's commitment to farmers and subsidies is very high. EU countries enjoy the benefit of dual agricultural subsidies, one in form of State Aid and another under CAP. In Karnataka, farmers get free (subsidized) electricity but the power supply is only for 3-6 hours.

7. Again, the precarious power supply position and high tariff / unit in the state could affect the functioning of the post-harvest infrastructural facilities, which are most crucial for any export activity.
8. Complex procedures for inspection, sampling and product testing, and non-recognition of Indian testing procedures and quality certificate.
9. Various quality control standards on fruits, e.g., tough fruit export norms.
10. Delay in clearance of flower consignments due to mandatory checks.

Opportunities to Expand the Exports to EU

1. Considering the volume of world trade in fresh and processed products as well as the geographical proximity of Karnataka to major consuming markets of EU, there is enormous potential for developing exports of horti-products.
2. There are off-season markets when the EU does not produce their own fruits and vegetables. These seasons have a short span and deliveries must be on time. If the state can concentrate on this segment, the chances of boosting exports would be high.
3. As Karnataka produces surplus volume of fruits and vegetables in recent years, the scope to export this to the EU is always there while considering a per capita consumption of vegetables per day for Karnataka at 120 gms. and per capital consumption of fruits per day at 45 gms, there prevails a surplus in both as shown in Table – 5.

Table – 5

Production surplus in Fruits and Vegetables in Karnataka (per annum in tones)

Vegetable	Present veg.	Volume of surplus	Fruits require -ment	Fruits produ -ction	Volume of surplus
2,309,747	4,493,868	2,164,120	962,395	4,038,618	3,076,223

Source: NHM, Action Plan for Karnataka

4. There is a demand for tropical horticultural products from immigrant population in EU, especially in countries like U.K., France, Germany, etc,. This is a sizeable segment.
5. The varied agro-climatic conditions of the state favours production of diversified crops suitable for export which is the strength of the state.
6. The grapes grown in Karnataka has an increasing demand in EU, along with papaya, mango, etc., both in original and value added forms.
7. In recent years the Government of Karnataka has evolved a horticulture policy which is pro-export. So the opportunities to expand the exports are always there.
8. The demand for organic products is increasing in EU, while in Karnataka organic farming system is becoming popular, so there is a vast scope for increasing the exports to EU in the near future.

Horti-crops of Karnataka Having Export Potential

1. **Mango**: Mango is popularly known as the king of fruits. The area for cultivation of this crop has been increasing in the state. Apart from the Alphonse variety which is familiar in global markets, other varieties which are likely to find favour in the export markets namely Banganapalli, Raspuri, Malgoa, Swarna Rekha, etc. are also grown in the state.
2. **Grapes:** Karnataka stands second in production in the country only second to Maharashtra. Grapes grown in the state has already established a brand in U.K. However, extra care has to be taken to supply it as per the quality standards of E.U.
3. **Cashewnut:** Presently cashewnut is exported to EU. To promote the export there is a need to establish more of the cashew processing units in the state. There is also the need to develop the Mangalore Port.
4. **Coffee:** Karnataka exports coffee to EU countries in raw form and to some extent to the MNCs in the value added form. Recently, the Coffee Board along with the Government of Karnataka has started to give incentives to the coffee growers to go for organic coffee production. This may increase the

demand in E.U. Apart from this, to promote the exports there is a need to develop a brand for Karnataka Coffee and to encourage exporters to export value added coffee products like instant coffee, coffee powder in packed form, etc.

5. **Black Pepper:** To promote the export necessary steps has to be taken with regard to Quality upgradation.
6. **Pomegranate:** Pomegranates grown in the state are being exported to U.K. and other EU nations. However, Quality and productivity are the two aspects that need immediate attention.
7. **Flowers:** The demand for cut flowers, seeds, bulbs, live ornamental plants, dried flowers, perfumes in EU countries has been increasing. The severe cold winter in European countries works to our advantage. APEDA has already established a market facilitation center at Aalsmeer in Netherlands, which is the world's largest flower auction center trading more than 30 million cut flowers and ornamental plants every day. So as to boost the export earnings further, it is needed to improve the quality.

Even though, Karnataka's export of horti-products to the EU countries has increased in recent years, the state has not yet grabbed the opportunity. Now, Indo-EU FTA has opened the venue for these products, so considering the opportunities available in EU countries the state has to overcome the prevailing challenges. If these challenges are addressed properly, the scope for export of horti-products from the state is immense. In this regard, the state has to remove all those barriers and bottlenecks that hamper the efforts of export of these products.

Contributors

Prof. Hartmut Elsenhans, Professor emeritus of International Relations, Institute for Political Science, Leipzig University, Germany

Prof. Rajendra K. Jain, Chairperson and Jean Monnet Chair, Centre for European Studies, School of International Studies, Jawaharlal Nehru University, New Delhi

Dr. Sudarsan Padmanabhan, Assistant Professor, Department of HSS, IIT Madras, Chennai

Prof. Subrato Mitra, Professor and Head, Department of Political Science, South Asia Institute, University of Heidelberg, Germany

Dr. Jayaraj Amin, Chairman and Associate Professor, Department of Political Science, Mangalore University, Mangalore

Dr. Bhaswati Sarkar, Associate Professor, Centre for European Studies, School of International Studies, Jawaharlal Nehru University, New Delhi

Prof. Kurt Hübner, Jean Monnet Chair for European Integration and Global Political Economy, Institute for European Studies, The University of British Columbia, Canada

S.Y. Surendra Kumar, Assistant Professor, Department of Political Science, Bangalore University, Bangalore

Prof. M.J. Vinod, Professor, Department of Political Science, Bangalore University, Bangalore

Prof. Sukalpa Chakrabarti, Professor, Symbiosis Institute of Media Communication, Symbiosis University, Pune

Dr. Gulshan Sachdeva, Associate Professor, Centre for European Studies, School of International Studies, Jawaharlal Nehru University, New Delhi

Dr. B. Krishnamurthy, Associate Professor, Department of Political Science and International Relations, Pondicherry University, Pondicherry

Jeeva, Research Scholar, Department of Political Science and International Relations, Pondicherry University, Pondicherry

Dr. Vigneshwara Vermudy, Associate Professor, Department of Economics, Vivekananda College, Puttur, Karnataka